Small Boat
in the Midi

Small Boat in the Midi

Roger Pilkington

J. M. Pearson
Tatenhill Common
Staffordshire

First impression 1989

by J. M. Pearson & Son (Publishers) Ltd.,
Tatenhill Common, Burton-on-Trent, Staffordshire.
Typeset by Character Graphics of Taunton, Somerset.
Printed by Penwell of Callington, Cornwall.

British Library Cataloguing in Publication Data

Pilkington, Roger
Small Boat in the Midi.
1. France. Midi – Pyrenees, Visitors' guide
I. Title
914.4′8604838

ISBN 0-907864-44-9
ISBN 0-907864-45-7 Pbk

Contents

Pierre Paul Riquet
Constructer of the Canal du Midi

FOREWORD

W hen Mr J Macgregor, MA, of Trinity College, Cambridge, and Barrister-at-Law set down his reason for taking to a holiday voyage in a canoe he was clear and concise. "A smash in a railway carriage one day hurled me under the seat, entangled in broken telegraph wires," he wrote. So he very wisely took to the water instead.

Not all become inland voyagers so instantaneously. I myself started with a canoe more than half a century ago, advanced through Banham's hire-cruisers on the Cam – two of which I ran into bridges – and graduated by purchasing an admiral's barge in a state of decay from the Admiralty. It, or she, became known as *Commodore*, and it was aboard her that I first crossed France to the Midi and so fell in love with the land of wine and troubadours that I have voyaged thither several times aboard her successor *Thames Commodore*. That area of France is one that for me and my wife has no equal, and when hundreds of miles away from it we can still see its sights in our minds' eyes, bask in its distant sunshine and imagine the scent of the pines and the sewing-machine sound of the cicadas. It is a countryside of sheer delight, but also of excellent waterways.

Just who it may have been that first took a voyage in the Midi for sheer enjoyment I cannot say. For the waterways of Provence and the Languedoc are a heterogeneous collection, some such as the Rhone having been navigated from Roman times, and others from the seventeenth century onwards, or even the twentieth. First in every case came the professionals, the *nauti*, the bargemen and the skippers, and yet I cannot help wondering whether even in earliest times some enterprising Gaul may not have said to his wife "Come, let us have an afternoon of lazing away in a boat, in a backwater of Rhodanus Flumen, or along the Fossae of Marius if you can risk the mosquitoes." We can be reasonably certain that the Cardinal Archbishop of Narbonne must have enjoyed his trip in a boat beflagged and accompanied by musicians when the Canal du Midi was opened, and one can think that some of the English knights appreciated the voyage when they sailed through the marshes to St Gilles on their way to cleave the Saracens very properly to the navel. Yes, St Gilles, which now lies many miles inland, an indication of how things shift in that land of changing areas of earth and water.

One of the epics of inland voyaging is the beautiful book by P G Hamerton, extra beautiful because of the hundred and forty-eight peerless drawings by himself and his co-voyager, Joseph Pennell. It was in 1866 that the pair pursued their voyage up and down the Saône in a donkey-hauled berrichon, a sort of long and narrow barge, and by catamaran. Like Robert Louis Stevenson a few years before them, they were, of course, arrested, the French authorities believing that any person travelling the waterways for alleged relaxation could in reality only be deranged or a spy, or both. And if he made notes in a diary or, like Pennell, sketched some broken-down medieval fort, then the suspicion of espionage was overwhelming.

Times have changed. Although as recently as 1958 everything possible was done by French frontier officials to prevent *Commodore* entering the country by water, France is now dotted with bases for hire-craft fleets. I have a paternal affection for their being there at all. It was in the winter of 1963 that I gave a talk to the Midlands Branch of the Inland Waterways Association in Birmingham, showing members a number of slides I had taken that summer on the canals between the Rhone and the Garonne. One of the members was so taken with the possibilities that he set out for the Midi to see it for himself, and soon afterwards the first of the hire fleets on the Canal du Midi came into being, originally based in the pleasant port basin in Toulouse (now ruined by being turned into a traffic roundabout). Since then the fleets have multiplied and grown, and when seventeen years later I passed for the eighth time through that fascinating waterway I met a hired craft every few minutes. Those aboard to whom I spoke at the locks were from many different countries, but every one of them was highly enthusiastic about the charm of such a voyage.

Then there are the yachtsmen passing through on their way from sea to sea, using the canal as a shorter and safer passage than Gibraltar, very much as was intended when the Canal des Deux Mers, as it was then called, was opened more than three hundred years ago. Very often they are in a hurry to reach a distant sailing ground, but the lure of the Languedoc is such that they may find themselves staying a while to see it in more detail, or even just to lie on deck in the sunlight filtering through the bankside plane trees and enjoy the beauty of the watery scene, touched as it is with the gently moulding hand of time.

There are also those rare inland explorers, who come back on their own boats. Some – like myself and my wife – are drawn back again and again to the area, merely to move gently along the canals and enjoy the brilliance of the flowers, the scent of the herb-laden countryside, the red earth shining through the rolling sea of vines which stretches almost to the horizon and invites us to explore on foot the white limestone hills which glint in the distant haze.

The Midi really means the South. It is not defined by any county boundary but more by appearance and feel, by an atmosphere which is sun-drenched and warm and by the bleached houses with vines around the door, by a very definite sensation of not being in Northern Europe. Hamerton considered that from Tournus downward the Saône Valley had this recognisable tang of the south about it, and I agree. But every voyage has to begin somewhere, and if I begin this one at the insignificant town of St Jean de Losne that is merely because all the water-routes from the northern lands to the Mediterranean converge upon it, or join the Saône not far below it. Besides, for the yachtsman from the north the most strenuous part of the voyage is over and he will have time to look around, relax, and enjoy the beauty of the broad, slow river and its mightier successor, the Rhone. Already a few roofs are less steep than further north, and the south is definitely within feel if not within sight.

This book is the product of voyages spread over twenty-four years aboard *Thames Commodore* and her fore-runner *Commodore*, supplemented by explorations on foot and by the local buses of which France has so many. My wife and I came to love the Midi so much that we were prepared to leave to others the delights of round-the-world package tours and guided visits to the Great Wall of China or Leningrad's museums. Year after year we voyaged through it with never a moment of boredom, and when, eventually, at seventy it seemed prudent not to risk falling off locksides or straining the back by working recalcitrant paddle-gear, we were content to find ourselves a cottage in that same area, with the same heady scent of broom, the same matchless outlook over the rolling country toward the distant sparkling snows of the Pyrenees. That is why the location which an author habitually puts at the end of his foreword is here set down as...

Roger Pilkington   Montouliers, 1989

I

The Upper Saône – the strategem of Queen Theodehild –
Chalon and Tournus – the River Seille – Solutrian horsemeat
– the fate of Cluny – Ile Barbe – the founding of Lyon –
mission of Pothinus – the end of Roman Lyon.

S t Jean de Losne is nowadays a place of no importance to anyone but a
bargemaster, and of such there are plenty to be seen sitting on the
steps by the end of the bridge or near the church, talking in a desultory
way about such matters as bargemen habitually talk of. Although they
may be in the town for days or weeks they have little contact with the
mere land-based citizens, the 'gens de terre' as they call them, except for
such simple needs as buying a baguette or a glass of vin de table. The
stone banks on either side of the broad River Saône are lined with their
barges, most of them empty and awaiting news of a possible cargo from
the nearest freighting bureau, some stopped for fuelling or repairs, others
merely for the opportunity of meeting casual barging acquaintances last
seen hundreds of miles away and many months past. Architecturally the
town is undistinguished, even if Pennell paused there to make two sketches
of its streets and one of a paddle-wheeler tug such as a century ago used
doggedly to haul the laden barges up the stream. But the yachtsman bound
for the Mediterranean from the north is inclined to breathe a sigh of relief
when St Jean comes into view, for ahead of him all the few remaining
locks will be modern, efficient and electrified. If he has come from Paris
by the Canal de Bourgogne he has already put two hundred and twenty
one behind him, most of them hand-worked and muscle-testing, and if
from the Baltic via the Moselle one hundred and sixty-six. It is surely time
to relax and look forward to the delights of the Mediterranean shores now
a mere week of voyaging distant – even if, as a Frenchman remarked to
me on the Cote d'Azur, one has to pay to get so much as a smile, and
even then it is not given.

The hundred miles of Saône upstream of St Jean are one of the most
idyllic stretches of river navigation to be found anywhere, but below the
town the curves and meanders, the faded villages redolent of cow manure
are left behind and the navigation runs off into a long and featureless cut
which leads all the way to Seurre, bypassing the charming and wriggling
stretches past Pagny-la-Ville and Glanon. The same correction has disposed
of the need for the next two locks also, and the way is open and unobstructed

to Verdun-sur-le-Doubs, so no longer can the boatman enjoy as previously
the unlikely experience of being welcomed to the lock of Le Chatelet by
a much amplified nightingale. That lock, now abandoned, was appoached
by a cut of a quarter of a mile above which a bend cut off the view from
the keeper's house, and as it was of some advantage to know if a ship were
approaching from upstream the ingenious engineers of the Ponts et Chaussées had mounted beyond the corner a microphone which would pick up
the sound of a distant hooter or the thudding of a heavy diesel motor. It
so happened that a willow bush at the foot of the microphone pole became
the favourite haunt of a nightingale whose amorous calling was picked up
and broadcast to any craft that might be patiently waiting for the lock to
be filled or emptied.

Once when I came to Le Chatelet lock the pen contained a pair of barges
going down river ahead. The craft were already at the bottom level, the
gates stood open, and there was nothing to prevent them from leaving.
Nothing, except that there was nobody aboard. I asked the lock-keeper
whether anything was the matter, and he merely pointed to a nearby pub,
shrugged and disappeared, leaving us alone with the song of the nightingale
which, I believe, could hear its own broadcast voice after a time-lag of a
second or two and so was stirred to further musical activity in an attempt
to shout down an imagined rival. After waiting for a while with no other
sign of life, I remarked to Fred Doerflinger, who happened to be making
the trip with us, that I thought some sort of action was needed.

"Sure," he said. "Why don't we go up to the pub and ask them to come
and move their craft?"

"Why not?" I had a slight suspicion why not, but I thought it was worth
trying.

We climbed the path to the eminence on which stood the bar-restaurant.
It was the familiar kind of French pub with a pungent smell of Gauloise,
the hideous plastic furniture bathed in the relentless glare of horrid strip-
lights. The landlord was an anxious-looking man who stood behind the
bar with a wet cloth in his hand, dabbing at the counter. At a table slouched
rather than sat two men, a burly and brown-stained individual of about
forty-five and a younger and thinner one with a rather simple face. Two
women of comparable ages sat more upright, with smaller glasses of
Chateau Plonque in front of them, half full.

"Messieurs?" The landlord stopped his dabbing, ready to attend to our
order for drinks. But there was none. Fred smiled pleasantly and indicated
that our only wish would be fully met by the two bargemen hastening to
remove their craft from the lock-pen. The tooter the sweeter, I added.
We wished to use the lock immediately.

Our request seemed to please the women, who evidently wanted to get
their husbands out of the pub while there was still some chance of their

being able to stand up and stagger to the lockside, but the combined effect of the wine, our demand and its approval by their wives, made the men somewhat defiant. Another glass, they said, and then they would oblige.

Fred and I realised however that another glass would become two and probably three, so I said No. They were obstructing the navigation and I would return to the lock and telephone to the regional engineer at Dijon. Of course, I did not intend to do any such thing, for I knew that before long a barge or two must certainly appear from the other direction and would not long tolerate having their use of the lock blocked. However, the suggestion had the desired effect, and amid a rain of oaths and imprecations the men stumbled back to the lock and the barges were removed, not to set out again on their journey but to be run into the bank below the lock so that the drinking bout could be resumed. The keeper now reappeared and locked us down, indicating amid the song of the nightingale that the men were of a violent cast of mind and it was for that reason that he had felt ill-equipped to tell them to vacate the lock.

His assessment of character proved correct, for just as we were about to leave the pen the two men and their wives reappeared, clambered aboard, and set off immediately ahead of us. It was not difficult to guess that they had some sort of unsociable intention, and we soon discovered that the idea was to drive us into the bank. The craft steered by the younger man was towed by the other, so they were at a disadvantage when it came to swift changes of direction. Besides, *Thames Commodore* was far more manoeuvrable than a pair of péniches steered by intoxicated dimwits, and the river being broad it was easy enough to dodge them and even to encourage them with our loud hailer when abeam, asking them to repeat more slowly some of the physiological terms which, we assured them, we were unable to find in the Concise Oxford French Dictionary. This seemed to irritate the front bargeman unreasonably, and in spite of the protestations of his wife he endeavoured to whirl a pit-prop round his head like an Olympic hammer-thrower to cast it at us. Of course, we were well out of range, and as he was not watching the wheel the only result was that the péniche ran hard ahead into the bank. This was of course hard luck on the ship under tow which had forward momentum and no means of reversing, but with much coffee-grinding on his wheel the younger man managed to avoid running the other down from astern and came to rest in some bushes. As we proceeded down the river the high-pitched angry screeching of the wives and the violent oaths of the men could be heard fuelling the flames of family quarrelling, and rather than stop and offer to tow the craft back into a more seemly position I decided that it might on the whole be wiser to run ahead and put another lock between ourselves and them.

This foolish sort of bargee behaviour was rare. After all, a skipper owning his own péniche could be regarded as an entrepreneur with a capital of between fifty and one hundred thousand pounds according to his ship, and so he was unlikely still to be in business if he was merely a soakaway. In thirty-five years of canaling I have only been cursed three times, and both the other occasions were understandably caused by the sight of people sailing past on a yacht, revelling in the sunshine and without an apparent care in the world whilst the unfortunate bargeman had been stationary for several weeks without income of any kind, waiting for some cargo to be allocated to him for carriage in his ship. In fact, it surprised me that the bargemen were not more frequently irritated, but perhaps they were thoroughly used to waiting and on the rare occasions of cursing and swearing it was merely that the appearance of a yacht sparked off an explosion which had its real origin in a smouldering domestic quarrel below decks.

If St Jean de Losne is now a barge town and nothing else, it at least has its heroic memories, for St Jean on the west bank and Losne on the east were joined by a bridge that was much more than a link between the two parts of the town, for the river itself was formerly the dividing line between the Kingdom of France (or Duchy of Burgundy) and the Holy Roman Empire. At the end of the bridge on the St Jean side a monument commemorates one particularly notable victory of the local people when the town became caught up in the Thirty Years War. The Imperial army was invading Burgundy and intended to attack Dijon, so in order to protect his rear the general decided to reduce St Jean de Losne, which commanded his line of supplies. Sixty thousand men were put to attack the place, which was defended only by its citizens and less than two hundred soldiers. When, after six days, the attacking artillery had breached the wall, two of the councillors and some of the citizens met together and drew up an agreement which stated that each of them would fire his own house and they would also fire the ammunition store in the town hall, and they would then retire over the bridge and destroy an arch behind them. The declaration was taken round and signed by the defenders, whose families then set about filling their living quarters with quickly inflammable materials.

The expected attack came with great violence, but just as the signal to set the town on fire was about to be given twelve men from Auxonne further upstream managed to reach the gate with news that a relieving force of cavalry was on the way. Helped by these dozen men, the defenders held firm throughout the day, and during the night the promised relief arrived. The attackers retired, thwarted, and the helmet and sword of the gallant commander of the citizens is still to be seen in the church at the end of the bridge.

Earlier, in 1273, a force of five hundred men was sent from France-Comté to carry out a surprise attack by the stratagem of dressing the men up as women. However, the locals were not deceived. They spotted them, perhaps either by their unusual numbers or their unfeminine way of walking, and after greeting the ladies courteously they invited them in – and then slaughtered the lot.

Forty-five kilometres below St Jean the wriggles of the Saône are over and the gentle valley gradually broadens into a wide plain. When first I travelled down the river in 1962 I thought it tame, sluggish, and by no means picturesque. In fact the height of the banks raised to save the surrounding land from flooding make the river somewhat uninteresting, and if the locks are now thirty or forty miles apart that in itself indicates a gradient which is extremely small and a flow which must be negligible except in time of flood. There is little to be seen after Verdun-sur-le-Doubs until Chalon-sur-Saône comes into view, another town of barges but a more considerable one. It has shipyards and a commercial port, and tall banks of masonry to conduct the river safely through the place. Chalon is pleasant enough, but it is probably seen at its best when dusk is falling, the outline of the towers and gables stand out mysteriously against the fading colour in the west, and the lights come on along the quay. Then the town looks infinitely more mysterious than it really is. Like the lady in "Trial by Jury" she might very well pass for forty-three in the dusk, with a light behind her.

At the time I first went down river, a favourite occupation of the Chalonese was to accost yachtsmen and enquire whether they already had a pilot. This would be followed by terrible tales of how the river was dangerous, full of rocks and submerged walls, and how only a week past an English yacht had been lost and its occupants nearly drowned. The catalogue of disasters was continued until the yachtsman, thinking he was receiving what the Admiralty Pilot Books call "local knowledge" rather than a whole pack of lies, agreed to take the man on as pilot as far as Lyon at an absurdly high price, only to discover next day that the dangers were imaginary and that the Saône could be navigated without difficulty by anyone capable of rowing a boat in St. James' Park.

On that first voyage I stopped to see the exhibition of the early works and apparatus of Niépce, who invented photography (later developed by Daguerre) but I knew nothing of the story of King Gontran and his resourceful queen. Back in the dark ages and before Burgundy had become a duchy it was a kingdom of some size extending all the way from Sens on the Yonne to Avignon and beyond. The capital of this realm was Chalon and at the time in question King Gontran was the ruler who resided there, his brother Haribert being King of Paris. Now it came to pass that when away from Paris on an expedition Haribert died and his wife Theodehild was therefore left a widow. Her ambitions lay somewhat higher than to be no more than an ex-queen, so she managed to lay her hands on all the royal treasures of her ex-husband, and when she had done so she sent a message to her bachelor brother-in-law Gontran at Chalon, offering herself to him in marriage and mentioning that she happened incidentally to be very well provided with riches.

Gontran seemed very pleased with her proposition and the messenger was sent back to Paris with a letter to that effect. "Let Queen Theodehild come to Chalon with her treasure and upon her arrival I will marry her and she will become a greater queen than ever," Gontran wrote.

So Theodehild set out for Chalon and reached the city with her lumbering baggage-wagons containing all the wealth of her former husband's kingdom. She was well received, the goods were carefully unpacked, listed by the chamberlain and his aides, and then put in a repository. Gontran next called his counsellors together. "Would it not be much better that this treasure should belong to me?" he asked them. "Surely that were much safer than that it would belong to a woman who has already shown herself unworthy to be my brother's wife."

The counsellors all readily agreed, which may well have been very prudent of them. So Theodehild was taken away under escort all the way to Arles, where she was quietly put away in the seclusion of one of those early religious foundations which so often served as dumping-grounds for the unhappy, the deserted or rejected. And Gontran kept the treasure, if not his word to the lady.

Just under the power cables which cross the river below the town is Port Guillot, not a port since medieval times but formerly serving the village of Lux, where the emperor Constantine is locally alleged to have seen the cross in the sky with the words "*In hoc signo vinces.*" However, the same is said of Neumagen on the Moselle, and as Constantine is known to have had his summer palace there it seems to me to be a more likely location, even if Chalon was the Roman Cabillonum. But as signs in the sky are by nature ephemeral, we shall probably never know. However, in this area the river is always crowded with thousands of blackheaded gulls, an unexpected sight so far from the sea, and I naturally assumed at first that modern pollution from factories had caused something to appear in the river that was either directly attractive to them or perhaps slew the fish in such numbers that they were to be picked up on every hand by hungry birds. However, no dead fish were to be seen, and I later noticed that a century earlier Hamerton had recorded exactly the same – at least, he observed vast quantities of seagulls without identifying the species or suggesting a reason for their presence.

Two hours below Chalon along an almost straight course down the middle of the wide plain Tournus comes into view. It has long been my favourite among all the towns of the Lower Saône, for its prospect from the river is really a delight. Along the cool tree-lined Quai du Midi and the Quai du Centre the houses once owned by wealthy vintners stand back

to survey the riverside where, in the days before phylloxera and over-production destroyed the local vintages, the barges loaded the heavy barrels
of local wine. Broad double doors lead back to pretty courtyards or to
deep, cool cellars, and even if the activity of wine-pressing is no longer
what it used to be the vines grow up to the eaves as though to emphasise
that the town could still produce good grapes and wines if it really wanted
to. And also to remind us that we have now really arrived in the south.

From those same quays little alleyways lead through toward one of the
most glorious and well-tended abbey closes of all France where the splendid
romanesque basilica of St Philibert towers up, hinting by its loopholes
and machicolations that it has stood through centuries in which it has had
to be prepared for all emergencies. The foundation goes back much further,
for it was in the second century that the Roman market at Tournus was
visited by an energetic Christian from the Middle East, Valerianus. Accompanied by his friend Marcellus who had escaped from prison in Lyon he
made his way up the river to Tournus, whilst Marcellus went on alone to
Chalon. He had not long been at Tournus, preaching and teaching, when
the provincial governor, Priscus, passed through the town and Valerianus
was ordered in the familiar Roman way to show his loyalty by worshipping
the emperor as a deity. Upon refusing, he was summarily executed just
outside the walls of the Roman citadel of Tenurtium, and on the place of
his martyrdom a church was shortly afterwards built in his memory. If
the abbey church which has taken its place is not named after him, that
is because the remains of the Gascon saint Philibert were later brought to
Tournus for safety by monks driven from Normandy.

The abbey itself was not begun until the tenth century, when St Philibert
was built as a fortified stronghold encircled with battlements which were
to serve it so faithfully that in the following centuries of brigandage and
religious wars the abbey itself remained almost unscathed whilst the town
around it was devastated and pillaged by whatever victorious army happened just then to be passing on its way. Tournus was also fortunate
enough to escape being the scene of a battle for the river crossing during
the Second World War. The posterns of its ancient defences still remain
even if the walls themselves have vanished, and the great church of St
Philibert stands aglow in a sun which already has something of the intensity
of southern sunshine in its light, and the two tall towers of rich Burgundian
stone look out over the five radiating chapels and away across the mellowed
creeper-clad buildings of the close toward the plain of the Saône with its
backcloth of the distant Alps, or west and southward to the warm slopes
of the vineyard hills of the Mâconais, which tumble right to the edge of
the town.

I had several times been down the river before curiosity prompted me
to push the nose of the ship cautiously into what appeared to be the mouth

of a smaller river entering on the left bank. In fact, it proved to be merely the run-off from a mill some way back across the meadows, but that in itself was encouraging, and a short way further downstream I tried another opening at the edge of a wood, which proved more rewarding. In the angle between the two rivers – for this was indeed the entrance to the little River Seille – the meadow was grey with the silt of floodtime, and it evidently contained some special delicacy which brought the elegantly plumed egrets to stalk across the grass, white and serene, shooting out a long neck to snap up a bit of food before stretching up to start in dignified surprise at a boat wishing to enter their own private stream. Right at the actual confluence there was something of a sand bar, but even in times of summer drought there would probably be a few feet of water over this because the curious little 160-ton craft which carried gravel from Tournus up to Louhans kept the entrance ploughed. Or at least they used to.

The River Seille is one of those curious and little-known streams that appear unexpectedly but immediately win the affection of anyone lucky enough to discover them and patient enough to deal with the obstacles they are likely to provide. I hope the little Seille barges are not extinct, for when I first discovered the river there were only three of them in existence and so each skipper had a reasonable idea of where the others would be and, of course, he was not expecting to meet any other boats. One of these barges met us unexpectedly emerging from a narrow lock-cut, and the sight so unnerved the captain that in his astonishment he ran hard on a shoal. On another voyage I found one of the old-timers abandoned for the Bank Holiday weekend in the entrance lock at La Truchère. However, the keeper's little boy had a cycle, and the present of some stamps for his collection sent him pedalling away into town to find the right pub and the correct skipper, who was very willing to back out to let us through.

These few little gravel barges appeared to provide enough reason for the Seille to be kept open to navigation. Otherwise it had no commerce, no ships beyond a few fishing punts, and it seems unlikely that it can ever have known much trade. Along the whole of its course from below Louhans to the Saône valley there was not so much as the remains of a loading wharf or warehouse. For all of its twenty-five navigable miles the river wound lazily to and fro, almost as though trying to be the Thames above Oxford. Not for a yard of its course above La Truchère was there a road or railway along either bank, and only a single inn was within sight of the river, where the road to Dôle flew overhead on a bridge. Quiet and green, and spread at the edges with waterlilies, the Seille was a stream of utter peace. The cows ambled over the meadows to stare narcissistically at their reflections until the accustomed picture heaved and crinkled in the impertinent wash of our unexpected passing. Unpolluted and unspoiled, the river moved dreamily between banks bright with flowers, or through copses

which were the safe haunt of night heron and harrier, and where the bright
slash of black and white on the wing revealed a little bittern darting swiftly
up the reach.

Naturally enough, the Ponts et Chaussées were not going to spend good
money on a navigation used only by three small barges, so the expenditure
on lock repairing was minimal. Indeed, the gates of the entrance lock were
so rickety and full of holes that to open them at all involved a trial of
strength between the head of water on the one hand and myself on a long
armed windlass on the other, aided by the keeper who had set up the kind
of winch one might use for hauling out recalcitrant stumps of oak trees,
and his six year old daughter who wound away valiantly at a similar but
smaller mechanism. It would take a lot of obstruction to thwart *Thames
Commodore*, and the only time she was frustrated at this point was when
one autumn she found the entire pound above the lock had been drained
so that at last the much needed repairs could be undertaken.

Above the second lock the village of Cuisery stood on its own hill,
obsequiously clustered at a respectful distance from the Chateau of Mon-
trepost with its turrets delicate and sun-blanched, its face unarmoured as
though it had always known this to be a countryside free of fear and strife.

The third lock at Loisy was unmanned. How long ago the last keeper
died and the house began to collapse I do not know, but now the building
was gutted and forlorn, its fallen tiles and plaster already vanishing under
a thicket of nettles and lilac and buddleia. The lock gates carried a weight
of herbage growing on the timbers, but they would still creak leakily open.
Like the others on the river, they were worked on the windlass chain-and-
hook system, an excellent one for gates so little used, because the power
that can be brought to bear when an upright capstan is turned with a long
steel pole is formidable indeed. Even then on my fourth voyage up to
Louhans I had to give a stout push of Perkins horses in the·mitre before
the gates would swing at all. Across the spit and above the sloping weir
a mill of soft grey stone still churned under the power of the water, whilst
behind the ruined lock-house the meadows stretched away, faded green
in later summer, but in June shimmering russet and silver with the sheen
of the snakes-head lilies which decked the whole valley. At night the
glow-worms signalled cool and green along the bank, chemically more
efficient than any light source of human devising, and the country was as
silent as only rural France could be. One more lock near Branges, and
Louhans was a mere twenty minutes ahead. There, at the tumbledown
staging, one of three Seille ships was unloading its thrice-weekly cargo of
gravel.

Louhans is a surprise, as are so many of those exquisite French towns
nobody has ever heard of. Its long main street, arcaded from end to end,
is preserved as an historical monument, but there is a very curious ancient

dispensary in the former Hotel Dieu. Somebody in one of the shops told me I must not fail to see it, and said that if I asked at the hospital they would certainly be delighted to show it to me.

So off I went to the hospital. I passed through the smart swing doors and came to the reception desk amid a scent of carbolic.

"Name, please," said the girl at the counter running her eye over me. I gave it.

"Complaint?"

"No complaints at all, I was just..."

"Sit over there please." She indicated a row of chairs mostly occupied by women of considerable size. It was some time before a tall and efficient looking sister came past, hesitated, and then spoke to me.

"Is it your wife?" she smiled pleasantly.

"Is who my wife?"

"Is she in here?"

"Not that I am aware of, mademoiselle. Why?"

She laughed. "This is the maternity department. Have you mislaid yourself?"

"I must have," I said apologetically. I was aware that some of the neighbours in the row of chairs began to edge away a little, taking me, no doubt, for a VD patient. "Please, I am not sick, I have no relative having a baby. I want to see the dispensary at the Old People's Home."

"Ah!" A ripple of amusement spread along the waiting queue. "Come," said the sister. "I will take you to Sister Martha."

We passed out of the smart new ward and crossed a sort of cloister to enter a mellow stone building of the seventeenth century. The sister tolled a bell and soon there came an aged nun to whom I was handed over. She had long since ceased to be active in nursing, but presumably nuns cannot retire elsewhere because they are retired from the world already. I followed her to the front of the building, where the great doorway was topped by a carving which showed a man helping a wounded individual on to an ass.

"The Samaritan," I said.

She stopped in astonishment. "Why yes! Do you know about him in England too?"

I assured her we did, but I did not destroy her belief that he was something particularly French. We passed in, and she drew my attention to a series of gigantic wardrobes or presses, fully ten or twelve feet high. Each had been brought in by a novice in times long past, to contain the whole of her worldly goods as well as her changes of religious clothing. There she hung the discarded garments from the life she was leaving. They would never be needed again, but they were stored there throughout her life. I could not help wondering if occasionally at dead of night a sister might not give way to temptation and open her cupboard just to run her fingers over the happy dress she had worn on that summer evening long ago when walking hand-in-hand along the flower-strewn meadows of the Seille with...

"Come. They will be having their meal." And Sister Martha opened a door at the end of the hall and led me into a long dormitory arranged as a series of cubicles in which some forty or more very old men and very old women sat either in their beds or beside them at little tables. Each bed had an enamelled plaque with the name of the donor in old-fashioned print. The family of a local manor might endow three or four beds, and would have first call upon them for their own tenants or servants. Others were given by individuals for the benefit of whomever might need a safe, sure place of care for their later years.

The inmates were indeed being served with lunch where they sat and the food looked so good that I wondered if the sick wards did as well. But what struck me so powerfully about this Dickensian scene was the tremendous, shining happiness and gaiety of the inmates. There was no sense of being shut away and forgotten. For they were not forgotten, but were one great family of the very elderly, tended with love.

That was how the place was when I saw it, but when, on another voyage, I took some cousins to see the hospital, this wonderful home for old people with its friendly dormitories and endowed bed-cubicles had been emptied of life. The beds were stripped, the enamel plaques a little dusty. Some official in a ministry or a county council had decided the place was not sufficiently modern. The formerly happy inmates had been cleared out, probably to be given soulless and sterilised bare walls and municipal sanitation. I doubt if there was much laughter in those new surroundings.

Sister Martha took me on to see the object of my visit; the former dispensary with its ancient volumes of herbal cures and simples and its unique and priceless collection of apothecaries' jars from Moorish times onward, the items having been given by grateful patients to the nursing sisters, who, being nuns, might evidently not receive money or other more personal gifts. And very fine this little museum was, yet what I remembered much more vividly was the cheerful, welcoming faces in the dormitory and I wondered if local authorities would ever learn to leave things alone, homely and old-fashioned, instead of replacing them with the modern for no other apparent reason than uniformity. By now the elderly have probably been reduced to mere coded numbers to be flashed up in quivering green letters on the screen of a data-machine.

The return to the Saône was easier, for a leaky lock aids rather than obstructs when locking down. Another couple of hours down the larger river Mâcon opened up to starboard. I have a personal interest in the public conveniences at that city, for on my first trip down river I was anxious to fill up with water, only to find that there was no such facility as a tap available. However, a glance into the quayside gents convinced me that water must be available there – something that cannot always be assumed of a French public facility. So I took my wrenches ashore and disconnected the pipe from the main. It is not very easy to fix a hose to the end of an unobstructed pressure main but I persevered, and a side effect of *Commodore's* watering was that the walls, ceiling, floor and other appurtenances of the public utility were pressure-washed as they had never been before. Twelve years later I fancied that I could still detect the beneficial results of such a wash-down as it had never known before or since.

There is often a market in the wide space at the Quai Lamartine above the gents. The poet was born in the town and his birthplace is on view for all those who find such connections inspiring, which, personally, I do not. I doubt if anyone will want to see mine, and if they do, they are in for such a disappointment as is usual. They would see (if it has not been pulled down) a store-room in an industrial testing laboratory. Mâcon's modern claim to fame is based on the wine trade, but in the sixth century it was the venue of one of the councils of the Church. The delegates – men only of course – spent some time arguing the question of whether women should or should not be regarded as human, an interesting subject for discussion which, I believe, proved inconclusive, and which in connection with ordination seems to have reared its head again and provided the Church of England with something about which to get itself worked up.

Mâcon is the capital of the Cote d'Or, the hills of which stand back from the wide flatness of the Sâone plain and are rich in vintage names. Clearly visible from the river is a great white bluff which rises to a height of several hundred feet, and after a steep climb up the cracked limestone of the counterscarp one looks out over the twin hamlets of russet stone whose names are known all round the world; Pouilly and Fuissé. The tall crag itself is the rock of Solutré which has given its name to one of the periods of the Upper Palaeolithic, to the time when men were producing fine implements from flakes of flint and using also the antlers of reindeer as working tools. These were in fact among the later prehistoric inhabitants of Solutré, and for centuries before the 'Solutrian' culture was evolved generations of early men lived at the foot of that same rock, people of the same Cro-Magnon type which extended in the Aurignacian period from Britain to the French Riviera, and in the later Solutrian age as far as Czechoslovakia. Some of them were buried at Solutré, their faces turned towards the rising sun in some faint and mysterious recognition of the place of man in nature, or perhaps some shadowy hope of things unseen, or another dawn. During the long time when these people lived at the foot of the rock the climate varied from the subtropical heat in which hippopotami lurked in the French rivers, to such cold that reindeer were widely distributed and provided the antlers which could be worked up into pick-axes and other serviceable tools, but one of the most universal and widely distributed creatures was the wild horse of the Pleistocene, a short-legged wiry creature which roamed Europe in small herds. So many of these were slaughtered by the men of Solutré that their bones form a mash which covers thousands of square metres to a depth of up to two and a half metres. Various estimates have been made of the number of horses needed to form so immense a kitchen scrap-heap, and certainly there must have been tens of thousands. If their remains lie at the foot of the cliff, along with those of reindeer and other beasts, it is because of the particular mode of hunting which our early relatives used, and which led them to choose Solutré as a suitable home.

The hunters would scour the countryside between the river and the hills, searching for a band of wild horses. Then they would drive the animals ahead of them, stampeding them with shouting and waving of arms, and probably with the help of fire and smoke as well, but they made no effort to attack the beasts. Instead, they merely herded them toward the long, narrow and sloping corridor which extended up to the summit of the rock, and from which there was only the one fatal escape. Once the animals were safely on the shoulder of the hill the chase became more vigorous and the horses, together with bison and other creatures which happened to have been surrounded incidentally, would flee in terror up and up, ever higher, until they had been driven to the edge of the precipice. There, screaming and bellowing in their fright, they were chased over the edge of the rock to hurtle and bounce down the face of the crag and land, crushed and bleeding, at the very hearths where the women were ready to slit them up with knives of flint, disembowel them, skin them, and dismember the broken limbs to roast them at the fire. It was an ingenious method of hunting and it was only possible because of the shape of that singular hill.

The fact that as many as one hundred thousand horses may have been herded over the summit of Solutré conjures up a fearful picture of an endless stream of terrified and whinnying creatures plunging one after the other to their fate in the primitive boucherie chevaline. Yet the site was occupied for many thousands of years; and even in one thousand years this immense mass of bones would have been produced if a herd of no more than eight horses were to have been manoeuvred on to the rocky shoulder once in every month. Nowadays the site is deserted, but lying at the very edge of the precipice to look down upon the fragmented rock far below it is not difficult to think oneself into the distant past when Solutré was a busy scene of cuisine, and Mâcon no more than a cluster of rude shelters.

Very different are the remains at Cluny, not far away. Only a fraction is left standing of the abbey church which was the greatest in all the world, not merely in its sheer dimensions but in its astonishing influence upon the life of people in many lands. For this abbey, the church of which even exceeded in size that of St Peter of Rome, spread its rule so far and wide that the dependencies of Cluny at one time numbered more than fourteen thousand.

The debt of the western world to this Rolls Royce of abbeys goes far beyond its religious importance, for in its heyday it furnished Europe with architects and theologians, professors and painters, doctors and philosophers, ambassadors and sovereigns. The French architect Eugéne Viollet-le-Duc wrote that if Cluny had been destroyed in the 11th century there would be little in Europe but darkness, ignorance and gross oppression, and he was probably right, but eventually the magnificence and power of the abbey began to lead to decadence, and as was so often the case, the abbots became interested more in opulence and ostentation. As these increased, so the influence of Cluny declined, and in the wars of religion the place was too fine a prey to be left alone. Time and time again, in spite of its stout walls, Cluny was pillaged and its treasures stolen. It merely remained for the Revolution to begin the final wrecking, selling the whole magnificent foundation to a hard-headed merchant of Mâcon who pulled down the nave for building stone and cleared as much of the site as he could. The sole piece of the abbey church which escaped his Republican hands, and which still stands today, is no more than one of the transepts, bearing one of the six great towers which set a style that can be seen right across France wherever the influence of Cluny was felt. But if nearly all the buildings have vanished, perhaps the best of what Cluny once stood for has been reborn only a few kilometres away in the modern community of Taizé, with the Church of Reconciliation founded by Roger Schutz and built by young volunteers from Germany.

Only fifty miles of the Saône remained before the great river poured its waters into that of the Rhone at the further edge at Lyon, but when two thirds of the way had been put astern, the stream decided to pull itself together and put on a better appearance. To port, the octagonal striped brick castle of Trévoux stood proudly over a town which seems to have been spilled down the steep hillside (the Rue Casse-Cou was probably rightly named) whilst to starboard, the hills of the Mont d'Or closed in until the river was confined within a narrower course with the land rising steeply on either hand and road and railway noisily flanking the stream. One more lock at Couzon, and the river began to wind tightly towards its final wriggles through a succession of bridges and past the Ile Barbe, which stood like a fortress in midstream. Said to have been in former times the Insula Barbara or wild island the eyot was well placed to house a monastery, and in the 12th century its abbot ruled over more than one hundred institutions. It accumulated great riches, and even boasted a library presented by Charlemagne and the alleged battle-banner of the mightly Roland. Yet here too as at Cluny, the monks became powerful and self-indulgent. Once this process has begun, it seems that nothing can arrest it. Perhaps the truth is that worthy young novices anxious to live a life of service and caring are no longer attracted to an institution which has lost its sense of direction and so they go elsewhere, with the result that numbers decline, the population of the foundation ages year by year, and the inmates lapse more and more into idleness. But at least in the case of the Ile Barbe the end was to some extent creditable. For in the 16th century the monks themselves with astonishing candour petitioned the French King.

'We are so bad, so sunk in turpitude and vice, so given over to wickedness, that we might better be able to achieve salvation if our monastery were dissolved and we were to discard our monks dress, associated as it now has become with an evil and licentious life' they declared. The King consulted the Pope, who agreed with them. He disestablished the monastery, only fragments of which incorporated into other buildings are now visible as one passes down the river into the great city.

To approach Lyon downstream is to some extent like steaming up the Seine into the centre of Paris. Soon one is passing long stone quays where anglers sit motionless in front of walls bearing *NON* or occasionally *OUI* red painted in letters six feet high – for there is always something in French political affairs with which some person can agree or disagree, or maybe both. To the right the hillside rises up to the great 19th century basilica of Notre Dame de Fourvière, from the pinnacles of which there is an astonishing view over the whole of Lyon, with, far below,the towers of the cathedral of St Jean, standing older and less flamboyant beside the river, straight across from my favourite free mooring close to the Pont Bonaparte.

I have always admired the enterprise of the French. After my wife and I had toiled the height of the basilica, turn by turn around the axis of a dark spiral staircase, we emerged breathless through a door on to the parapet, bathed in the brilliant summer sunlight. A man stepped forward, holding out a metal dish with a notice which told us not to forget the service. It did not refer to service in the sense of mass or matins, of course, but to – what? I asked the man, kindly, what service he had, in fact, performed for us, but he seemed to think the question one of those idiotic ones that haunted the parsimonious English mind, and with a shrug he walked away to tackle the next arrival.

The special appeal, for me, of the quayside opposite the cathedral of St Jean lay largely in the fact that there was always a busy vegetable market under the trees beyond the parapet, and it was no bad place for shellfish either. Once I noticed a tramp dangling a small hoop of wire on a string over the quayside and I saw that he had a few square inches of net stretched

across the frame. On closer inspection, I found that he had a small piece
of rotten meat attached to this, and what found the lure irresistible were
crayfish. I had never suspected the centre of Lyon to be a haunt of these
delicious miniature lobsters, but I very soon fixed up a wire net of my
own and by the time we set off again we had thirty of the crustaceans
cooked and rosy and ready for our lunch. And there was no savour of
diesel either.

Lyon is so fine a city that the Michelin Guide *'Vallée du Rhone'* devotes
fourteen pages to it, and its specialities are best discovered in that excellent
description. The Roman and medieval city is on the slopes of the hill
behind the cathedral, the next later one on the tongue of land between
Saône and Rhone and the third and most modern beyond the Rhone itself.
Certainly the beginnings of the city (Lugdunum to the Romans) go back
a long way and some authors have dated its origin to one Lugdus, a
descendant of Japhet who turned up in Gaul seven hundred years after
Noah's flood. That, according to the ingenious biblical time scale of a
former Bishop of Armagh, would place the beginnings of the city at about
1,700 BC, but a more modest fable recounts that Lyon was founded by
two valiant Rhodians chased out of Marseille by the Ionians about 393
BC. Hardly had they begun to establish themselves at the confluence of
the rivers than a flock of crows (lug) arrived and settled in the trees of
the hill (dunum) at Fourvière. One of the Rhodians happened to be something of an expert in augury, so he knew at once that he and his companions
must have chosen the right place to settle.

Toward the end of the century, two violent events shook the flourishing
capital of Roman Gaul, and from the windows of the excellent Museum
of Gallo-Roman Civilisation one can look across the ruins of the amphitheatre which was the terrible scene of the first of them. The background
to what happened can be traced back to its beginnings before the Christian
era, when sailors and shipwrights, traders and workmen from the middle
east visited the Rhone and its developing towns, and many of them eventually settled there. Within the first years after the death of Jesus, Christians
must have been found among the immigrants of Marseille and Arles,
Vienne and Lyon, and also among the minor civil servants, the builders,
and particularly the slaves of the Roman power which administered the
territory. Then, round about the year 150, there arrived in Lyon a party
of Christians from Smyrna, headed by Pothinus, who was only one generation removed from those who knew some of the apostles personally. His
particular mission was to strengthen and develop the church in the Rhone
valley.

It must be remembered that the central point of Christianity was a
dangerous one – the resurrection of a God sentenced to death under Roman
authority, crucified between two thieves, but raised to rule over another

world where the poor, the outcasts and even the slaves enjoyed a paradise of bliss which could only with great difficulty and change of heart be attained by the wealthy, the bureaucrats and the entrepreneurs.

Wisely, the emperor Trajan had advised the local governors not to attack the Christians but when Marcus Aurelius took over later in the second century the full fury of Rome was turned upon the church in the Rhone valley. The details of the horror are known from a contemporary letter written by an eye-witness and repeated by Eusebius, Bishop of Caesarea and a member of the Council of Nicea, and the torments of the church in the Rhone valley were to leave a permanent mark upon the history of the whole of southern France. For the Roman leaders of the second century were as accomplished masters of brutality and torture as the Soviet leaders of the twentieth.

The tortures to which the Christians were subjected are too frightful for me to relate them in detail, but amid all the horror, one figure above all others stood out, perhaps because such superhuman strength was not expected in a person of her kind. This was the pale young slave girl nicknamed Blandina. 'Not only her mistress, who already lay in prison, but all of us feared that this particularly frail, gentle and delicate creature would give in to the tortures. Yet all the while she only spoke softly the words, "I am a Christian. There is no evil done among us",' the letter recounted.

Apart from her nickname, nothing is known of this gentle girl. She may have been a local maid, or perhaps from Smyrna. But the memory of her is still very much alive in the city where she met her death. Every day while the tortures and burnings lasted, Blandina and a young lad named Ponticus were brought into the arena and forced to watch the end of their fellow-Christians. Each day they refused to recant, and the sympathy of the crowd for the two teenagers at last turned to fury. On the final day the fifteen year old Ponticus was tortured to death but died without a mumur of complaint, his courage continually sustained by Blandina. Last of the prisoners, the young girl was finally despatched by the executioners.

To the people of Gaul gathered together for the entertainments of a public holiday this was something new. They had burned with lust for the blood of the Christians, and the forty thousand eyes which stared at Blandina as she suffered one frightful inhumanity after another were afire with hate. Yet now some of them began to have second thoughts and this girl above all the rest was to make the beginning of a transformation in these rough people. 'Even the pagans declared that they had never seen a maiden bear such sufferings with so much courage.' They talked and talked of the frail slave girl, and of the radiant serenity which surpassed anything in their experience. From her death the eventual triumph of the church was assured, and Gaul was never the same again. Every year the second day of June is celebrated in Lyon as the day of the Saints Blandina, Biblis, Pothinus, Maturnus, Sanctus, Ponticus and Attalus.

From the point of view of the historian, it may have been inevitable that such an orgy of cruelty signalled the coming fate of Roman Lyon. The end of the second century was a violent time for Roman emperors, and when Marcus Aurelius was succeeded by his son Commodus, that emperior was murdered and his successor Pertinax also, leaving the empire to be fought over by three rivals, Niger in command in the east, Septimus Severus in Hungary and Jugoslavia, and Albinus in Gaul. That was in 197 AD. Septimus quickly defeated Niger and sped across Switzerland to cut off Albinus who was trying to get to Rome ahead of him. Albinus retired into Lyon, and in the course of a violent battle he had to fall on his own sword to escape the ignominy of being captured alive. Still gasping, he was dragged before his rival who promptly had him decapitated, the head being sent forward to the imperial city as a warning to any other possible opponents. The victor then celebrated his success by firing the houses and razing the whole of the city of Lyon except for a few imperial monuments. He had many of the citizens strangled, to leave no doubt that his name of Severus was well earned. Thus, after two glorious centuries the capital of Gaul ceased to be, and in its place Trier and Arles became the new centres of Roman administration. Centuries passed before a new and different city arose from the ruins of the old at the confluence of the two great rivers.

II

The Échelle de Chasse – the King's Rock – Viviers – up the
Revestidou – Avignon of the Popes – Bénézet's bridge – the
mistral – Jeanne's bargain – Petrarch and Laura.

I t was in 1962 that I swung the old *Commodore* round above the Pont
Bonaparte to draw in at the quayside across the river from the cathedral
of St Jean to make everything ready for a descent of the Rhone a few days
later. The preparations included such uninteresting jobs as emptying and
cleaning the fuel filter, but also the equally important one of ensuring that
there would be somebody aboard who was familiar with the Rhone. I must
admit to a slight sinking feeling which was not diminished by taking the
bus down to La Mulatière, where the last of the Saône locks released the
shipping into what appeared to me as an endless stretch of seething and
swirling water.

My anxiety was partly due to my not as yet having made all the observations which were to result in Pilkington's Law, an empirical guide which
runs as follows:- *The true speed of a river is one third of that given by a
yachtsman in his memoirs or a yachting magazine, and one quarter of the figure
stated by the same yachtsman in the members' bar.* I had read several accounts
of the terrors of the Rhone including one by a well-known boating man
who was swept through Avignon at such a speed that he could not even
pause there to visit the papal palace. Later I developed the habit of flinging
a stick into a river and walking along the bank abreast of it, which is a
simple and reassuring way of discovering that the flow is much slower
than it appears, but in the case of the Rhone in Lyon it would have been
difficult.

So I betook myself to the office of the Ponts et Chaussées along the
river bank and asked in a vague way whether it was in order for the
Commodore to descend the Rhone. The engineer said maybe, but first he
must consult the Échelle de Chasse, and he would telephone immediately.
So saying, he left the room, and I patiently waited. I wondered who this
person could be. Edward Lear's lines about the Akond of Swat came to
my mind. Perhaps the Échelle de Chasse was a similar mysterious being,
ruling over her own equally obscure territory. For the name sounded
feminine. I began to wonder.

Is she roundish and heavy, tallish and thin?
Is her preference whisky, or vodka, or gin
                                    or Bass,
        The Échelle de Chasse?

Does she wear regalia only to dance?
Does she travel by SNCF or Air France,
                                    or SAS,
        The Échelle de Chasse?

Is her word always truthful or does she tell lies?
Is her husband a cityman, wealthy and wise,
                                    or an ass,
        The Échelle de Chasse?

At this moment the engineer returned. The Échelle, he said, thought it would be possible to descend the river. Only there was not much water and personally he would advise me to take a competent pilot because the river was strewn with rocks and other encumberances. He suggested I should enquire for Monsieur Pariset, a man of incomparable ability, and evidently the king pin of Rhone pilotage. Yes, I would be safe to come to an arrangement with Monsieur Pariset, who would be found in the Café de la Marine – a standard address, as I had discovered in the course of a dozen voyages in France, for any person having what the Admiralty Pilot Books described as 'local knowledge'.

I did not need to go to the pub. Monsieur Pariset arrived at our berth unsought, radiating bonhommie through a strong odour of garlic, Gauloises, and vin as rouge as his face. In fact, he had behind him a lifetime of piloting barges and yachts down the Rhone and he knew what he was about. And because there had been a drought and the Rhone was low in water and the level was still falling, it was imperative to leave on the following morning, he said. That is, if the Échelle de Chasse were agreeable. He would telephone the Échelle and report back to us. And with a grave shaking of his head and clicking of his tongue he rode away on his cycle to consult this supreme authority, or oracle, or whatever it might be.

Again I wondered as I waited for his return. Perhaps the Échelle was not a female but a male, a sort of aquatic échevin.

Does he fight with his neighbours with sabre or foil?
Is his mansion illumined with candles, or oil,
                                    or gas,
        The Échelle de Chasse?

Is he served by a butler, a footman and cook?
Does he cast a lascivious, covetous look
                      at a lass,
    The Échelle de Chasse?

I was well aware that the Reformation had not reached France, so he (or she) would almost certainly be a Roman Catholic, I thought.

Is his thinking religious, shallow or deep?
Does he peep through his fingers or nod off to sleep,
                      during mass,
    The...

At this moment Pariset reappeared at the quayside, breathing heavily from his exertions. He shook his head diagonally, neither positively nor negatively. There was no time to lose, he explained. The Échelle gave us permission, but only just, I gathered. And he or she or it might change its mind later. He would go and fetch a colleague and then we would set off immediately. Start the motor, prepare to cast off. Buy bread and any other supplies at once. He cycled away, returning shortly with a younger man who had such a pronounced squint that I asked to see his piloting certificate, which indeed he had.

The voyage proved so fascinating that I soon forgot all about the Échelle de Chasse and it was not until a few years later that I came across her. I was steering down the fast section of the river below Lyon and when we were some thirteen miles below the city and speeding down a section where the channel was near the left bank my wife pointed toward the shore.

"What is that?" she asked.

It was the Échelle, a tall, grey structure with its feet firmly in the water. A limnograph, in fact, an automatic recorder of the depth of the river at that point, from which, of course, the probabilities elsewhere could be oracularly predicted.

Back in 1962 there was a sense of crossing a line of no return when the lower gates of the old lock at La Mulatière opened and Pariset moved out, with ourselves and the second pilot following astern. Gone was the placid water of the regulated Saône. The Rhone rushed in, unbridled, chilly and steely grey, swirling and tumbling as it rocked us on its shrunken bosom toward the first of the three modern locks ninety miles ahead. From there the long, deep pounds above the locks at Le Logis Neuf, Chateauneuf, and St Pierre gave a welcome respite of a few hours before another stretch of bouncing river which carried on as far as Arles, where it seemed to become tired and gradually lose its pace.

I am sorry indeed that no boatman can ever again have that experience of the wildness of the Rhone. From the voyage astern of Pariset I soon realised that the trick was to keep on the roughest water (where the river was at its swiftest and deepest) and in the following years I ran the Rhone many times, using my own judgement and without difficulty. And each time there was less of the river left untamed. First came the great lock at Lyon itself, and then others further down river at a frequency of one in every two years until in the early eighties the Rhone was finally harnessed, a magnificent waterway with gigantic and handsome engineering works along its course, but very different from the breathtaking stream of earlier times, with its shoals and backwaters, and rough grey rocks projecting from the surface like so many seals.

We were lucky to leave Lyon when we did on that first trip. In the evening we approached a defile between two villages, and high on the rocky hillside behind the one to starboard three empty crosses stood out boldly. This of course was a calvary, but local legend preferred them to be erected in memory of three lovely and noble daughters of Andance, the village at their feet, who threw themselves into the Rhone in the despair of awaiting the return of their loves from a crusade. We drew in against an American yacht which was abandoned there, being too deep going to proceed any further up the river for lack of water, and when Pariset went ashore to consult the oracle of Chasse he found that behind us the navigation was now closed, the weirs as far up as Switzerland shut down. The last trickle of Alpine water was on its way down to us, and in the first light of morning we could see that a mark scratched on a stone by Pariset the evening before was now ten inches above the level of the water. As soon as the mist had lifted sufficiently we were off again, running for the safe deep head-water of the lock at Le Logis Neuf.

The next time I descended the Rhone the old lock at La Mulatière had been bypassed and lay disregarded at the side of a vast sheet of water, the great new inland port of Lyon into which the two rivers poured their unequal contributions to mix gradually so that after a few hundred yards the steely grey of the Alpine Rhone and the turgid brown of the Saône no longer had a sharp boundary between them but united in a colour nearer to that of the Rhone than of its tributary. Giant pusher units lay against piles and jetties, awaiting their turn at the efficient new covered loading bays, and none would very easily have recognised the new port as the site (in one corner) of the former entrance to the unbridled Rhone. In the basins of the Port Edouard Herriot the transporters from Marseille were unloading beneath sleek modern cranes, and the inland harbour stretched all the way to the splendid new lock of Pierre Bénite, three kilometres below the older pen. Whilst awaiting an upcoming tanker I went up to the tower of the structure and found a school class being given a demonstration with models and diagrams in the lecture room of the

Compagnie du Rhone.

The stream of the Rhone disappeared through a power station to the right of the new structure, and did not rejoin the navigation until ten kilometres or more ahead, when the deep cut of the lock outfall was united with it once again as it swept in, sucking and gurgling exuberantly a short way upstream of the Pierres de Ternay. Formerly these had been a dangerous collection of rocks which sometimes showed their smooth backs like so many dolphins, but now they were marked with a row of black-and-white striped poles. Romance was already disappearing in the face of determined engineering, but there was as yet no other lock before Logis Neuf, and Andance was just as I had known it seven years earlier except that there was more water in the river.

Andance was on what boatmen still called the *réiaume* and I heard this term for the right bank of the Rhone used as lately as 1985. It is a corruption of *royaume*, and in the same way the opposite shore is the *pèri* (*empire*, that is), a reminder that for centuries the Kingdom of France faced across the water boundary toward the Holy Roman Empire. And we had long since passed the first place of any size on the *pèri*, though it was not until a year or two later that I drew in at its quay on the sharp bend opposite the fourteenth century tower of Philippe de Valois.

That place was Vienne – a town rich in Roman remains and with a great theatre cut in the hillside of Mont Pipet. About half a mile downstream of the cathedral it was possible with luck to glance up across the autoroute and along a side road to have a fleeting view of a curious pyramid standing alone in a small square. Probably it was once surrounded by the Roman circus, but legend came to endow it with being the tomb of Pontius Pilate. There is probably no truth in this, even if it is certain that Pilate was recalled from Jerusalem for his bungling of local affairs and was semi-exiled, demoted to a civil service job in Vienne where, according to belief, he was so overcome with remorse (or perhaps a sense of failure) that he flung himself into the Rhone and was drowned.

The gradual taming of the Rhone has meant that levels have changed, and below Andance the Rocher du Roi is nowadays just awash but marked with a tall red-and-white pole. This large and flat mass of stone was once the subject of a quarrel, for being more or less in mid-stream – though definitely on the *pèri* side of the centre – it was claimed by the riparian owners on either bank. Not that it was of much use, but then landowners are not always concerned about the usefulness or otherwise of their property. However, one of the claimants heard that King Louis IX was to come down the Rhone valley on his way to launch a crusade, so he quickly and respectfully invited the monarch to a reception and dinner. The water being at that time sufficiently low, the whole event was arranged to take place on the rock, which thereafter was endowed with its royal name.

Louis was charmed with the unusual event and he asked how he might give adequate thanks for the hospitality of the evening. The resourceful host had the answer ready in the form of a royal certificate of ownership of the rock. It only needed the monarch to be good enough to sign on the dotted line, he pointed out. This Louis obligingly did, evidently not noticing that he was bequeathing a piece of imperial territory which was not within his jurisdiction at all. But the paper was signed and sealed, and the Holy Roman Emperor Frederick II probably had more important matters to occupy his attention than to dispute the rights and wrongs of the ownership of a rock usually under water.

One of the more attractive stops on the way down the Rhone is at La Roche Glun, at a small jetty now situated some thirty or forty feet above where *Commodore* swept past beneath the walls in 1962, for it is only a very short way above the huge modern weir. In spring the nightingales shout their love songs from the acacias beside the mooring, as though wishing to be heard right across the village where little remains of the castle of the Rogiers. The day after dining on the rock in midstream, King Louis made another halt, not for further entertainment but to teach the Rogiers a lesson. They were in the habit of waylaying merchants and pilgrims and robbing them, and that was something young Louis would not tolerate. He stopped, drove the Rogiers out, and razed their castle to the ground.

Although Valence and St Vallier are possible stops for the boatman and have approachable quaysides, they suffer too much from noise of autoroute or wash of passing ships. Tournon has a proper little harbour on the outside of the sharp bend opposite the famous vineyards of Tain-l'Hermitage, but it is hard of entry – and even more of exit – because of the way the river current is deflected through its piles. Yet it is a quiet and confident little town with a chateau perched on a rocky knoll, and at the end of the port a statue of Marc Seguin, who invented the tube boiler which made it possible for locomotives to get up steam efficiently. In fact he even wrote a book on the influence of railways. "In our own valleys and across our hills wind and spread long ribbons of iron along which rush, rapid as thought, those formidable machines which seem to eat up space with spontaneous impatience and which appear almost alive in their breathing and their movement." And that was as early as 1839. Later he constructed – as did many others – a wing-flapping flying machine or ornithopter which, like all the rest, never flew. He also tried his hand at a helicopter, but these failures are not mentioned on his statue, where he is rightly praised for inventing the suspension bridge, such as that close to the harbour, which connects his home town with the opposite shore across the powerful, swirling river.

La Voulte is another town of some charm with a chateau, and mooring is just possible against a severely sloping wall. Cruas also is moorable for anyone who has no objection to having the boat filled with the cement dust which covers the whole locality with a shroud of ghostly grey. But best of all is Viviers, a cathedral city tucked away unexpectedly in what is now a backwater below the lock of Chateauneuf but was formerly the main stream of the Rhone. Standing opposite the great limestone cliffs at the head of the Donzère gorge it is not large as cathedral cities go, being no more than two or three hundred yards across and having a mere three thousand inhabitants, most of whom appear to live in houses so rickety and run down that one cannot be sure whether or not they are ruins. Not that the people are slum-dwellers. A rotting door may creak open but there emerges a lady with neat coiffure, elegant clothes and shoes and bag, to go her way through streets too narrow for a car, to shop at the grocers or the bakery.

It was when climbing the hill outside Viviers to see the commemorative cross put up there by a Monsignor to illustrate the Knight of right and truthfulness (that is, the Allies) slaying a particularly nasty (German) dragon that I came upon a vintner tending his vines who told me about the attack upon Pont St Esprit, a town now bypassed by the redrawn river but having a most strategic bridge built in the thirteenth century by the Brothers Pontiff and nearly a kilometre in length. During the advance of the French forces up the Rhone valley it was judged essential to put out of commission this ancient structure and also the suspension bridge at Viviers, in order to impede the German retreat, and the attack on Pont St Esprit was entrusted he said, to the USAAF, that upon Viviers to the RAF. So inefficient were the Americans, he alleged, that they knocked down half the town and killed scores of local people. But the RAF – well, never could one find such brilliant exactitude of aim. Bang, boom, poof, and the bridge was gone, and the only loss to anyone in Viviers was that one old gaffer in the pub jumped so violently at the sound of the bombs that he broke his denture. I could not help noticing that he told me this ingenious tale after first enquiring whether or not I was English. Maybe if I had been American the story would have been changed to one split denture in Pont St Esprit and doom and desolation in Viviers.

One evening my wife and I walked up the avenue from the port and climbed up the alleyways and steps to the plateau at the top of the village, where stood the remains of the castle and the quiet but sombre bulk of the cathedral of St Vincent. Apart from the swallows and martins the place seemed silent and deserted, but when we tiptoed in through the door and came into the dimness of the vaulted nave we found ourselves in the presence of something which moved us greatly. By the light of two candles on the altar an elderly priest was conducting the vespers. There was no congregation, not another single body or soul, but the fine old man perse-

vered, his face shining with devotion as he held up the chalice toward his
father in heaven. Viviers was presumably watching the TV or shopping,
or cooking supper perhaps, but he was there as the sole representative of
the faithful, a latter day Elijah. "I, only I am left."

The priest did not turn round at the creak of the hinge of the heavy
door, but carried on with his celebration, oblivious perhaps of everything
earthly. Then he knelt in prayer, and we could only do the same before
quietly leaving him in the decaying cathedral that was his life.

The two mile gorge of Donzère ends as abruptly and magnificently as
it begins, the navigation cutting away to bypass Bourg St Andéol and
Pont St Esprit with nearly twenty miles of long and rather dull cut spanned
by the hydro-electric works of La Bollène which are passed by Europe's
deepest lock, the Écluse de St Pierre with its maximum drop of more than
eighty five feet. This is an experience in itself, and fortunately one can sit
back and enjoy the descent into the cool and clammy depths because there
is no need to tend the lines, no risk of being left hung up at a terrifying
height above the quickly descending water. The bollards move up or down
with the ship, as they are mounted on tanks sliding in vertical slots, and
it was here that this system was first ingeniously developed.

St Pierre is not the easiest of moorings, but above the lock one can
penetrate behind the stagings and go ashore without risk that the boat will
be pulled and pushed by the outfall of the power station beyond it. It is
possible to walk a short way along the service road away from the lock,
to where a culvert with a narrow path alongside a stream leads under the
motorway to the village, which in itself is not in any way interesting
although it has a pleasant little restaurant where one can eat under the
trees on a summer's eve. But the road leads to a lane which winds up to
the village of Barry, a walk of about an hour and a half. This extraordinary
village is completely deserted, and consists of houses and chapels cut out
of the soft limestone, the stone removed being then sometimes tailored
and re-erected to form the front of the building. The houses date from
Gallo-Roman up to late medieval times, and on the summit of the hill are
the ruins of a castle strong-point with a view across to the sometimes
snow-clad Mont Ventoux, and in clear weather all the way to the Savoy
Alps. But who were these people who lived up in Barry under such peculiar
circumstances? All I could get by way of answer in the village of St Pierre
was that they were troglodytes, cave-dwellers, and that was already obvious.

St Pierre was for many years the last lock on the way down the Rhone,
and it was so when the *Commodore* went down river with Pariset. It led
out into a long, deep and featureless cut to where at the foot of the castle
at Mornas the Rhone came sweeping in again, fresh from its course through
the medieval arches of Pont St Esprit. Before long we were at the passage
of Revestidou, which then was the fastest section of all the Rhone except

for the gap at the ancient Pont d'Avignon.

To gallop down the narrow, turbulent mile or two of the Revestidou was pleasant enough. To the side the hills of Provence shone white, dry and very Mediterranean, with the little village of vintners and sparse remains of the papal castle of Chateauneuf-du-Pape spread along the slope and facing across to Roquemaure and the tower of the castle of Hers. There was no risk of running down approaching craft for the channel was reckoned to be too narrow for two-way traffic and was controlled by traffic lights operated from the port of l'Ardoise at the upper end. Several years later I was returning upstream from Avignon aboard *Thames Commodore* when I came to the light at the lower end, which was set at red. A notice warned that mariners were under all circumstances to obey the signals, so we had no choice but to stop and wait, but this was easier said than done in a current so swift and where the bottom of smooth cobbles provided no holding ground for an anchor. So I moved cautiously toward the shore to starboard where a tree was leaning far out over the water and threw a couple of lines over it, made fast and went below for supper. We would be safe there if need be until morning.

Dark had just fallen, supper was at a comfortable end and I was considering turning in when unexpectedly the signal lights were turned from red to green. Not particularly pleased, I started the engines, loosed the lines and plunged with full power into the noisy swishing and sucking and swirling of the Revestidou. I could dimly see from the passing trees that we were making headway, but it was not more than one knot against the stream. That did not surprise me. More remarkable was the fact that when, eventually, we arrived off l'Ardoise and I drifted her in to the quay there was something like a reception committee of Rhone-ship skippers drawn up on the quayside as though expecting royalty. The explanation was soon made clear. Everyone (except me) knew that the Revestidou was never navigated in the dark. Such an undertaking was far too dangerous. Never in human memory had such a thing been done but here, ma foi, was a boat which had done that very thing! An anglais, of course. One of the race of formidable, mad, persistent inhabitants from beyond-the-Channel. Magnificent! Extraordinary! And so forth. It seemed that our arrival by night was the greatest event that l'Ardoise had experienced since 219 BC when Hannibal crossed the river there with forty astonished elephants ferried across on rafts supported by inflated skins – a much more hazardous undertaking than ours.

The songs of praise and gasps of amazement were interrupted by the advent of a man in an official cap. He turned out to be the signal operator, hastily summoned from his vin rouge in some nearby Café de la Marine. He was as surprised as the rest at the news that a ship had come up in the dark and he asked me in a not unfriendly way why I had done so.

"But the notice said the signals were to be obeyed under all circumstances," I explained. "Did you not turn the light to green?"

Yes, yes, yes, yes, he had done so, he agreed. "But that was for tomorrow!"

The Revestidou exists no more. Its kinked and narrow section of river has been cut off, short-circuited with a bow-string of broad and straighter cut, and the signal lights have, of course, also gone. Added to that, the new lock at Caderousse has taken the pace off the river, and none could imagine that not so many years ago this was a difficult stretch for shipping, and not without its dangers, but giving a tremendous sense of exhilaration when one galloped downstream over its swirls and whirlpools at a speed which at the same time seemed almost frightening. It sounds like one of those yachtsmen's tales told while propping up the club bar, but I remember travelling swiftly round the bend at Condrieu, now bypassed, with one engine full speed ahead and the other hard astern to keep the ship straight.

Chateauneuf-du-Pape is only a few miles upstream of the Avignon of the popes, a city which in its papal days had a port or quay just as it has today, with the curious exception that the port was not below the walls of the city at all but on what now is the navigation branch of the river, on the further side of the Ile de la Barthelasse which splits the great stream into two. That position was not very convenient for the merchants of the city, so in course of time they removed it to their own side of the river, more or less where the long quayside is now. And there it became a victim of Coriolis.

The Coriolis effect is due to the rotation of the earth. Any movement tends to go ahead in a straight line, but as the meridians of longitude are turning away from west to east as the earth spins, so a moving object in the northern hemisphere will tend to swing right-handed relative to the surface of the earth, and in the case of a motion due north or south this effect will be at a maximum. If that sounds too complicated, it can be forgotten, but as the Rhone flows south, the result is that the river tends to flow down the right-hand of the two branches, scouring it out and leaving the left-hand branch to become more and more silted. As the shoals forming in the Avignon branch threatened to close it completely, the river was forced over again to that side by building a sill of rocks at the top of Ile de la Barthelasse, high enough to send most of the water round by the city, and it was only in the 1970's that navigation was returned again to the Villeneuve branch with the construction of the lock.

In 1962 we did not draw in at Avignon, but I did so on many other occasions. On one of these, before the Villeneuve lock was built, we had company down the Rhone of three other yachts, two of them travelling at modest speed and trailing us as a free pilot, the other a smart and overpowered craft from Duisburg owned and operated by just such a man as one would expect to own a smart and overpowered yacht from Duisburg. Each time we passed through a lock he would forge ahead at great speed leaving the other craft far behind him, and then he would chafe and fret at the next lock because he was obliged to wait for us. He was in a hurry to reach the Mediterranean, so much so that he was not inclined to waste time in studying the state of the water ahead. So, as we came round the upper tip of the Ile de la Barthelasse we found the German speed-yacht high and decidedly dry on the long shoal at the approach to the city. I had no particular animosity toward the man either as a German or because he was so foolish and careless so I drew over as near to the shoal as was prudent, turned, and stemmed the current.

Various attempts to throw us a line were of no effect, if only because the lines of the yacht were, as usual too short, and in the end the owner's son, a tarzan-chested individual of about nineteen, came on deck clad in bathing trunks and the announcement was called to us that he would swim over with the end of a succession of lines tied together. To this I immediately replied with the loud hailer that if the strapping young ass jumped in I would leave them there, as I had no wish to be delayed by having to attend an inquest. Eventually I cast a heaving-line over their craft, told them to haul a light line across from us, then two very stout ropes. When all was ready I whipped up all our fourteen score of Perkins horses and dragged the yacht right over the bank. Then I pulled in the lines and left them to proceed at a more sensible pace.

Half a mile ahead we could swing round to slide in against the long quay wall of Avignon, and soon the Duisburgers came sailing past, still travelling rather fast. They passed within twenty yards of us. Did I expect them to draw in and present us with a bottle of sekt? Or even a can of Dortmunder Union? Or just a pleasant nod and a dankeschön? If I did, I was disappointed, though perhaps not altogether surprised when without so much as a wave of a little finger they aimed past us and on toward the Mediterranean marinas where sheep might safely graze – and would certainly be fleeced.

Avignon, with its mighty ring of crenellated walls pierced by fortified gates, is such an astonishing city of treasures that Monsieur Michelin devotes seven and a half pages to it in the green guide "Provence", and for any boatman wishing to explore it from end to end there could be no better companion. Whenever I have called at the city I have made my way up the long cobbled incline past the astonishing and somewhat grim palace fortress of the popes (who resided in the city for 70 years from the time of John XXII in 1309 until the Swedish firebrand and visionary St Birgitta persuaded Gregory XI to return to Rome), up and up to the summit of the Rocher des Doms, the immense and sheer bluff of limestone dominating the port and the bridge below. There is an ingenious sundial there invented by a monk. Walk up the central line until standing on the right date, and one's shadow points to the correct time. This is a reasonable kind of sundial too, for in Avignon the sun is usually shining.

At one corner of the rock is a cosy little nook for lovers, from which one can look down directly upon the famous bridge of which plenty still survives. The original structure was brilliantly designed with strong but- tresses to protect it from floods and ice, but unfortunately the bridge-build- ing Brothers Pontiff (who were probably responsible for the structure) left the maintenance to the civil authorities, who did little more than replace arches one at a time when they happened to collapse. Much of the repair work was done in wood and altogether the state of the crossing became so poor that as early as 1226 it was too weak for the tramp of the forces of the king of France and several arches collapsed into the Rhone with a loss of life estimated – perhaps with chronicler's licence – at 3,000 men. Again repairs were made, and throughout the centuries that the bridge was in use the ravages of fire, battle, sapping, ice, storm and flood were continually but not very effectively made good. The Sade family poured money into repairs, and Pope Clement VI reconstructed the four great arches which still survive to this day, but by 1679 the decay was proceeding faster than the maintenance and the bridge had finally to be abandoned, except as an occasional setting for dancing, as the once popular song reminds us.

The legend of the building of the Rhone bridge, probably the most astonishing engineering feat of 12th century Europe, relates that in 1177 there lived near Viviers a woman who sent her twelve year old boy to watch her sheep. Bénézet was engaged in this humble pastoral activity when one day he heard a voice calling him three times from heaven. Samuel-like – for the tale of Eli as well as the boyhood of Moses may surely have left their mark upon the account – young Ben answered and was astounded to hear the voice announce that the speaker was none other than Jesus Christ himself and that he had an important piece of work for Bénézet to undertake.

'I want you to leave the sheep you are looking after, because you are to make for me a bridge over the river Rhone,' the voice said.

Bénézet protested that he could not leave the sheep, he knew nothing of the Rhone, he had only three farthings, he was the last individual to be capable of such construction work. But the voice insisted that he was to do as he was told, so the lad made his way to Avignon, where he found the bishop preaching a sermon. Obedient to his charge, he interrupted the discourse and boldly announced to prelate and people that he had come on the special order of Christ to build a bridge.

The bishop was not accustomed to having his sermons so rudely inter-

Top: On the Saône
Bottom: A Rhone tanker; the deckhand is sounding the depth

Top: Canal d'Arles à Bouc, van Gogh's bridge
Bottom: Martigues, the Mirroir des Oiseaux

rupted, and he had the lad seized and conducted to the provost of the city with the suggestion that he be flayed alive or have his hands and feet cut off – or perhaps both. Ben obstinately repeated his tale and explained that he had only come to build the bridge over the Rhone which was so much needed, but the law officer was unwilling to take him seriously. How, he asked, could such a simple, common villain, a penniless good-for-nothing hope to bridge the Rhone where not even the great Charlemagne himself had been able to succeed? And sarcastically he added that he happened to have a stone at his residence; if Bénézet could carry it down to the river then he would perhaps believe the lad capable of building a bridge after all. The stone in question was part of a Roman column, and according to local accounts it measured more than four metres by two and needed thirty men to lift it.

Taken to where the stone lay, Bénézet braced himself, lifted the stone and carried it to the river bank, to set it where the first arch was to be built. Amid the tumult of astonishment the provost flung himself on the ground before Bénézet, and promptly made the first contribution of three hundred sous to the bridge fund. The authorities and people alike took up the cause of the bridge with enthusiasm, working so energetically under the guidance of the shepherd lad that within only eleven years the bridge of nineteen great arches was complete. As for Bénézet, he was never to see the great work brought to completion, for, in 1184, he died at the age of only nineteen. A chapel to hold his remains was built above the fourth arch, and it naturally became a place of considerable pilgrimage. Within it Bénézet remained buried for nearly five centuries, until the arch beneath the chapel was so seriously threatened by ice floes that his remains were removed.

That the bridge was begun in 1177 and finished within eleven years is undoubted, and curiously enough the story of Bénézet, his vision and his arrival at Avignon to set about building the bridge is not an invention of later romantic ages. It is recounted in detail by no less than six chroniclers who were either alive at the time or within a decade or two, and the origin of the bridge was even the subject of a law suit between a French King and one of the Popes. And the story was always considered remarkable, if not incredible. In the year 1230, forty-two years after the completion of the bridge, an investigation took place into the origin of this extraordinary tale, and fifteen witnesses who were alive at the time the bridge was built were questioned closely. Every one of them either confirmed part of the story, or deposed how they had seen miracles of one sort or another at the tomb of Bénézet, most of them healings. Enough crutches were left there to provide two or three donkey-loads, some of them said.

Of course, we live in a sceptical age and modern historians brought up in a much more materialistic way have sought to explain the whole story as an allegory. Bénézet was not a shepherd but a pastor, chief of the Brothers Pontiff. The sheep he abandoned were the faithful, when he left the fraternity to become a constructional engineer. The great stone represents the obstacles which previous bridge builders had not been able to overcome. And so on. Maybe, but it is not necessary to debunk the beautiful merely for the sake of mundane plausibility. Nor do I think there is any evidence that contemporary chroniclers and witnesses wrote or spoke in riddles. When they said shepherd I suspect they meant a person minding sheep, and by a large stone they meant a large stone. Anyway, I like the story of Bénézet and I always shall, and whatever the truth behind that tale the bridge, originally more than half a mile in length, is in itself a sufficient wonder for me to sit on the bench in the lovers' bower and ponder the amazing enterprise of the men who could construct it eight centuries ago in the middle of such a fiercely swirling and majestic river as the Rhone.

Avignon is now in a backwater. Years ago, I sat in the lovers' bower on the Rocher des Doms and watched a canal péniche, a 38.5 metre craft, coming up the river. Bénézet's bridge is nowadays only half there, but the part of the river under its arches is shoaled and blocked so that the whole force and volume of the Rhone used until recently to race through the remaining gap. This was the fastest section on the whole river, and even if it were only a cable or so in length it demanded power, and skill too. The barge came steaming upstream, reached the gap, and was unable to push through against the current. The skipper floated her back a hundred yards or so and tried again. Once more he reached the gap, and opposite St Bénézet's chapel he again found his ship stationary. The next time he took a real run at it, backing off for a quarter of a mile and roaring up the river near the opposite bank, taking advantage of the slack water below the arches and developing such a momentum of mass times velocity that when he sidled his craft a little to port to miss the last of the bridge pillars it carried him through the narrows to the slower water above. *Thames Commodore* had the edge of a couple of knots on all but the sleek Rhone barges specially designed for the river, so she was able to visit Avignon even before the current was taken to the other side of the island.

Approaching Villeneuve lock from upstream one sees a striped wind-sock possibly hanging but more probably streaming from a mast. In this latter case it may be difficult to void crashing into the wall, and the fact that some of the huge dolphins have been knocked over is a hint that the big ships may have their difficulties too. The dolphins are not aquatic mammals, but *Dalben* as the Germans say; or – such is the linguistic confusion – *Ducs d'Albe* to the French. (Somebody who was translating a French nautical work once asked me in the greatest perplexity why so many Dukes of Alva apparently had their tombs in the harbour.) This sudden headlong rush toward the wall is caused by waves driven up from astern, and what drives them up is the mistral, a wind quite different from anything to be experienced in northern Europe because it is a wind that blows out of a clear sky and blows without passing for breath. The wind-sock is for the benefit of those who have not noticed the gale.

Parliament, the mistral and Durance are the three scourges of Provence, so runs the old saying. Parliament has vanished, the capricious river Durance which flows into the Rhone just below Avignon has had its floods contained by modern engineering and is now an agent of good rather than evil, but the mistral remains as the sole surviving scourge. And no human agency can do anything about it. In northern lands gales are usually of short duration and are always involved with bad weather, so it is a surprise to come into an area of howling and sometimes freezing wind without a cloud in the sky and with the sun shining so strongly that out of the wind one can bask in brilliance and warmth. The wind was already remarked upon by Strabo in the earliest years of the first century when he wrote that the whole plain around Arles was swept by a very cold wind which would whip up the gravel, fling men from their mounts and strip them of their weapons and clothing. He called it the 'black northerly' whereas the people of Provence call it the mistral – which means the magistral or master wind.

And a master wind it certainly is. Strabo did not exaggerate, and the mistral can make things difficult for an inland boatman and positively dangerous for those sailing on the Mediterranean under the lure of travel posters showing a calm, unruffled sea. The first time I met the mistral was in Sète, when I was walking down a street and an electric sign of some size was torn off the roof of a building and dropped on the pavement behind me. The second occasion was on a freighter trying to berth in a Marseille basin. The wind obstructed the captain's efforts so completely that he had to call a naval tug to the rescue. The mistral is a wind which commands respect, and caution too.

It is not just a breeze; in 1845 the mistral blew the Rhone bridge at Tarascon into the river. It has destroyed whole crops, it often uproots grown trees and has occasionally halted trains on their tracks. Lorries may be overturned, and if one wonders why so many houses in Provence have large rocks sitting on their tiles, it is to prevent the mistral carrying the whole roof away.

The areas where the mistral blows most violently are on Mont Ventoux, east of La Bollène, where speeds of more than one hundred knots have been registered, and across the desert-like plain of the Crau south-east of Arles, which is a desert for that reason. The wind is brought to life when the hot sun of the south strikes upon the low-lying salty and sandy regions of the Rhone delta and the air close to the ground becomes super-heated, and then expands and rises quickly. Something has to rush in to fill the partial vacuum, and that something is the heavy, cold air lying over the Alps, the Massif Central and the Cevennes. Sliding down the slopes into the Rhone valley and the lowland areas toward the coast this cooler air gathers speed and reaches its maximum force between Avignon and the coast, to turn along the shore and die out over the sea as it fills up the gap in pressure. It can blow furiously as far as Toulon and even reach Cannes and Nice and Corsica on occasion.

I have heard local people say that the mistral blows for three hours, three days or three weeks – though not, I am happy to say, for three months. There is no truth whatsoever in this beyond the fact that the mistral sometimes blows for longer than it does at other times. Usually in the summer months it is a matter of a few days, and its breath will then be stopped by high pressure in the south, or low pressure further north, or both. There may be stretches of mistral-free weeks in the summer, and the times of its most frequent occurrence and greatest strength are when the temperature *difference* between the mountain summits and the coastal area is at a maximum – that is, in the winter and spring.

Avignon's history has been turbulent indeed. Sacked by barbarians, attacked by Clovis, occupied by the saracens, besieged by Charles Martel, fought over by the counts of Toulouse and Provence, it eventually set out on the brave course of being a republic and fortified itself accordingly. Unfortunately it was ready to support the Albigensians, whom we shall meet later, and this gave Louis VIII a pretext to attack it under the guise of a holy war on behalf of the Pope Innocent III. After a terrible siege the walls and most of the houses were torn down, the knights of the northern lands pillaged everything they could lay their hands on, the defenders were slaughtered, and King Louis showed his pious horror of a successful conquest by processing through the corpse-strewn streets, bareheaded and dressed in grey sackcloth. Thus originated the Brotherhood of the Grey Penitents. The same king also had the mighty fort of St André raised on French soil at Villeneuve on the further side of the river, just to make sure that the Republic should never forget that to have truck with heretics was imprudent.

Oddly enough, Villeneuve is so hidden by high banks that from the river one has no idea it is there, and a friend of mine lived for a year on a barge beside the Ile de la Barthelasse without any notion that one of the most spectacular of medieval fortresses was with within half a mile of him. But from the Rocher des Doms the view of it is splendid and one can at once understand that it is a favourite backdrop for films or television programmes about the middle ages. One expects a sortie of knights in armour at any moment. Villeneuve itself began as a sort of overflow for papal dignitaries and one after another the cardinals had built for them the handsome little mansions which spill down the hillside into the main street. From there it was a convenient ride across the bridge so obligingly built by Bénézet to reach the more congested area around the papal palace.

As to how the city of Avignon came to belong to the Popes, that is an intriguing story. The French King gave half the territory of the republic to the papacy but kept half of the actual city for himself. The other half (one quarter of the whole, that is) belonged to the king of Naples, who happened to be the Count of Provence. As each piece was passed on from hand to hand in succeeding generations, the time came when both quarters were in the possession of a brilliant young woman, Jeanne of Naples, Queen of the Two Sicilies. Clever, artistic, learned, passionate and beautiful, she was married off early to a Hungarian prince, but quickly getting tired of her husband she persuaded her lover, Louis de Tarente, to murder him. However, to marry the man of her choice presented difficulties. It was necessary to achieve a declaration of innocence and at the same time to thwart her dead husband's brother, the King of Hungary and Poland, who had designs to revenge himself by seizing Naples, and who further demanded that Jeanne should be tried publicly for the murder.

But Jeanne was astute. The papal court was at Avignon, and thither she came in splendour to be received by the enthusiastic cheers of the crowd, her lawful subjects. They loved pageantry, and she gave it to them. Although she was still only twenty, she knew what she was about and so magnificent was her cavalcade that no less than eight cardinals were dispatched to receive her outside the city and lead her through the streets under a baldaquin of cloth of gold embroidered with jewels. They swiftly succumbed to her charm and beauty, and when she appeared in all her elegance before the Pope and presented her own defence in a four hour speech in Latin, who can say that the heart of Clement VI may not have beaten a little faster at the sight of one so beautiful, so able and exhaling all the best of feminine charm? Even if officially the church was still scared of women – had not Adam and Solomon and David all been ruined by female seduction? – Jeanne was irresistible and the pope gave her everything she wanted. The murder went unmentioned.

In return, and knowing that the Pope was anxious always to enlarge his possessions, she sold him Avignon for a mere 80 thousand florins – accompanied by a properly attested absolution and an instruction to the king of Hungary to go home with expenses paid and leave Naples alone. So Avignon became papal, in 1348, and Jeanne was free to marry Louis de Tarente. But the money was of course never paid.

The popes had resided at Avignon for nearly 40 years before they acquired the ownership from Jeanne of Naples. They were, as Petrarch pointed out, 'loaded with gold and clothed in purple'. Clement VI, who was responsible for much of the fine building still to be seen, used more than a thousand ermine skins for his personal wardrobe. So much money was acquired by selling benefices that the city contained 43 branches of Italian banking houses. It was a good time to be a pope, but in 1415 the last of the Avignon popes (by that time mere 'antipopes' in competiton with Rome) was deposed by the Council of Constance. It is interesting that every one of the Avignon popes was not only French but an Occitan (Languedocian), and that they gave asylum in their territories to Jews – though this magnanimity was certainly not without its commercial advantages.

Petrarch was no admirer of the popes. Just because they had a scrap of purple on their shoulders they despised the rest of the human race, he wrote. They covered themselves with gold like Asiatic despots and received none except those who payed for the privilege. Overdrinking, lavish living, 'infamous' pleasures, maintaining suppliers who beat the country for pretty girls and carried them off to the palace, those were just some of the faults he attributed to them, and he told how one of the cardinals put on his purple robes before raping a young girl. There is no doubt that some of them indulged in these activities. The beautiful Countess of Turenne and the equally lovely Countess of Périgord were very familiar with the papal bed and chamber of Clement VI, but the same pope did much to protect Jews and also moderated the worst features of the Inquisition.

The mention of Petrarch inevitably brings to mind the fair Laura de Noves, the lovely girl whom he is said first to have seen at church in Avignon on 6th April 1327. She was then seventeen and legend says that he never spoke to her but worshipped her in secret, pouring out his heart in poetry inspired by her. She is believed to have been married to a member of the Sade family when only twelve, and eventually to have had twelve children. Petrarch roamed over Europe but when he returned to Avignon he continued to pour out sonnets to Laura, and after her death he loved and worshipped her memory and wrote as before with Laura as his sole inspiration.

Less romantic historians say Laura was born, lived and died in Vaucluse, where at the age of eighteen she was discovered by the poet. He was twelve years older and walking up through the woods towards the source of the Sorgue he was suddenly confronted by this fair and beautiful creature. He told her of his love, but never married her. Instead, they wandered through the woods, lost in poetry and thought and carried away by a love which was idealised and purely spiritual.

Did I say less romantic? Perhaps nothing could be finer, more romantic than all-consuming love such as that. But whatever the truth of the matter the locality where Petrarch lived and wrote under her inspiration is no dull building devoid of interest but the quite extraordinary village of Fontaine de Vaucluse, a bus-ride eastward from Avignon up the valley of the Sorgue, a stream which once worked silk mills, oil crushers and other curious pieces of machinery which still lie scattered along its lower course.

The time to see Fontaine de Vaucluse is in the early spring, before the crowds arrive and the stalls of toffee apples and tourist junk are opened up, and when the Fontaine is a truly mighty fountain. Rain falling upon the limestone plateau of Vaucluse and on Mont Ventoux percolates through the porous stone to form underground the River Sorgue which here bursts out into the open, issuing from a natural siphon of great depth at the foot of a sheer and overhanging cliff-face a thousand feet in height. After periods of heavy rain the stream forms a mighty torrent which bounds over the boulders in sheets of spray, but in midsummer there may be no water whatsoever at this point. In spite of its banalisation and the necessary swamping of the village by car parks, one can still feel the magic of such an extraordinary place and understand as one sits over a glass of *pression* that to walk with a girl of outstanding comeliness in a woodland of such loveliness beside a stream of so emerald a clarity roaring exuberantly from a cavern of such unfathomable mystery might even now cause the heart of a poet to leap and transcend new heights of sonnetry. Petrarch was too carried away by emotion to pause to estimate the flow, which a few weeks after heavy rains can reach one hundred and fifty cubic metres *per second*. And that is a very mighty flow indeed.

III

St Ronan's Abbey – René the troubadour – child marriages –
better than burning – the *"droit du seigneur"* – the terrible
Tarasque – the Alyscamps – beauties of Arles – waterways to
the sea.

M y reason for not stopping at Avignon on the voyage down river with
Pariset was a purely economic one, with which anyone will be familiar
who has ever taken a pilot. Such men are often paid by the hour, and so
the slightest dalliance became as expensive as to walk round a city while
leaving a taxi with the meter ticking. In fact, we had agreed a price for
the trip with Pariset and it was not expensive, so decency prevented our
keeping him an extra day on the way while we explored the papal city.
We sailed past, heading for the end of his run with us at Beaucaire, where
the Canal du Rhone à Sète leaves the river. At least it did in those days,
but the building of the Rhone lock just upstream of the canal entrance a
year or two later meant that the river level was dropped and the entrance
lock to the canal was left high and dry. To reach Beaucaire quay a couple
of hundred yards distant nowadays involves, as we shall see, a voyage of
forty miles to reach the town basin on the other side of the unworkable lock.

From Avignon to Beaucaire the Rhone is now a splendid lake curving
through a dry countryside of thorns and scrubby pines and box bushes,
with whitish hills to either side stretching away toward the Luberon (port
side) and Cevennes (starboard). The little River Gardon, fresh from its
passage under the Pont du Gard, has now been transmuted into the weir
stream of the Rhone lock, and above it is a curious little box-clad hill on
which some ruins of walls can be made out. These are all that remains of
the abbey of St Ronan, which can be reached from Beaucaire. The site
has been cleared and excavated in recent years by the Historical Society
of Beaucaire and once again it proves to be a place inhabited by troglodytes,
and the whole church together with the small cells for the monks and the
more ample domestic offices have been hewn out of the limestone. The
pillars of the nave have become eroded by the wind into curious shapes,but
the abbot's chair or throne and the smaller one beside it for the prior are
beautifully preserved in situ and are in fact unique in France, carved as
they are out of the surrounding stone.

The second surprise is on top of the rock, for its flat summit is entirely
excavated into a cemetery, one hundred and forty-eight neat torso-shaped,

tailor-made tombs about a foot deep having been chiselled out of the rock. None of them can be dated for certain, for all were empty and uncovered when excavations began, largely because the abandoned abbey – said to date back to the 5th century – was in later turbulent times partly remodelled as a castle stronghold. The abbey is documented in the 11th century as belonging to that of Psalmodi near Aigues Mortes and the 'tomb of St Ronan' (who died in 463 but was in fact buried elsewhere) is said to have been in the nave of the subterranean church and to have contained two very prized relics in the form of part of the right hand of St Ronan himself, and part of the right foot of St Trophimus of Arles. Pilgrimages to the place persisted until the 17th century, and undoubtedly it was considered a fashionable place in which to be buried.

It is particularly annoying that the Rhone Company, which has undertaken such enormous works in order to harness the great river for hydroelectric power, should care not a fig for those who might like to pause at some of the towns strung along it. Beaucaire and Tarascon face each other and are linked by a pair of bridges, but each is hidden away behind a high flood bank and there is no quay, no staging, nothing other than a rockstrewn foreshore at either of them. Only the splendid castle at Tarascon rises square and mighty from its rocky foundation in the edge of the stream. The castle has had its fair share of horrors, and if reaching Beaucaire by the inland route one can walk across the bridge and pay to climb to the roof from which the associates of the infamous Robespierre were flung down into the river in 1794. More pleasant is the recollection of the troubadour King René of Anjou, who in the fifteenth century built up the castle to its present magnificence and vested it with much of its romance. And as the signal lights are set at red and we have to wait for an upcoming pusher, there is plenty of time to think of the Languedoc of those far off times.

The worthy René of Anjou was married at the age of twelve to a bride of ten. There was nothing unusual in that, at least among noble circles. The second daughter of Louis VII was only three years old when she was married to the Count of Blois. Marriages were entirely the matter of the parents on either side, who struck the bargain, announced and recorded it, then left the little darlings to grow up sometimes in their respective homes, but more often the girl was moved over to the castle of her future parents-in-law to prevent such a valuable prize being abducted. By the time the young people were teenagers they may well have been thoroughly tired of their little playmate, but when the girl was about fifteen or considered 'nubile' there was a big party and a procession of friends and relations marched through the bridegroom's premises up to the bridal chamber, where they saw the couple properly tucked up in bed. Under the circumstances one can imagine that a couple might be sick of the sight of

each other, and several cases are known of the man decamping for good
on the morning following.. (The girl could not decamp so easily; it was a
man's world in which she lived.)

But the lower orders did not marry, at least not in the high middle ages;
they merely mated and reproduced. A serf was bound to his master in an
oath of loyalty, and so if a man living in a simple cottage brought in a girl
from another estate, that was a matter of importance to the seigneur, and
it was the natural custom for the worker to seek the approval of his lord,
from whom he in turn regularly received his food, his livelihood and
protection. The seigneur then gave his blessing in appropriate cases by
entering the marriage room and placing his hand, or sometimes his foot,
on the marriage bed. This pleasant custom was known for precisely what
it was, a sign of approval, until after the French Revolution. Then it
became the custom to denigrate anything to do with the aristocracy, a
habit taken up gleefully by the socialist current in education in schools in
modern Britain. If schoolchildren today learn anything at all about the
French aristocracy it is sure to be about the "*droit du seigneur*", which was
the right of the lord to authorise a "marriage" by entering the bedroom
at the head, no doubt, of a modest procession of retainers and signifying
his approval. Under socialism it is of course taught that the "droit" meant
the right to have the first go at the bride, and that it was not a hand placed
on the bed but another part of his anatomy placed within it.

With medieval marriages being arranged between children and only
consummated years later, it is not likely that a bridegroom was passionately
or even mildly in love with his wife. That was beside the point. The young
couple were part of an arrangement made for very practical reasons, or to
consolidate the ownership of land, or (following St Paul) because the
bishop thought it better for a young man to marry than to "burn with
lust" – which is hardly likely to have been the case for a twelve year old.

It is easy to imagine (the lights are still at red on the lock signal) that
marriage was not very attractive. One shove into bed, a conception, and
finis – that was hardly a thing to commend itself to most young knights.
Nor indeed to their ladies. Had not Queen Eleanor, wife of Henry II,
been enthusiastic and free on the bedroom front?

So young men and women among the nobles grew up betrothed; that
is, married but not yet in the 'carnal' relationship the church decried. No
wonder they became romantic, 'burning', indeed the younger knights
had every reason to want to make love wherever they could before they
were chained down to an already contracted marriage. Adultery was only
a female sin; men could do pretty well what they liked. But the women
were enthusiastic too, in spite of the dangers.

It was love, real love, sensual and sexual and exciting that was sung by
the troubadours, and obviously it had nothing to do with marriage. These

often travelling minstrels and poets sang and dreamed of beauty, of valiant fights, of chivalry certainly, but above all of love, a real burning love of the kind Paul recommended one to flee from into marriage. Love was secret, dangerous. It drove men to great deeds of chivalry and women to take enormous risks for the sake of romantic love, for a wife whose fidelity or honour were suspect might be ejected, and even killed by a jealous husband.

It seems likely that the enormous flowering of romantic dreaming and poetry which eventually came with the troubadours was really a compensation. If you burned with desire for a woman but knew that sex was out, forbidden and perhaps even dirty or disreputable (the priests were often harping on the number of snaky and sexually scheming females in the Bible from Eve onwards) then you could lift the whole to an ideal plane and sublimate it into a state of a romantic adoration. How else explain a troubadour falling in love with a noble lady of Carcassonne whom he had never set eyes on, and his struggling thither all the way from Sicily to find her, and then expiring at her feet in mute but satisfied adoration?

So the chivalrous love sung by the troubadours accorded to certain rules, but cases arose which needed the competent advice of experts in romance. 'Courts of Love' were established, of which those held by René at Tarascon were among the most famous. To them, and to the brilliant and romantic individuals who formed the bench of judges, lovers brought their problems for adjudication and advice. And these judges were not men but women, who no doubt had personal experience of chivalrous loving and perhaps secret sexual adventures. The cases they advised upon involved matters of principle in which romantic love was supreme and marriage was relatively unimportant – one might describe the court as a Non-Marriage Guidance Council.

The good René of Anjou at whose castle of Tarascon such proceedings were often held, was a kindly man, well read and generous, a linguist and a mathematician, a poet and painter, a lover of good wine, a ruler simple and philosophical, a peaceable man in an era of violence, and above all, a troubadour himself. His subjects adored him – a thing rare enough in those days – and it was for their amusement and gaiety that he commissioned the construction of the first model of the fearful beast which gives its name to the town. And as the pusher is coming out of the lock and the lights are green for us, we can leave the troubadours until we meet them again at Carcassonne, and can run in, drop down, and steam out down the gently bouncing river to pass René's castle and keep our ears open for hideous and threatening bellowings.

Below the rock upon which is built the castle of René of Anjou there seems once to have been a hole, and in it lived a monster, a dangerous creature of the type of a Leviathan. It wrecked ships and ate the mariners, and generally held the land in a grip of terror.

A river such as the Rhone was certain to have monsters. At least they could be heard easily enough before the engineers of the Compagnie du Rhone regulated the course of the river. At Tarascon the fierce current swirling around the rock may well have produced sucking noises which could easily be assumed to emanate from the coarse throat of some strange beast, and if a ship were sometimes overset that would naturally be seen as the work of the same evil creature. The beast concerned was born in Galatia and had as its father the same Leviathan described in such intimate detail in Job xii, it was believed. When he began to grow up he left his parents and lumbered down to the coast to fling himself into the Mediterranean. The sea at once began to boil, which is perhaps not so surprising when we remember that his father was that Leviathan who, according to Job, could 'make the deep boil like a pot'. Swimming westward, the creature forged ahead until one morning he found the water actually pushing against him. Unknowingly, he had arrived off the Rhone delta, and the current of the great river seemed to challenge him. He turned into the river, beat furiously against the stream of cold and alpine water and swam vigorously against the current. By the time she had covered ten leagues she was rather enjoying it, and she decided that the land where she found herself might not be such a bad place for a monster to live after all.

The reader will have noticed that the creature has changed sex in the course of its ten leagues swim up the river. I cannot really explain this, but there is no doubt about it; in Galatia the beast was masculine, but on arrival at Tarascon it was *la* Tarasque, 'a dragon half beast and half fish, larger than a young bull and longer than a horse', as a medieval writer described her. Naturally, she proved a nuisance, killing everything within reach and wrecking the ships on the river.

Things would have gone badly for the people of the Rhone valley had they not been unexpectedly liberated from the ravages of the monster, which had already accounted for innumerable victims. The saviour of the local people was not St George but a woman. Legend relates that during the first persecution of the Christians in the Holy Land a boatload of refugees escaped to Provence. According to some, they were forced into a leaking boat without food, water or sail, and pushed out to await their fate, whilst others suggest they fled by sea of their own free will. The passengers vary somewhat, but generally included Mary Magdalene with her brother Lazarus and sister Martha, Mary the mother of James and John, Mary Salome, and two servants. The people of Provence are quite convinced that this is so, and that the boat reached their shores. I see no reason why they may not be right.

St Martha is remembered at Tarascon. The tenth century church where she is buried stands close to the end of the bridge, and even though it was rebuilt in the twelfth and heavily damaged by British and American bombardment of the bridge in the twentieth century, there is no reason to doubt that the lady who lies in a renaissance tomb of marble in the ancient crypt is indeed Martha of Bethany. Every year there is a pilgrimage on 29th July, the reputed day of her death.

The legend of Provence attributes to Martha herself the defeat of the monster. She was making her way up the valley of the Rhone when she came upon a crowd of people weeping and wailing. On her enquiry they told her about the Tarasque, and said that their high priests and magicians had failed to persuade it to depart, the warriors had blown their trumpets in vain and clashed their shields to no effect. Armed knights had courageously sought to fight the beast, and such as had returned were not anxious to try again. Meanwhile the Tarasque continued to sink the ships and ravage the countryside just as before.

'Weep no more', said Martha. 'Pray to the only God who can vanquish dragons.' And with cross in hand she followed the trail of bones (for the Tarasque was a messy eater) until she came upon the beast in a wood. It was still engaged in its horrid meal, with part of a young man hanging from its jaws we are told.

At her approach the beast reared, flapped its wings, cracked its tail, and uttered such a cry that the whole countryside shook. Martha held up the cross, and the Tarasque at once became so docile that she could put her girdle round its neck and lead it, meek as a kitten, into the town. There the people in their fury despatched the beast with lances and stones without its putting up any resistance.

And that might have been the end of the terrible monster which lived in the hole under the rock and roamed the forest in search of prey. But it was to be reborn, made of wood and cloth and with eight young men inside it to propel its fearsome body through the streets. That genial ruler René of Anjou first resuscitated the Tarasque in this way, and from time to time a new one was built – as in 1742, when there was some kind of riot during the annual procession and the poor Tarasque (without the young men) was thrown down a well. Naturally, the Revolution had to interfere with it, for socialism is the sworn enemy of romance or imagination, and the national guard was sent to hew the dragon to pieces and burn it in the street, so that the happy people of Tarascon might not have their attention diverted from the more urgent business of class hatred. Since then, the Tarasque has been again reincarnated, but for many years she no longer roamed the streets at Whitsun, knocking people down with great flicks of her powerful tail. Instead, she lived in a little house near the church of St Martha, and was tamely shown to visitors on request. Now she has returned to activity once more, and on the last Sunday of June she comes out of her lair as large as life, and brings back to Tarascon

something of the gaiety that it knew under René, Count of Provence and
Duke of Anjou, King of Sicily and Aragon, Hungary and Jerusalem.

Beaucaire's castle is tall enough to be visible over the floodbanks, but
we shall reach it later. Otherwise there is nothing to be seen from on board
but the dried or shallow entrance cut to the lock with its huge gates no
longer used but high enough to keep out even a major flood of the Rhone
and save the town from a watery fate. In 1962 I bathed in the clean Rhone
water which then circled into the cut, and nearby on the bank of the river
sat an individual who was fishing in the most ingenious way I have ever
seen – though now the changed level has ruined his chance of a catch. He
had set up a comfortable arm chair in which he reclined, sheltered from
the mistral by a wind-break of reeds. Beside the chair was a basket and
he had erected a yard or so out over the stream a water-wheel some eight
or ten feet in diameter, equipped with paddles of which the leading edges
were continued as scoops of netting. The wheel turned slowly in the
stream, and every now and again the man would stir sufficiently to throw
some ground bait into the water. Occasionally, a small fish of the kind
the French call *friture* would be scooped, carried up and tipped sideways
into a chute which delivered it still flapping into the basket. When at the
end of a somnolent afternoon the man had enough for supper, he rose,
put on the brake, lifted the basket and went home.

Half an hour downstream the Little Rhone (which we shall also later
follow) leads off to starboard. Already on the next bend the arched walls
of a huge Roman arena and the tower of St Trophime stand up above the
crowded clutter of pantile roofs. This is Arles, an impressive mixture of
ancient and modern, if one understands modern at Arles to be ancient by
the standards of many other places. And as though wishing to pay tribute
to this famous city the Rhone narrows and puts on a final burst of impressive
speed, swishing and swashing through the two bridges which link Arles
on the left bank with Trinquetaille on the right. Once again, there is not
much in the way of facilities for stopping in the river, but fortunately
there is the broad cut leading up to steps at the foot of the huge lock
leading in to the Canal d'Arles à Bouc. It is a corner into which all kinds
of unmentionable and odoriferous rubbish is driven, but the mooring is
a good one for those who are persistent enough to discover it.

In 1962 I decided to visit Arles after Pariset had left us at Beaucaire,
and with considerable and justifiable trepidation launched out into the
Rhone again to be swept down between the groynes and training walls,
eyots and shoals, until I could turn and steer into a narrow cut at the
further edge of the city. This channel has now disappeared under the
approaches to the bypass bridge but at that time it led to a small and
primitive lock through which we passed into the safety of a small canal
basin with a rough quayside. Twenty years later I had to seek for some

time before discovering a building which I could identify by a distance-plaque on the wall as having been the original lock-house and bureau de déclaration where I had duly declared myself as having arrived but going no further.

In 1962 they were busy marking out the fate of that canal entrance but a newer and larger one was already in existence further downstream, leading to a vast modern lock which could accommodate half a dozen Rhone ships at once, for although it only led in to a very narrow canal there were dreams of enlarging that cut into a proper Europa-ship-sized waterway for the Marseille shipping. It was only in 1984 that when lying at the foot of the lock, I noticed that the whole pen and its bullnoses were constructed of tooled masonry, and marble at that, and in places it appeared unfinished. This intrigued me so much that I sought out the lock-keeper, who was delighted to settle down for a chat because nothing ever passed his lock in these latter days, the further end of the canal having been filled in.

Why, I asked, had they just constructed this enormous lock and in masonry too. Were they about to enlarge the whole waterway regardless of expense? The lock was not new, he explained. Work on it had been stopped as long ago as 1916, if I remember correctly, and in those days of course labour was cheap. He opened his filing cabinet − and pulled out pictures of locomotives puffing smokily on a railway track which had been laid to facilitate the removal of the vast quantities of gravel and rock excavated by wheezing steam-shovels. The lock was actually brought into use, and he had photos of tugs and steamers and masses of long thin barges in the pen. Those parts of the bullnoses where the stone work was unfinished, as I had noticed, had remained like that for nearly seventy years. The Great War stopped the work, and after that the canal was used but for many years only by the old lock I had been through in 1962.

Once when we wanted to explore the country around Arles, we turned out of the main river and I selected a suitably firm sandbank along the shore of the bay leading up to the lock, dropped an anchor on the line astern to keep the ship aligned and ran the bow up on the bank so that I could put down a ladder for us to walk ashore. The situation was pleasant as such places go, though the refuse from the slaughter-house gave an unusual tinge to the surface of the still water.

We were sitting on deck in the evening sun and my wife was wearing one of those charming flower-ornamented hats such as one finds in every French street market. To our great surprise the mighty lock gates began to open and out came a small sailing yacht with the British flag. It must have been one of the last craft to use that canal, for they were already preparing to fill in the further end near Fos. At the same moment an aberrant flurry of mistral came round the corner and took the beautiful flowery hat with it, dropping it some way astern of us. I ran to lower the dinghy, but the Englishman shouted to me.

"No, no! Leave it to me. I'll fetch it."

The perfect English gentleman, I thought as he leaned over the edge of his boat and picked up the hat. He turned and began to steer towards us.

"Don't run over that anchor rope," I called.

"No. That's all right. I can see it. We don't draw much, you know," he called back.

"Go round the other way," I advised him. "Then you can come alongside."

But no, and a moment later the yacht was held fast with a few turns of rope round the propeller and a sufficiently heavy anchor to hold her there.

"Don't jump overboard in here," my wife advised him. "We can back out and tow you into cleaner water." Her years of hospital work had given her a distaste for the idea of bathing in a mixture of sewerage and surplus entrails.

"No, no, I wouldn't hear of it," the perfect gentleman replied, and although his wife backed up our suggestion he took off his shirt and jumped in. He expressed lengthy regrets that he would have to cut the line, so I threw him a bread-knife attached to a string. A bread-knife is much the best implement for cutting a tight rope, and when locking with those who were inclined to day-dream I always made it rule that everyone knew where the bread-knife was kept.

The good man sawed and pulled and tugged, submerging from time to time so that he vanished under the scum. At last, he had his propeller free and we had the hat and the anchor. We also had a shower available on board but the perfect gentleman declined it.

"I don't want to run you short of water," he said with a smile. And with that he started the engine, waved us a courteous goodbye, and set off into the Rhone.

The Canal d'Arles à Bouc was cut as part of the inland route to Marseille. The Rhone emerges into the sea about twenty miles further west and where it does so it loses speed and becomes extremely shallow. No ship drawing more than a foot or two of water can pass out of the river straight into the sea, and I myself have run aground on a sandbank when at least two miles off the coast and out at sea. The inland barge route left the Rhone at Arles and headed for Port de Bouc on the gulf of Fos, where it entered the ship canal (the Canal de Caronte) by which the big tankers reach the Étang de Berre, the huge salty lake with its refineries. There the route skirted the southern shore behind a stone dike until it turned suddenly to run beneath the mountains of the Chaine de l'Estaque in the Souterrain du Rove, a mighty tunnel four and a half miles in length which led to the Marseille docks but unfortunately collapsed in 1963 and was blocked by a roof fall far under the hill. Rumours come and rumours go that the tunnel is one day going to be cleared again so that barges do not have to make the somewhat risky voyage round the Estaque mountains by sea, a trip of two or three hours along a shore which is at the receiving end of any swell or gale-blown waves from the direction of Africa. But meanwhile the industry at Marseille has expanded and has settled around the Gulf of Fos to such an extent that a new cut through from the Rhone has been made and there seems little reason to extend the inland route further than there and the refineries at the Étang de Berre.

But to return to Arles, it is of course a city of wonders of which the Roman arena is the most impressive. Capable of holding more than twenty thousand spectators it is like some vast Olympic stadium, and the three towers added to it in the twelfth century are a reminder that after the fall of Rome it became a fortified town in itself. Even nowadays it is used for entertainments and (I am sorry to say) even for bloodthirsty bullfights in the Spanish style. There is the Roman theatre too, the remains of which have a strange and melancholy beauty of their own, and are still used during the summer for concerts or classical plays. The church and cloister of St Trophime recall that Arles was one of the very earliest bishoprics of Roman Gaul, Trophimus having been a companion of Paul on his last journey (2 Timothy, iv) and personally consecrated bishop by the apostle. Believed to have been a cousin of Stephen, Trophimus was sent to Arles in AD 45 and is said to have brought with him the skull of Stephen. *The Pilgrim's Guide* to St James of Compostella, a detailed Baedeker of the routes thither published in 1140, states that Trophimus died in 94 and was buried in the Alyscamps, which the author recommended as a place that no pilgrim should miss. I can only confirm that recommendation, even for non-pilgrims.

Although much of this great ancient cemetery was boorishly destroyed to provide a railway cutting to the locomotive repair workshops, that which remains is strangely beautiful, nostalgic, haunted by many centuries of loving and of dying. Les Alyscamps (or the Champs Elysées, the Elysian fields) was an important burial ground as far back as the time of the Roman occupation, and it achieved such prestige that three separate layers of sarcophagi came to lie one above the other as the centuries passed. More than a dozen chapels served it, and their remains are still to be seen, bordering the quiet avenue that runs between the tombs.

The Alyscamps burial ground, originally pagan, seems to have achieved renown through St Genest, a local Roman clerk to the court who refused to write out an edict ordering the persecution of the Christians. Condemned to death, he fled over the Rhone to the marshes of the Camargue but was overtaken and beheaded under a tree, which quickly became an object of pilgrimage. However, the continual plucking of leaves and bark as souvenirs eventually killed the tree and it was replaced first by a column, then by a chapel of pilgrimage. It was the continual threat of attacks by the moors which led to the body of the saint, and the pilgrimage also, being transferred across the Rhone again to the greater safety of Les Alyscamps.

The cult of Les Alyscamps became so popular that Christians as far up river as Vienne and Lyon wished to be buried there, and their bodies made the journey by water. A corpse would be placed in a coffin on a raft, or in a barrel sealed with pitch, and the float bore oil lamps at each corner so that its arrival would be noticed if it should happen to approach Arles at night. The cemetery staff and the guild of boatmen at Trinquetaille on the opposite shore had the duty of bringing the bodies to land, and for this service they were paid by means of a gold piece inserted between the teeth of the deceased and held there by the rigor, or with a purse hung round the neck.

One of the chapels is that of the Porcelets, an Arlesian family dating back to the crusades. Their peculiar name is said to derive from a curse laid upon one of them by an aged hag who swore that the lady would have as many children at one birth as a sow would have in its litter. The sow in question turned up nine piglets, and the lady is alleged to have had nonetuplets (if that is the right word) the very same day. Naturally, the family came to be nicknamed The Piglets, and eventually took the name instead of their original title, which later was forgotten.

A place such as the Alyscamps cannot fail to have its own legends. One of them tells of a wealthy man of Lyon who was dangerously ill. Certain of his approaching death he gave away all he possessed to his family, took leave of his wife and rode off down the towpath toward Arles so that he might die in the city and be sure of burial in the Alyscamps. Yet when he at last reached the place he found Arles so enchanting that he felt continually better and better, and as the weeks and months went by he began to live in some style. At last his money was all gone, and yet he had never felt better than now. Mounting his faithful steed he rode back up the towpath, living on the generosity of the bargees and monks whom he met on his way.

Arriving at Lyon, he found that his wife was now remarried and his family were generally embarrassed by his return alive and well. Deprived of the welcome he had expected, he wisely but sadly set off once again for Arles to enter the abbey of Montmajour, set on a rocky knoll outside the town. And there eventually he died.

An earlier tale is that of the lovely Arcella, a girl of seventeen whose actual sarcophagus was found in one of the chapels. She was so famous as a dancer in the Roman theatre that crowds would attend the performances in which she was to take part. On one occasion a young Roman officer was so overcome with passion for this graceful girl that he rushed up the steps which led to the stage and lifted her up in his arms to carry her before the statue of Venus, where he vowed to love her eternally.

Wonderful to relate, Arcella's heart was stirred by his bold action, and faced with the choice before her she eventually decided to abandon the theatre and become the wife of her gallant admirer. But a few days before her marriage the lure of the dance became so strong that she decided to dance just once more, not before the adoring crowd in the theatre but alone, under the clear moonlit sky, and in the solitude of Les Alyscamps. There she danced the night away, swept up in the delirium of her own grace and motion. She danced until she could no longer stand, then collapsed against a stone sarcophagus and fell gently to the ground, where next morning the attendants found her dead.

Arles has long been renowned as a place for female beauty, the dark handsome faces of the girls being said to come from their Greek forebears two thousand and more years ago. So far as I am aware none has ever alleged that the male inhabitants of Arles are particularly handsome but l'Arlésienne is of great repute and not only because of Bizet. Indeed, Charles Wood wrote enthusiastically about them when he visited the city in 1899.

"Fair women? They are indeed fair women. We had long heard of the charm of the Arlésiennes, but our imagination fell short of the truth. We never anticipated such a galaxy of beauty – beauty of a noble and splendid type ... Their forms are magnificent; they hold themselves like queens, walk like queens, their heads are set upon their shoulders as though they were mistresses of the world." He went on for two more pages, so impressed was he with Arlesian beauty. Indeed he went to the arena not to see the course de cocarde, at which he apparently never cast a glance, but merely to watch spellbound the graceful ladies of Arles.

Even Charles Lenthéric, chief engineer of the Ponts et Chaussées, commented upon the matter in his monumental work on the Rhone published in 1892. "Their beauty is very real", he wrote, "and some of them are real living statues that appear to give a glimpse of the Greece that has vanished." And he went on to add that beside the natural and refined beauty derived from the Greeks, there might be added touches of the Roman and Saracen. "But what is quite certain is that Greek beauty really exists at Arles, and that it only exists among the women. The men there are heavy, small, vulgar, coarse in shape and movements and above all in the sound of their voices. The woman on the other hand has kept something of her native delicacy. Tall and supple, with grace that is a little proud, with the profile of a cameo, the gaiety of life appears to quiver in the undulations of her figure. Her nose is straight, her chin very Greek, her ear fine. Her eyes, admirably shaped, have about them sometimes an indefinable expression, and their sudden and vehement look are tempered by a sort of Attic grace, the precious gift from her mother which she too will know how to pass on to her own children. The inferiority in shape of the men is obvious...they have kept nothing of the elegance of the race from which they are descended." And that is certainly true even today.

It is not easy to imagine that Arles was once a seaport. In fact, it originally had two ports. One was on both sides of the Rhone, much where the small amount of river traffic draws in nowadays, but the silting of the river mouth meant that Arles was only accessible to ships drawing less than three feet and already in the 17th century the great engineer Vauban declared that the mouths of the Rhone would always be *incorrigibles*. Long before that the merchants of Arles had solved the problem by constructing a second port on the other side of the town, connected by a channel to the lagoons. This, as Petrarch related, made it possible for fully laden vessels to come and go between the city and the Grau de Galejon, a deep-water, sheltered inlet on the coast.

I was fortunate enough to pass the large lock on two occasions and make for the Gulf of Fos by way of the Canal d'Arles à Bouc while it was still open. Originally the waterway had two intermediate locks along its thirty miles of straight and somewhat uninteresting cuts, but these had already been taken out. It was the site of the first one that interested me, however, a mere mile and a half down from the entrance, for the bridge across this pen was none other than the double bascule of Van Gogh's famous painting "Canal en Provence". Years earlier I had rung the bell for the bascules to be raised at the bridge in Albert Cuyp's seventeenth century painting of Dordrecht which I had seen in the Kenwood Gallery, but I had never expected to take *Thames Commodore* through the middle of a Van Gogh.

It may seem strange to have a small canal running parallel to a broad and navigable river, but its origin goes back to Roman times when Arles was a port not too far from the sea, which has moved back about fifteen miles since the days of Constantine. Roger de Howeden described in his travelogue of 1191 how, on their way to join King Richard in the Holy Land, the English vessels followed the Mediterranean coast as far as Marseille, touching successively at the ports of St Gilles and the episcopal city of Arles.

In the days of the Romans the whole area was one of marsh and shallow lagoons, and it was the commander Marius who undertook the work of cutting a new channel through the soft and partly water-logged ground. Three factors were against the shipping coming up the Rhone. First, the bar at the mouth. Second, the adverse current, especially in time of flood. Thirdly, there was the mistral. The Roman cargo-ships were somewhat clumsy and had no more than a lugsail, and if the full force of the mistral was added to the current of the Rhone the upstream journey was impossible.

Marius hit on the very sensible idea of cutting a canal through the flat land to the nearest point on the coast, so that the ships could be bank-hauled in still water.

The canal of Marius consisted of cuts (fossae) which joined the meres, and channels through shallows. There were of course no locks, but the present canal is a direct descendant of the Roman waterway – a fact that is hinted by the name of its destination, Fos, where the Fossae Marianae reached open water. Marius later ceded the canal and its upkeep to the Greek shippers in Marseille as a reward for their help in supplying his army in his initial campaign against the barbarians who were intending to march along the littoral to Rome itself. It was on the flat hill top at the end of the Alpilles hills only three miles from Tarascon that he encamped during that fateful campaign in 101 AD, and it was a good position. His forces were safe on the hill top, the plain of Arles was an excellent source of provisions and he could watch for the enemy arriving in the Rhone valley. When the barbarians appeared, he followed them eastward toward Aix and then descended upon them with such success that the name of *campi putridi* (now Pourrières) attached to a locality in the plain of the small river Arc is a fearful reminder of the massacre. According to Roman authors, who may well have exaggerated, 200,000 were killed and 86,000 taken as slaves in the battle and the weary legionaries had to drink water from streams red with blood.

On the map, the canal looks straight and dull. It was indeed remarkably straight but it had a real character of its own, for it ran across a pebbly waste splattered with thorny bushes and scrub, and brilliant with the colours of such flowers as could thrive in these surroundings. This area, the Crau, is a vast extent of shingle and pebbles which in places is fifty feet in depth. It was formed by floods of the River Durance, and by the mistral which prevented vegetation taking root. An alternative explanation is that Hercules happened to pass that way when on his errand to the garden of the Hesperides, the three female guardians of Hera's precious golden apples, and that on his way back with the oxen of Geryon he was attacked when near to the Rhone by a pair of terrible giants. Almost at his last gasp in his struggle with them he was pitied just in the nick of time by Zeus, who saved him by sending a rainstorm of round pebbles. Being larger than Hercules, the giants suffered more direct hits, so the hero was able to subdue them, but the pebbles were left as a stony desert. Some of this barren area has been tamed by irrigation and by planting the endless wind-breaks so distinctive of the area around Arles, but much of it is still a genuine desert which is best seen from the canal. However, here and there the now disused waterway passed by wild meres, with coots and ducks, white egrets by the dozen, and here for the first time on the route to Marseille the herds of heavy black bulls could be seen roaming the wasteland, and groups of the greyish or white horses of the Camargue stood on the bank to watch curiously the rare sight of a boat going by. But I soon discovered that it was unwise to spend the night in this canal, for at dusk the mosquitoes rose from the ground like a cloud.

The alternative route – and in the nineteen eighties the only way – from Arles to the sea was of course to continue down the Rhone, which quickly dropped its speed and flowed ahead down a rather featureless course toward Port St Louis. Unfortunately its banks were so high that I found it hard to believe that the wonderful nature reserve of the Camargue was often no more than a hundred yards from the boat. The river seemed devoid of life, and there were no birds on the water – probably because the terrain behind the bank was so much more interesting to them. There was not a single bridge below Arles, but eventually the motor ferry leading to a salt factory on the right bank was a sign that civilisation could not be very far away. Four miles further down, Port St Louis du Rhone came into view, a straggle of small town on the left bank ending in a faded ancient light-house. Here the navigation ended, for although the sea was still several miles away the conflict between wave and current, salt water and fresh, resulted in the river being made to drop the load of silt it had carried all the way from the Alps or received from tributaries such as the Durance. This amounted to at least four million cubic metres each year added to the delta, which meant an average annual addition of one hundred acres to the land of Provence, and a corresponding withdrawal of the sea. The area below Port St Louis is strewn with shoals, and their names such as Éugene, Annibal, or St Antoine reflect the names of ships which stuck fast and were swiftly buried in silt to lie there entombed for evermore.

As a town, Port St Louis has little charm, but local teams of water-jousters are sometimes engaged during summer weekends in thrusting and lancing in the approach to the lock. On the edge of the town there is an arena for bull games (as opposed to bullfights) and I had the good fortune to be perched on the ground floor windows of a bank in the main street when the guardians on their sturdy little horses ran bulls down the roadway and pavements in what is called an 'abrivado'.

The first abrivado I saw was at Trinquetaille, over the river from Arles. Crush barriers were erected across the side streets and eventually a few young bulls appeared, accompanied by the local lads who ran to and fro in front of them or pursued them from the rear. It was all harmless fun, and it became unusually entertaining when one of the bulls cast a curious glance at a woman standing in the doorway of a block of flats. It then turned and rushed toward her, and she fled indoors, foolishly omitting to slam the door behind her. The bull followed her eagerly and the noise that began to come from the building suggested that the creature would have been thoroughly at home in a china-shop. Not even the young men with all their bravado, nor the gendarme by the barrier seemed inclined to venture inside and we all watched and waited expectantly until, after a minute or two, a ginger cat came out of the door like a rocket, with the bull a yard behind it. Of course, the cat escaped easily through the legs of the onlookers behind the barriers, and with much shouting and waving of arms the bull was re-routed down the street. When the woman reappeared she looked a little pale, but I admired her for laughing so gaily at an incident which must have been somewhat alarming as well as unexpected.

At Port St Louis one has to swing round and double back through an old-fashioned lock into the broad basin of the port, one of those rare and pleasant places where one may lie more or less where one wishes without paying a penny or centime. From there the ship canal with coasters lying at its quays runs straight as an arrow for a couple of miles to emerge into the wider, open, and sometimes rather bumpy expanse of the Gulf of Fos. For me this was always a great moment and I would turn round the point light on the mole, drop the anchor in a fathom or two and leap overboard into the clear, clean, blue, salty, delicious and genuine Mediterranean. We had arrived.

IV
Marignane and Marseille – the betrothal of Gyptis – the Petit Rhone – Aegidius the hermit – St Gilles' Abbey - the Cathars – murder of the legate – the Maries – Fair of Beaucaire – Aucassin and Nicolette

The Gulf of Fos is nothing more than a wide bay in low-lying country, but it is an anchorage for big ships and above all tankers. Whenever I crossed it the roadsteads were dotted with these great bulk carriers, some of them high and barnacled and empty and with their bulbous noses breaking the surface, others deep laden. There might be a dozen or more of these giants lying at ease, awaiting a berth at the refineries of the Étang de Berre or at Lavera, prominent with its tall chimneys on the further shore. A forty minute crossing aiming to the left of these stacks and we were in the Canal de Caronte, another ship canal which ran straight to the town of Martigues at the entrance to the Étang de Berre, a former gulf of the early Mediterranean.

Monsieur Michelin does not allot a single star mark (meaning "intéressant") to Martigues, which I think is a pity, for it contains one of the most picturesque corners in all Provence. It is no wonder that Corot so much admired it, and for the boatman it has a special charm for here is a real town of the Mediterranean with narrow streets of ancient houses with sun-blanched shutters, with a profusion of flowers and an all-pervading odour of fish. The little town is cut through by three canals which have successively served the needs of ships of ever increasing size. The second oldest is now a pleasant fishing port, attractive in the scruffy messiness which makes such a place so alluring, but the oldest is the Canal St Sebastien, a humble waterway which turns a corner to an idyllic miniature harbour where families sit in the brilliant sunlight before their faded houses, knitting, chatting, playing hopscotch, and in general living as people very well might in the colourful sunny south. This charming corner has the romantic name of *Le Mirroir des Oiseaux*, and it is a blessing that (so far as I know) such a really beautiful and peaceful place has not been boutiqued or filled with drop-outs pretending to make bracelets and leather belts. I hope that it may always remain so, and that the birds will still look at their reflections.

The third, largest and newest canal drives straight through the town and enters the Étang de Berre under a huge and elegant double bascule bridge, and to either side of the buoys marking the deep-water channel for the tankers a fleet of small boats appears at first light every day to fish for an hour or so, that being apparently the time when the fish are either hungry or off their guard. Then the fishermen retire, the market opens along the quay and an occasional Rhone ship comes sweeping round the edge of the Étang, travelling in a channel sheltered from the ravages of the mistral by a long stone dyke.

The only place on this canal that I ever stopped at was La Mède. It was not really a place at all, but there is a shipyard there, and an exit through the dyke beside some tall pillars of rock standing in the edge of the huge expanse of the Étang de Berre. I had not intended to go that way but it was the result of my own foolishness. We happened to have aboard an acquaintance who had a boat of his own on the Thames, was President or something of the sort of the River Thames Society, a small shot if not a big one in the Inland Waterways Association and a man who, with gold rings galore up his arms, had commanded an RAF rescue launch in the Bristol Channel. My particular foolishness consisted in assuming that anyone with all these attainments would be capable of steering a boat, and when after leaving the last Rhone lock at Beaucaire he asked if he could relieve me at the wheel I said "Yes, certainly."

Within a minute I had to tap him on the shoulder and say he was aiming far too much to the right. The channel here was down the middle, I pointed out.

"That's all right," he said genially. "Plenty of water."

"The channel is over there," I said forcefully pointing. "To port, at once." And I leaned round him and took off most of our speed, which was fortunate for a second or two later we went up on a bank of boulders with a terrible clatter, and when I jumped overboard to walk round the ship I could find that one stabiliser shaft was bent so that the fin was jammed against the hull, one rudder bent, and both propellors, though still present, felt as though they had been chewed by a savage dog.

It took us a while to get her off, though I knew we should succeed eventually, even if we had to wait for the winter rains or the thaw of the Alpine snows in the following spring. And as we could still proceed under our own power we did so, and it was at Port St Louis du Rhone that we were advised that France's largest floating crane was busy by day constructing a new tanker terminal in the Étang de Berre but returned every evening to La Mède. Which she did, and she picked us out of the water and landed us on the quayside as easily as a porter placing a suitcase on the airport scales. The shipyard was efficient beyond belief, and on the third day we were away again. But I held the wheel myself.

It was a year or two later that I decided to follow the same canal to its end, because we had friends who were arriving from Sweden at Marseille airport to join us on our voyage. The airport happened to be at Marignane on the Étang de Berre, which in turn happened to be where the entrance cutting to the collapsed Souterrain du Rove was situated. It hardly needs to be said that their taximan had no idea that there was a canal in his home town, nor that there was a tunnel which had collapsed, so in spite of the map I had drawn for his benefit it was a long time and many francs before he located it – precisely where I had marked it. I only mention this because it illustrates the extraordinary mutual ignorance that exists between the land-based and water-based communities. Land-livers passing over a canal bridge never give a thought to whence the waterway comes or whither it wends its winding way, and those living and working on barges seem to regard the world around them as a sort of waste land which serves only as a surface in which their route is cut. They rarely go ashore except to the bakery and the Café de la Marine, and they are not anxious to make acquaintance with the land any further. Ashore and out of sight of the quay they feel lost, and if there is one fear that haunts the owner of a barge it is that his daughter might marry a *gens-de-terre*, a danger which is not very likely, for she has little chance of meeting such a one and is in any case always on the move. Sometimes I have bought the *Journal de la Navigation* at a lock, and have been surprised to look down the list of engagements and weddings to see that almost invariably both partners hail from péniches. Surprised, because for better or worse the television has opened up the world even for the family in the wheelhouse cabin. But then, the programmes are always land-based and may well be accepted for the fairy tales and irrelevant glitter they usually are. Certainly the news bulletins appear to be of no interest whatsoever to the skipper of a 38.5 metre automoteur chugging up the Canal de l'Est or through the Midi.

Marignane has a loading basin for Rhone ships carrying phosphate, and from its end the deep cutting which now serves as a harbour for local yachts and motor boats runs a short distance to the steep hillside where the canal disappears into the blackness. Marseille was until 1963 only an hour and a half away, but now involves a passage down the Gulf of Fos, round the corner and a couple of hours along the shore outside the hills bored through by the tunnel. But as strictly speaking the city is (or was) the end of the inland run it must have a mention.

The mere appearance of the city from afar is a reward for any rigours of the voyage to reach it. Dominated by the great basilica of Notre Dame de la Garde set high on the hillside above the port, the city lies at the foot of coastal mountains so utterly dry and devoid of all but the most precarious vegetation that at first one can mistake the brilliant white of the limestone for snow. In the commercial harbour freighters great and small lie along the tideless quays, and what was once the older port of the Phoceans and Romans and Greeks is guarded by the massive twin forts of St Jean and

St Nicholas. Offshore the famous Chateau d'If stands solidly on its own white rock close to the dazzling ridge of the Ile Ratonneau, and to the south the high cliffs by the narrow strait inshore of the Ile Maire hide the route to the nostalgic, scented Isles of the Levant, to the fashionable resorts of the Cote d'Azur, to Monaco, Italy and beyond.

Marseille has nothing to do with the French national anthem beyond the fact that when Captain Rouget de Lisle had knocked up his song for a banquet in Strasbourg, the tune was a catchy one and when first sung by soldiers on the march those troops happened to be Marseillaises. It is obviously a very ancient town, and if Greeks from Phocis found and settled in the excellent natural harbour which is now the old port they later found it also to be an ideal place for producing salt by evaporation of sea water. It became known later as Salt Farm, Mas Salia. Marseille has long been celebrated for its dark-eyed female beauties, and some like to trace the origin of so much feminine grace back to the beginnings of the city itself as told in the romantic story of Gyptis, the lovely daughter of Senannus, King of the Segobrigi.

It was in 599 BC that a small flotilla of Ionian ships from Phocis arrived in the bay which nowadays is the Vieux Port, under the command of a young adventurer named Protis. As soon as they had landed in the bay the Phoceans very wisely decided to place themselves under the protection of the local tribe, and Protis set off with suitable gifts to Arles, where the King had his headquarters. By good fortune Protis arrived there on the day when Senannus had invited all his redoubtable chieftains to a feast. During the dinner his graceful daughter Gyptis was to select one of them as her husband, and according to custom she would advance toward her chosen man and hold out to him the goblet of wine from which – if able to stand – he was to drink. Protis arrived at Arles unexpected, a complete stranger, but Senannus had the goodwill to invite him to the banquet. His courtesy, his elegance and charm, his good manners and no doubt his behaviour at table too, were so much in contrast to the tough vulgarity and coarse boasting of his companions at the feast that the girl, passionate and determined and perhaps lured by the attraction of something so unusual and exotic, and an escape from a less attractive fate, advanced straight toward him, and in spite of the protests and belchings of the warriors proudly held out to Protis the goblet which was the symbol of union. He took it from her, looked into her eyes and drank the cup to the bottom. The betrothal was sealed.

When they saw the courteous treatment Protis showed to his bride, a number of the friends of Gyptis were quick to escape and seek out other young men among the Phoceans at Massalia. The happy couples quickly put up a few houses and some sort of stockade. This was a wise precaution, for more and more of the wives and daughters of the tough Segobrigi defected to the civilised ways of the new community. Naturally, their former menfolk became worked up into a state of fury. Craftily, the warriors from the surrounding country came in great number to one of the Ionian festivals in the new town. They arrived smiling and friendly and obviously unarmed – for they had sent all their weapons ahead of them in market wagons cunningly covered with foliage.

Yet the romantic charm of the men from Ionia was to save the infant city, for a daughter of one of the warriors who was about to take part in the slaughter revealed the plot to a young Phocean with whose mere appearance she had instantly fallen in love. Swiftly his companions raided the wagons, seized the arms, and inviting the rough and hardened Segobrigi to enter the gate they inflicted such a slaughter upon them that they never again attempted to conquer Massalia. More and more Ionians arrived by sea to swell the population, and we may assume that fresh waves of beautiful girls managed to escape over the arid country to join them. In this happy way, if we can believe the legend, Marseille was established, a city founded on brains and beauty.

However, a boatman anxious to reach the Mediterranean has no need to run down the Rhone as far as Port St Louis. Especially if he wants to have a leisurely voyage through one of the most curious and alluring parts of France. Just as Arles comes into view downstream the Petit Rhone leads off to the right, disappearing round a bend between thicketty banks of trees. It was brought into order when Beaucaire lock became unusable, and is now the way of reaching the Canal du Rhone à Sète. I must admit to liking the Little Rhone, partly because it is a placid stream that flows through nowhere at all. A haunt of coot (in moderation) and heron, especially the purple heron, it carries the rare barge heading for the port of Sète and is utterly different from the hurrying, bustling, swashing Rhone whose offspring it is. The stream has very little current, and it moves so slowly that a number of groynes have been added to make it drop its fine sandy silt in the right places. It is an easy navigation, devoid of anything but trees along the high banks, and perhaps in summer a family or two picnicking on the sandbanks, put there is not a house the whole way until twelve miles down the river the entrance to St. Gilles lock leads off to the right. Beyond this point the river is not dredged or marked or buoyed.

St Gilles lock is vast and impressive. But it is a friendly place, and the basement which contains all the magnificent machinery is also stocked with wine, red, white or rosé, for sale to anyone passing through. It is perfectly drinkable vin-de-table, but there is no need to get carried away with excitement. More than one hundred miles of vineyards lie ahead, and some of the wines produced there are much too good to be wasted on export to other nations.

The town of St Gilles is half an hour away round the next corner to the right. It is a quiet place, a little town in which the houses are simple rather than notable and lie tumbled pleasantly about the slope without the least regard to convenience or planning, and with an air that there is really no hurry. At the same time they are sparkling as can be, their doors and windows painted in the bright hues of the Mediterranean, the sills gay with flowers that seem almost to shout the brilliance of their tints, flaunting them in the certainty that no such gaiety could be displayed in the damper and colder climes of the north. It is a place of little alleys and queer corners, and of cats watching intently for something which never seems to arrive.

As it lies only a mile from the Petit Rhone one can guess that St Gilles used to be a seaport. In fact that branch of the river once flowed at the foot of the hill on which the town stands, safe from floods. What are now marshes were once a roadstead, and there would lie the ships from Venice and Tyre and Alexandria. In the 12th century two popes disembarked at St Gilles, and it was there also that Bertrand, Count of Toulouse, embarked for the Holy Land with a company of four thousand knights and forty vessels. But the construction in the following century of the new port of Aigues Mortes further west spelled the end of St Gilles as a place of shipping. Not even the coming of the canal in the 19th century could restore it to maritime prosperity.

Standing in front of the somewhat ruined facade of one of the greatest abbey churches of France, it is not easy to realise that the little town with butcher and baker, fruit packing station and wine co-operative was once an extremely important point in international communications. It all began with the burial there at the foot of the hills which edged the salty lagoons of a hermit, a certain Aegidius, Gilles or Giles, who set out on his wanderings in the seventh century, and leaving his native Athens eventually reached the forests near the mouth of the Rhone. It was there that he was to become one of the many European saints associated with deer. He did not hunt a stag as St Hubert did, nor was he saved from an untimely and involuntary marriage, as was St Notburga. But he had this in common with the others, that his deer was an albino. It is said that he lived alone with it in the forest, and that in return for the hospitality of his rough shelter the doe nourished him with her milk. News of the white doe, which by reason of its albino genes could hardly escape being seen, eventually reached Wamba, King of the Visigoths, who at once decided that he must hunt it down. A party was got together consisting of one hundred and forty dogs and an even greater number of huntsmen, and as this immense force accompanied the king through the forest a white flash among the trees showed that they were on the right trail.

Fleeing before the hunt, the doe led the chase deeper into the forest, and as she drew near to where Gilles lived beneath the trees the din of the pursuit roused him from his prayers. He hurried out, to see his faithful friend and provider cornered, cowering in terror. At this moment one of the royal huntsmen drew his bow and shot, but Gilles stretched out his leg and the arrow lodged in his knee. He pulled it out, the tale says, and prayed that the wound might never heal, so that he should always be reminded of the sufferings of Christ.

This curious incident so surprised the King that he asked his chaplain to enquire of Gilles who he was, where and what his dwelling. The hermit told his tale and the king immediately offered to give him a position where he could live in comfort and honour. Gilles declined, and returned to his lair with only the doe as company, but now that his hiding place was known he was constantly sought out by the poor and needy. At last he accepted the repeated offer of the king to build him an abbey, and the institution was erected on the spot where he had been pierced by the hunter's arrow. Gilles still slept on the ground rather than in a bed, but he was persuaded to accept the role of abbot. So good and saintly was he that Charlemagne himself is said to have been willing to confess only to Gilles, and in Chartres a window shows him doing do, but as the abbey was founded in 673, Gilles lived in the eighth century and Charlemagne in the ninth, the tale is not altogether convincing.

More certain however is that the sanctity and reputation of Gilles was such that the Pope John VIII attached the abbey directly to Rome in the year 878. Its fame increased, miracles were reported, pilgrims came there in ever greater quantities. King Robert the Pious went thither in 1031. He was brother of Henry of Germany, canonised for his abstinential marriage to Cunigunde, and he was known as the Pious because he confessed to the abbot of St Benoît that he had lain with a lady who was related to him spiritually and physically, for which offence he prayed, fasted, and mortified himself – and then proceeded for the all important matter of raising a male heir to have three wives. Not long after, Wladislas, Duke of Poland sent a mission to Saint Gilles to pray in the abbey that an heir might be born to him, which in due course happened. Soon the abbot could compile his "Book of the Miracles of St Gilles" containing wonders wrought for pilgrims from as far away as Germany and Denmark.

Some of these pilgrims had come to St Gilles itself, but many were on their way elsewhere, whether to the great church of St. James at Compostella, or to the Holy Land. They needed fresh horses perhaps, and provisions for the journey by land or sea, and a market arose to provide for their needs. Outside the abbey a busy commerce grew up, which reached the proportions of a trade fair throughout the town on 1st September, which was St Gilles' day, attracting such a throng of merchants from other countries that there were more than one hundred bureaux-de-change active in the town. Wool and silk, spices and perfumes of the orient joined the stocks of wine and fish, grain and salt produced locally, and the town which grew up to service the trade prospered. Ideally situated on a branch of the Rhone and on the channels connecting the lagoons as well as on the coastal road from Italy to Spain it was accessible to sea-going ships and to pack trains alike. St Gilles flourished, but today none of that great activity survives, and it is doubtful even that a Scotsman pausing for a moment to buy souvenirs in the little square in front of the abbey would realise that St Gilles and St Giles of Edinburgh are named after the same hermit.

This little square or market place is dominated by the steps and facade of what is left of the abbey church, once one of the glories of Christendom but now looking for all the world as though it has just been struck in an air raid. It is not just that the portals are chipped and scarred, but that the nave itself runs off into a profusion of broken pillars and tumbled masonry, cracked monuments, blocks of stone and heaps of crumbled rubble. It was a Sunday morning when first I saw it, and seated among the debris were an old woman eating olives, a vendor of balloons blowing up his wares, three lizards enjoying the sunshine, and a little girl in her Communion dress, but on most days there will be a bus load or two of visitors. For the abbey church is noted for its sculptures, including the famous Kiss of Betrayal over the portal, and even more for its role in an incident of medieval history.

The abbey of St Gilles has had its half wrecked appearance for centuries, ever since the zealous if over-vigorous reformers of the Church attacked the monks and threw them down the well, burning the abbey over them. But the magnificent front still remains, and is said by some to be as fine as anything in France. Certainly it must have been a thing of glory before the Revolution interfered with it and made many of the mute statues pay with their heads as though they were real fellow-citizens worthy of proper socialist class-hatred. Even now it is a thing of great beauty with its classical columns and flutings, and groups of medieval people viewing with very natural alarm the fearsome beasts which seem to want to drag them down and eat them.

Below the church is a deep, dark, but most impressive crypt, laid out in such a way that the pilgrims would pass through it in an orderly fashion on their way to St James's at Compostella or to the quay where they would board ship on their way to the Holy Land. They would file past the tomb of St Gilles himself, as did Count Raymond VI of Toulouse on the fateful day that was to unleash one of the most fearful and protracted episodes in the history of the Languedoc. And before we sail on eastwards to Beaucaire we must meet the Albigensians, for their terrible story still pervades the air of the sunny, scented Languedoc.

One thousand years after the onslaught by the Roman authorities upon the Christians of the Rhone valley, the Languedoc became a breeding ground for deviant beliefs, or heresies as the orthodoxy called them. "Orthodoxy is my doxy. Heterodoxy is another man's doxy," William Warburton once remarked. And of course this is true, but the heresies which grew up toward the end of the twelfth century were more than just differences of opinion. They rocked the whole foundation of Church and society. There were two main heretical movements. The Waldensians, who were centred more toward the Alps than the Pyrennean foothills, were the followers of Pierre Waldo of Lyon, a wealthy merchant who had the scriptures translated from the Latin and who then renounced his wealth and position to live according to the example of Christ and in charity with the poor. Shocked by the abuses and pretension of the Roman Church, Waldo and his friends attempted to live like the Apostles in poverty, preaching the gospel as they wandered from place to place. They recognised no ecclesiastical authority but God, and they not only rejected the Pope and the corrupt priesthood but much of Catholic doctrine and dogma, too. They could not accept the idea of purgatory, nor transubstantiation, and they ruled out praying to relics and to saints. Indeed the Waldensians were the first breath of the Reformation, and a serious menace to the authority, power and revenues of the Church of Rome, which they unhesitatingly identified with the Great Whore of Babylon. The danger from the Albigensians or Cathars, however, was of quite a different order.

Apart from attacks along the coast by Arabs, or further north by Viking raiders, Europe had long been living in a period of comparative peace which has had no equal either before or since, and the reason for this was the pyramid of fealty and loyalty upon which it was constructed. The serf had his master to whom he was bound by oath and from whom he received security, shelter and payment of some kind even if only in a patch of land to cultivate. Big lords had little lords and lordlings as vassals beneath them, and above them there might be the Duke of Burgundy, the Count of Toulouse,the King of France, or whoever might be the top dog in the area. On the whole rulers did not fight. They may have abducted women in order to get their dowry, but quarrels were in general taken up to the Pope, to whom the protagonists were both bound by oaths of loyalty, and he would adjudicate, usually on rather sensible lines. The system was an excellent one, and even if the power of the Pope was in many ways limited, the general arrangement in terms of a caste system or power pyramid with the pontiff at the top worked extremely well. Everything was peaceful. Yes, provided nobody rocked the boat or flouted the rules of the hierarchy of loyalties. And that is precisely what the heretics did. There they stood and they could no other, like Luther hundreds of years later.

The Albigensians were so-called after the region around Albi, one of many where they flourished. Their real name was Cathars, or 'pure ones'.

The Étang de Berre

Top: The Canal des Étangs near St Gilles
Bottom: Abrivado at Les Saintes Maries

Some of the beliefs of the Cathars have been lost forever, because the crusade against them endeavoured to destroy every trace of their Church, but certainly they emphasised the wisdom of Christ rather than his sufferings, and they aborred reverence for the cross. If one's son was slain, they logically demanded, surely one would revere his memory for what he was, rather than glorify or worship whatever weapon or accident had killed him.

But there was much more to the Albigensian heresy than that, or a feeling of revolt against the abuses of the Catholic clergy, great though they were. The movement came from the Bogomils (or beloved of God) who flourished in Bulgaria in the tenth century, and spread across to the Languedoc as a theology which contained various elements from the East. The chief 'heretical' point was the Cathar insistence that the world was under a sort of dual control, everything physical being the work of Satan, alias (oddly enough) Jehovah. The good God sent Christ as a Mediator, but because it was unthinkable that he could have had a genuine or Satanic body, Christ was not 'really real'. From this it followed that he could not genuinely have suffered or died, but the Devil cleverly founded the Roman Church to make believers think that he had done so. No pope was likely to take well to this idea.

The notion that everything physical was created by an evil deity led the Cathars to abhor anything associated with reproduction. Eggs and meat were banned, and so was milk. The Cathars themselves had a horror of sexual relations as aiding the Devil in his creative activity. How far these notions were understood and accepted by the *credentes*, the rank and file of adherents, is another matter. Probably much of the doctrine was far above their heads, and certainly the great majority of them were married, but the *perfecti* were well versed in their theology, and true to it. These *perfecti* were those who had accepted the only sacrament the Cathars recognised, a laying-on of hands which conferred the Holy Spirit. This was only given to a person after he had spent a year or two in study and preparation, and when he had received it he thereupon became a *perfectus*, a bonhomme. From that moment he gave away all his goods, he ate no food of animal origin, he lived ascetically and sometimes starved himself to death, or he gave his life to prayer or preaching and service, and dressed in a black robe. Whether man or woman, the *perfectus* swore never to retract for fear of death by fire or any other means, and amid all the barbarity of their persecution there is only one single recorded case of an initiate recanting.

The *perfecti* or ministers of the Cathars thus lived in a state of poverty and purity and dedication which stood in complete contrast to the affluence of many of the Roman clergy. Inevitably they were respected, and their logical and liberal preaching based on the Gospel of St John blended easily with the romantic ideas of the troubadours to make the Languedoc an area of such freedom that Jews held official posts and professorships, Arabs taught in medical schools, women were largely emancipated, and capital punishment was regarded as barbarous. But there was no place in Cathar thinking for obedience to the pope as head of an institution which they regarded as the work of Satan, and so it was inevitable that against this splendid flowering of justice and equality and faith Pope Innocent III, a sincere and fanatically enthusiastic defender of the faith, was to announce a crusade.

Generally it seems that the Cathars were liked – their name of 'bonhommes' indicates as much – but some of the practices were easily misrepresented. For instance, their complete rejection of sex led the *perfecti* sometimes to live together in mixed communities which could easily be misrepresented by the clergy as sinks of sexual vice and aberrant practices.

In the year 1207 the Cathar heresy was by no means new, but it was in that year that St Gilles was the scene of an event which was to have the most terrible consequences for the Languedoc. At that time Pierre de Castelnau was Legate to the Languedoc, and his particular charge was to contain or put down the heresy which was growing so alarmingly in the domains of the Count of Toulouse. Count Raymond VI openly gave shelter and encouragement to those who did not agree with the dogma and practices of the Church of Rome which, within his realm, had reached an almost unbelievable state of corruption. Pierre de Castelnau set about inciting the lords of Provence to rebel against Raymond, and as this was not successful, he publicly excommunicated him and outlawed his territories, pronouncing in advance a blessing on any who should strike the Count dead. Either from real fear for the fate of his soul, or more probably to make an appearance of subservience and so avoid the worst result of the interdict for his people, the Count came to St Gilles to make formal submission to the authority of Rome. The scene in the abbey was a victory for the Legate, and certainly it was his day of triumph. But it was also his last, for as he left the town to cross the Petit Rhone, one of the Count's officers ran him through with a sword. That was too much for Pope Innocent III, and he gave the signal for the forces of Europe to be launched against the Albigensians in a war of extermination.

The final destruction of the last strongholds of the Albigensians was not to be achieved for nearly forty years, but only two years after the murder of the Legate the crowds were gathered again at St Gilles to see Count Raymond VI humiliated a second time. He was forced to submit in public to the supreme religious authority of the Pope. More than a score of bishops had been summoned to see Raymond submit to whatever the new Legate demanded of him.

There was little that the Legate did not require. A collection of relics (which the heretics despised) was set outside the door, and grovelling before them the Count had to swear obedience to the officials of the Pope. Stripped to the waist he was then led into the church with a rope round his neck. At each step the clergy beat him on his bare back, and still stripped and bleeding he was forced to pass through the crypt where not only St Gilles but the Count's own former mortal enemy Pierre de Castelnau lay buried. Even this was only a beginning, for the outward humiliations were no more than the formal seal set upon eight conditions which he had to accept, each of which involved either submission to the clergy of his domains or some restriction of freedom for his subjects – such as that all Jews were to be dismissed from holding office in his territories.

Probably the Count thought that by appearing to accept these indignities he would hold off the storm which threatened his people, but he was mistaken. He was a tolerant man, and there was no place for tolerance in the world of Innocent III. When, thirteen years later, Count Raymond lay dying, he was refused the Last Sacrament – a thing that may or may not have been so terrible to his mind but which showed unambiguously the extent to which the Church of Rome knew his submission was not genuine. And not content with that, they refused him burial, and for years his coffin remained above the ground until finally his remains were eaten by rats. Yet even this was as nothing to the fate which was dealt out to those throughout his domains who dared to accept teachings which had not the stamp of papal approval, and in one locality after another they were slaughtered without mercy and their homes razed to the ground.

So much for the events in the abbey church of St Gilles. The heretics were duly exterminated, and the *ignorami* of the French Revolution eventually succeeded in smashing most of what was beautiful on the facade of one of the finest medieval buildings in all France. Perhaps it is no accident that the kiss of Judas has remained unscathed as a monument to socialism.

When first I drew in at the quay after entering the canal at Beaucaire, the waterfront was lined with tanker barges and a purple stain extended over the quay, across the road and up the walls of the houses. And this was wine, or at least the colour from the grapes, for what appear to be the storage tanks of a refinery are in fact full of wine, the Costières du Gard of the vintners' co-operative. In the street behind is a doorway where one can enter – preferably with a bucket in hand – and see local people buying their wine in jars, jerricans, carboys, any receptacle which can be weighed before and after filling. The wine is dispensed much like petrol at a filling station. There is a flexible hose for each of several varieties, and the wines have a good strong flavour.

It is a good place to take on board a few cartons of wine if homeward bound within a week or two by boat or car. That is, if one likes the good earthy wine of the Languedoc, which personally I do very much, especially the red with its strong tang of the south. But I must admit that a flagon for lunch is as much as I buy at St Gilles, for the vineyards stretch ahead for a hundred miles and a day or two of voyaging will bring us to vintages which in my opinion are very much better. However, the Gilles co-operative has a curiosity in that its best vintage of Costières du Gard has the unlikely name of Cuvée Gagarine. It may seem strange to see the victorious Yuri Gagarin, recently returned from outer space, in martial uniform decked out with all his medals staring at one from the label of a wine bottle, but the explanation is that when the first cosmonaut was given a heroic welcome in France he was taken on a tour of all the familiar tourist sights ranging from the President himself to the tomb of Napoleon, Notre Dame, the tomb of the unknown soldier and I know not what besides. But at the end of the few days he was still there, his stamina unbent and courage undaunted, and they had to do something to entertain him. He was accordingly sent down to St Gilles, a long and exhausting journey it was supposed, and led around the hillsides of the Costières. Then they plied him with their best wine and when the hero licked his lips appreciatively they duly honoured him with giving his name to that particular co-operative mix.

But wine is only part of the local trade. Between the two canal bridges is a fruit packing station, and in high summer it is a real wonder to see the fresh peaches delivered from the farms cascading down gentle slopes, being sorted for size, taking trips on aerial conveyors and ending up neatly positioned in trays from the mountain of empties stacked high up the end wall. But it is not just a wonder. More than once I have bought a tray of top quality specimens and eaten them all the way along the canal.

It is from St Gilles that one comes most easily by bus across the marshes of the Camargue to Les Saintes Maries de la Mer. In summer time the town is high on the list of tourist traps, with stalls selling cowboy hats and bags made of horse-hair, but I personally think it worth wearing blinkers and making straight for the ancient fortified church, for the memory contained within it is believed very possibly to be that of the first Christian community in France. According to legend it was here that the boat landed which carried St Martha and her companions, and it is where the two Maries settled after Lazarus had gone to Marseille, Mary Magdalene to the Massif of the Sainte Baume (Holy Cave) behind the coastal hills towards La Ciotat, and Martha to Tarascon. The Maries in question were the mothers respectively of St James the Major (of Compostella) and of St John, and of St James the Less and St Jude. They are said to have erected here the first Christian altar in the whole of France about the year AD 42, but to have lived a quiet and secluded life, unrecognised and undisturbed, pondering the amazing events which they had witnessed at the Crucifixion and immediately after.

The two women are also said to have had a girl servant named Sara, who later became the great patroness of the gypsies. None are quite sure whether they took to her because her statue had a black face, or whether the Sara in the church was given the black face later to please them. But she is there as large as life, in the crypt. Not being a saint she is not allowed upstairs, only emerging on 24th May for the two days of celebration and pilgrimage attended by the Camargue *guardiens* (or cowboys), by gypsies from all over Europe, and of course a great crowd of visitors. The reliquaries of the Maries are brought out, the charming statues of the two women in their little boat are carried round the town and out into the water, where priests wading out to their armpits (provided the sea is calm) bless the sea and the fishermen. It is a most extraordinary and exuberant Camargue occasion, and perhaps most easily witnessed if wearing a swimsuit.

Even if Les Saintes Maries in summertime seems ready to sink into the sand under the weight of junk – for tourism is its only trade – it is worth turning a blind eye to all the trading just to enter the cool, dark vault of the fortified church which rises up like a castle among the houses. It can be a most moving experience, for an air of age-old devotion pervades the building. On the left of the nave are the figures of the two Maries, waiting in their little boat for the next blessing of the sea, and under the east end a few steps lead down to where the figure of Sara stands arrayed in one of her glittery dresses, illuminated by the flickering light of the hundreds of candles provided by her devotees. Indeed, the whole church is blackened on the ceiling by centuries of waxy smoke, yet there is something about the place which is not just tawdry and superstitious but sincere and not easily forgotten.

Much research has gone into the matter of the Maries. It has even been suggested that they have been derived from Marius the Roman canal builder who was said by Plutarch to have had a female Syrian soothsayer in attendance upon him, named Martha. This is the disadvantage of living in a hypercritical and sceptical age. Much that is beautiful and romantic is missed, and in this book I shall un-blushingly tell the tales and legends that have been handed down, for very often they have a charm and poignancy of their own. It is possible to explain the colours of a sunset over the Camargue entirely in terms of refraction and absorbtion of various wavelengths – to say nothing of retinal pigments and optic nerves. But I like the sunset all the same for its glory, and the uplifting feeling it imparts. And the same is true of the legend of Les Saintes Maries. Besides, I suspect that the tale may well be founded on fact.

Back on board, from St Gilles to Beaucaire is a run of about three hours, including the time needed to pass the speedy automated lock on the way. It is not the most spectacular of canals but it is a pleasant one just the same, with views across the wilderness of the Camargue on the right and up to the foothills of the Cevennes on the left. As the canal runs to a dead end there is little traffic if any, and even if at the approach to Beaucaire a highly odoriferous chemical works and an unpleasant dusty cement factory lie by the canal, it is worth holding the nose and persevering to reach the broad open basin of the port of Beaucaire, a mere hundred yards from the now regrettably inaccessible Rhone.

Beaucaire has always been one of my favourite inland ports. It is asleep from midday for three or four hours, but it has a modest market, and many very picturesque and unselfconscious streets and alleys, some of them spanned by arches to prevent the place collapsing altogether. Near ruins alternate with dwellings of great charm, and curious statues, carvings, doorknockers and the like are to be found unadvertised throughout the town. My first arrival at Beaucaire was accompanied by a sense of enormous relief. We had run the unbridled Rhone with its swirls and whirlpools, we had swept past sun-dried villages and proudly impregnable fortresses, and now quite suddenly we were in still and stagnant water, in the easy ambience of the world of canals but with something new – the easy-going, spicy, pine-scented world of the Midi. We passed the lock, and a short cut running out into the canal basin, to face a town of very real charm and innumerable cats. Later that sense of achievement was absent, for the approach from St Gilles was straight and easy, and one merely arrived. Even if the town was the same it appeared more gradually, half asleep as usual in the summer sun.

It was in the final week of July that I last drew in at Beaucaire and moored close to the footbridge and on the side of the canal away from the rather noisy and dusty traffic which sweeps past on its way from Tarascon to Nimes. During the course of the day some workmen appeared on the bridge and others came to moor a work-boat in midstream close to where we lay. Their foreman courteously greeted us, removed his cap, and recommended us to move to the further side of the bridge because, he said, the wind was from the west and we would be smothered in smoke. Besides, when the merchants arrived by water we should have a better view of the proceedings.

In the early evening the merchants duly arrived, a half dozen dressed in elegant costumes of the eighteenth century. They stepped ashore from the small work barge that had been lent to them, were greeted by an official in sumptuous robes and followed a horseman and a brass band to disappear down a side street toward the town hall. The Beaucaire Fair had begun.

The fair is nowadays no more than a nostalgic relic. Shops push their wares out on to the pavements, and some knock down the prices. The streets are hung with banners, the majorettes are of course in evidence, and the Champ de Foire behind the massive flood wall of the Rhone, which rises as high as the second floor windows, has the usual collection of shooting galleries, roundabouts for children and stalls of sticky nougat, whilst a few Avignon drop-outs sit on the pavement pretending to fashion with their own hands the bracelets imported from Hong Kong. After dusk the canal basin became the scene of a splendid firework display which ended in the footbridge being transformed into one long waterfall of silvery fire. The foreman was right; we had an excellent view, whereas our original position was shrouded in acrid smoke.

But this same Sainte-Madeleine fair was, until the coming of the railway to the Rhone valley, one of the greatest in Europe. Begun in 1464 it continued to grow until it rivalled those of Cambridge and Nijni-Novgorod and certainly flourished much later. A whole town of tents and booths and stalls would fill the Champ de Foire for an entire week, and as many as fifty thousand people came to the town, comedians, sharpers, pick-pockets, clowns, ruffians, prostitutes and the eighteenth century equivalent of twentieth century drop-outs, together with half the police force of the Languedoc. These of course were all no more than incidentals, hangers-on of the very great trading that took place. Thousands of carts converged upon Beaucaire laden with goods of all kinds, and more than a hundred sea-going ships laboriously hauled up the turbulent Rhone were moored along the wall. Traders from Provence, from Alsace and the north, from Switzerland and Italy, Catalonia and the eastern Mediterranean, they brought jewels and ironwork, fine timber, bales of English cloth and the latest fashions, wines, cattle, sugar and spice and all things nice. And if it was the railway which eventually put an end to this activity that was because it killed the shipping, and when the Rhone was later tamed for larger transport the powerful Rhone ships had no business with Beaucaire but with Lyon and Marseille. The Champ de Foire became more used as a boulodrome and the mighty flood wall is now a place where one can take a pleasant stroll in the evening, chat with the occupants of the upper floors of the houses as they take their glass of wine on a flower-decked balcony, or admire the fine bronze of a life size and charging bull, its horns shiny with the fondling of generations of children's hands.

At the back of the town the tall, imperious keep of the castle stands on tip-toe at the top of a hill clad with pines, as though trying to show how much it can look down upon the castle of Tarascon across the stream. The last time I toiled up the steps to the roof to look out toward the row of the Alpilles hills, I was stopped by a rather crippled young man wearing the hat of guardian of the ancient monument. We talked awhile, and then with a sigh he asked me if I could guess what his life's dream had been, and always would be. This was a puzzle quite beyond me. A loving wife? No. To study some special subject, perhaps? No. To travel far away to exotic lands? No, not at all. His dream was to be the owner of a Morgan Four-four.

I was surprised that he had heard of that car, which I personally regarded as the only one still manufactured (in very small numbers) which actually looked as a car should, and when I told him that some thirty years previously I had personally owned one his enthusiasm knew no limits. He knew far more about the car than I did and having extolled its virtues in terms of wonder he told me to sit by him on the step.

"For you, I shall sing," he said. "You have talked to me of my one dream. I shall sing, just for you, a song I learned long go."

It was a song about a defeat of the fearful Duke of Marlborough, and as his gentle voice sang out the verses even the cicadas seemed to stop their zizzing to listen.

The mighty keep of whitish stone is inseparable from that great tale of Aucassin, son of the Count of Beaucaire, and of the captive slave girl Nicolette, a prisoner taken in battle against the Saracens. Who she was, none knew, for she had been taken from home as a child. But she was beautiful in the eyes of Aucassin, her hair curling and golden, (somewhat surprising in an Arab, perhaps) her eyes blue-grey and full of laughter, her lips of vermillion richer than ever rose or summer cherry wore, her form so slender that one might clasp her round with one's two hands. So white were her feet, for all their colour, that the daisy blossoms broken by her gentle tread seemed black beside them. No wonder that Aucassin should have loved her so deeply that his only joy was in waiting upon her, or thinking of her. This he much preferred to joining in the wars, and fighting his father's mortal enemy the Count of Valence from further up the Rhone.

But this notion of making love not war so angered Aucassin's father that he forbade his son ever to see the lovely Nicolette again, and to make sure that his wishes should be obeyed he ordered the girl to be shut away in a lonely tower with only a slit for a window. There she was to stay with none but an old woman to watch her, and if Aucassin should try to reach her or to speak to her she was to be burned alive.

When Aucassin learned of the fate of his beloved he retired to his room and wept without ceasing. Meanwhile the terrible Count of Valence came to lay siege to the place, and Beaucaire was under bombardment with stones flung by every possible engine of war available at that period of time. At the height of the attack, Count Garin ran to summon his son to defend the family castle, but all Aucassin could do was to weep. He would never bear arms again, he said, unless his father allowed him to come to his beloved Nicolette and to marry her.

Never, never would he be allowed to see the girl, his father declared in his fury. But the sound of the onslaught made some sort of compromise seem desirable, and with the enemy thundering terribly at the gates a formula was agreed upon. Aucassin would fight to defend Beaucaire, and if he returned alive from the encounter he would be allowed to see Nicolette, but once only, and for long enough merely to exchange a few words of love and to share a single kiss.

So great was the joy of even that limited expectation that Aucassin began to daydream of his love even in the thick of the battle, and stripped of his shield and lance he was being led away captive from the battlefield when he most fortunately came to his senses, ran down furiously upon the Count of Valence and gave him so lusty a clout with his sword that he stunned him and could lift him up to carry him off as a prisoner. The battle was won, and Aucassin rode home triumphant to claim his prize of the single kiss upon Nicolette's lips.

But the Count of Beaucaire had no intention of keeping his part of the bargain. He would never allow his son to see the wretched, low-born, worthless Nicolette, he stormed. And Aucassin, helpless before his blank refusal, promptly freed his prisoner the Count of Valence and retired to his chamber to give himself up to weeping.

This everlasting crying seems to have worked on the nerves of the Count of Beaucaire, for soon it was Aucassin's turn to be dragged away and thrown into a dungeon. Nicolette came to hear of how he wept and suffered for her still, and one warm night of May as the nightingales sang sadly outside her tower she could bear it no longer. She waited until the woman set to watch her was asleep, then swiftly knotted together her bedclothes and coverings to make a rope down which she could glide. Being so slim she could squeeze through the narrow window, and so find her freedom.

Fleeing through the moonlit alleys of Beaucaire, Nicolette came at last to discover the dungeon where her true love lay imprisoned. She managed to squeeze her head through a hole, and sure enough she could hear her beloved Aucassin weeping the night away, still sobbing helplessly in his love for her. But already her escape was discovered, and the guards were out looking for her. Warned by the kindly night watchman she hid behind a pillar, then fled barefoot from the town and out to the forest. And there it was that Aucassin came to her when his father, thinking Nicolette dead, at last released him.

Now the joy of the lovers was complete. Together they reached the coast and sailed away to a castle where they were received with kindness and sympathy. But alas, one day the ships of the terrible Saracens appeared, the castle was overrun, and many of its defenders slaughtered. Aucassin and Nicolette were seized and carried away to slavery, each on a different ship. The two craft were driven asunder in a swift and dangerous storm, and Aucassin came to the coast of Provence. Free at last he reached Beaucaire and discovered that he had succeeded to the title. As for Nicolette, she was taken to Carthage. And there to the great joy of all the people she was identified as their long lost princess. She had no lack of rich suitors; but no, Nicolette would not stay. Once more she set out on her travels, and with blackened face and in the guise of a troubadour she crossed the sea to Beaucaire.

Troubadours were always welcome, so in the castle of the new young Count she sang to him the true tale of Nicolette and of the Aucassin she had lost and to whom she would for ever be faithful. And of course her song brought back the tears to Aucassin's cheeks, but when the troubadour threw off the disguise and her tears of happiness began to wash away the blackening his own weeping also changed to tears of joy unbounded. The next day the two young lovers were married, to live for many years in such a state of ecstatic love as only a troubadour could sing – even if they seem to have been an exception to the rule that love could never be found in marriage.

V

Aigues-Mortes and Louis IX – the autumn fête – bull games
– Le Grau du Roi – birds of the Camargue – Palavas jousting
– the fair Maguelone – Frontignan – Sète, town of wine and
sardines.

L ong before the Canal du Midi was built to connect the Mediterranean
and Atlantic, the land west of the Rhone delta was linked to the
Rhone itself by a system of waterways through which boats of modest
draught could pass from one mere to another. Some of these channels had
been cut for the boats engaged in the salt trade – for the shallow and briny
lagoons have always been a source of salt produced by sun-drying. After
1500 there was the Beaucaire fair too, to which produce from the area
could be taken by small craft plying throughout the southern part of what
are now the provinces of Hérault and Bouches-du-Rhone.

But waterways had their opponents. When a landowner of Béziers tried
in 1618 to build a link from Béziers to the sea, paralleling the capricious
course of the Orb, a powerful league of carters, merchants, and landowners
saw their interests threatened by imports of cheap grain by water. They
roused those living near the course to object on health grounds to the
dangers of excavated mud, and their combined opposition stopped the
idea at birth. In 1644 Brun, an engineer of substantial means began a
canal from Agde to the Rhone (more or less the later Canal du Rhone à
Sète) and he put hundreds of men to work on the course, but the same
interests persuaded the States of the Languedoc that the possessions of
the church and gentry were under threat – so the assembly instructed
contractors from Nimes to go and fill in such sections as had already been
dug.

Later, when the Midi barges were able to ply from Bordeaux and
Toulouse to Sète, it was obviously of great advantage that they should
also be able to reach Beaucaire and the Rhone. The States of Languedoc
took the matter in hand and constructed the Canal des Étangs eastwards
from Sète, enlarging the medieval channels and linking together the lagoons
and salt marshes almost as far as Aigues Mortes. After various failures by
private individuals to cut a canal from there to the Rhone, the waterway
was at last opened in 1808. It has not changed much since that time, and
from the one lock of Nourriguier to Sète it is all on the same level as the
sea and lagoons. But it is a pleasant waterway, with the grand chain of

the Cevennes standing clear, purple-topped and mysterious to starboard. Over the banks lies a patchwork of fields, rich red and decked with vines in the glory of their spring buds or autumn leaf, or in places black as the Cambridgeshire fens. There are nightingales in the bank hedgerows, and groups of Camargue horses alongside, and perhaps a herd or two of solid looking black bulls.

And the Camargue which the canal skirts is of course a bird watchers' paradise. The hoopoes and bee-eaters lie further ahead, but watching over the banks as the boat glides past there will be black-winged stilts, looking awkward and very much over-legged as they search about among the pebbles or the watery weed. There are purple herons, larger than their humbler grey relatives, and egrets of both kinds wearing red or black boots respectively, and flamingoes. But these astonishing great birds are only seen in distant flight. It is beyond Aigues Mortes that we shall meet them intimately and by the hundred or thousand.

The run to Aigues Mortes usually took three or four hours, but already after three hours the bulk of the Tour de Constance was visible right at the end of the final straight cut. Somewhere off to the right lay the site of an abbey with the pleasant name of Psalmodi – though in fact it was salt and not plainsong which gave the place its name. Its monks, who lived entirely on the fish which abounded in the marshes, sold some of their land to Louis IX when he needed a base for his operations against the Infidel. Upon it he built the astonishing town of Aigues Mortes.

When Louis IX assembled his force of sixty thousand men, the walls had only just been begun, but planning for a protracted war with the Saracens he had devised a fortified town which could serve as a permanent point of assembly and supply, and the building of it was finished by his son. And while a fleet of Genoese vessels was being assembled in the grau, royal quartermasters were preparing dumps of supplies in places as far away as Cyprus. No previous crusade had been more carefully conceived, or more magnificent. Each involved nation had its encampment around the little town – for the great walls were not yet built – and the various flags showed which they were. There was the leopard of England, the lion of Brabant and the lion of St Mark for the Venetians. The Genoese vaunted a red cross, the papal contingent a triple crown. Altogether, sixty thousand warriors are said to have been assembled, but personally I doubt this estimate, for such a crowd could hardly have found standing room on the ships of that period assembled in the grau. Yet it was certainly a long procession that filed through the little church to receive a blessing upon their undertaking, for the special envoy of the pope had come to bestow on each knight a particular benediction as the warriors filed and clanked through the chapel which is still there, very much as it was at the time but mellowed by age. The year was 1248, and some of those who received the benediction bore titles newly taken from the heretic lords of the Languedoc whose people they had so recently slaughtered.

Even now one can almost see them embarking, each knight with a chest to serve him as travelling trunk, as a bed, as a coffin if he should be unfortunate enough to die at sea instead of cleft to the waist by a Saracen scimitar on the hot sands. And notable perhaps by his simplicity amid all the pomp and glitter was the rather dreamy figure of Louis IX, the future saint. Thin and fragile, pale and with his refined face framed in locks of long fair hair, he moved about with gentle confidence and an almost unearthly surety in the rightness of his mission. Cheers greeted him, we are told, wherever he was seen, but always he remained humble, the very epitome of gentility. Yet it seems that he had a tougher side too, for a hagiography which I acquired from a bouquinist at Aigues Mortes itself mentions that he was so pious that if anyone should blaspheme he had their tongue bored through with a red hot iron, declaring to the unfortunate victim that he would most willingly suffer the same torture himself if by doing so he could rid his realm of cursing and blasphemy. But now his thoughts were fixed only on wresting the Holy Land from the Infidel, as he stood with his fair hair streaming from below his helmet, beside the queen and her ladies aboard the royal galley to receive a final blessing, and the soldiers, bareheaded, raised the great strain from *Come, Holy Ghost, our hearts inspire*, and then the sails unfurled, and the heavy vessels slowly lumbered out to sea – the *Reine*, the *Montjoie*, the *Damoiselle* and their thirty-five companion ships. The banners streamed in the salty air and after some hours the fleet was hull down on the horizon. The Seventh Crusade was on its way.

Months later, Louis leapt ashore at Damietta and would have attacked the Musulman host single handed. Then came the costly victory of Mansourah, and after it the capture of Louis himself. He was ransomed in gold to return to France with such few of his soldiers as survived.

The queen who stood beside Louis as the fleet sailed from Aigues Mortes was the striking and talented Marguerite, eldest of the four remarkable daughters of Raymond-Bérenger V, Count of Provence and of Forcalquier – in which little provencal town there is a monument with an inscription in English to remind the visitor that the eldest of Marguerite's sisters, Aliénor (that is, Eleanor of Aquitaine, the province she collected through her first marriage) spouse of Henry Plantagenet, was born there. Beside the voluptuous Eleanor, whose funeral journey was one day to be marked by the erection of crosses such as Waltham Cross and Charing Cross where her cortege rested overnight, there was Sanche, who married the brother of the English king, and Béatrice who espoused the brother of the French monarch.

Marguerite's confessor related that the nineteen year old King Louis spent three whole nights in prayer before consumating the marriage with his bride of twelve. Yet in spite of the frequent lack of love in arranged top-drawer marriages the historian Joinville, who was himself on the expedition that sailed out from Aigues Mortes, told that the king himself and his beautiful Marguerite were so passionate that the king's mother, the domineering and jealous Blanche of Castille, was continually trying to keep them apart. The servants however were on their side, and when the lovers were at the chateau of Pontoise the staff arranged that they should have rooms one above the other and connected by a staircase hidden in the wall. When Blanche appeared, the footmen who patrolled the passages tapped discreetly with their staves so that one of the lovers could flee before Blanche came bursting into the room. "You never let me see my husband, alive or dead," Marguerite was later to scream when, after the birth of a daughter, Blanche drove the young king from her beside.

This passionate girl was the only spouse aboard the flotilla which set out from Aigues Mortes. By this time she was twenty-five, and the mother of three children whom she left behind in France. Louis had forbidden the nobles to take their wives with them, and it seems likely that he took Marguerite to keep her safe from her terrible mother-in-law. Yet it proved a wise decision for quite a different reason. With the king and his brother captured by the Turks, the army in retreat and the Genoese skippers about to up anchor and away, it was Marguerite who rose from her bed of childbirth to inspire the forces with fresh courage, negotiate the release of her husband and save Damietta. She eventually reach Aigues Mortes again with another three children, and it is perhaps tragic that the king's ardour began to wane so that he came to dedicate himself totally to a religious life instead of to the Marguerite who had done all for him. To be the wife of a future saint cannot have been easy.

In 1270 Louis was again at Aigues Mortes, to launch the Eighth Crusade. This time there was less enthusiasm, and the knights were in no hurry to leave. But their king led them on, and as they crossed the sea toward the African shore an epidemic of cholera broke out. Upon landing, Louis himself assisted with burying the dead 'not holding his nose as did the others', but he was already too old and too sick to see the campaign through. Below the walls of Carthage he died, and the role of Aigues Mortes in history was over.

Details are known of the ship upon which King Louis set out upon his ill-fated expedition. There was a stern-castle which contained a private room or cabin for the king, a boudoir for the queen, a small cabin for her attendants and a chapel or oratory. The historian Joinville wrote that all the ships in the fleet had as many as twenty-five anchors, a thought that would give a yachtsman a nightmare. However, this great number was probably needed, for the ships were of large draught and had to be able to hold their position securely in storms driving toward the land.

Less grand ships transported ordinary travellers and pilgrims. The latter could travel at a reduction in the bilge, where they camped on the ballast. By regulation each was nevertheless allowed to demand a minimum personal space for himself which measured in modern terms about six square feet. There he kept himself, his stock of water and provisions, a lantern, and his bed-coffin, so he must certainly have been glad when after several weeks or months in such cramped conditions the shores of the Holy Land hove in sight.

It is from the channel which runs to Le Grau du Roi that one can best see the town, one of its longer sides rising from the reeds in medieval might as a third of a mile of formidable grey wall broken only by five posterns. No building inside the place is so tall that it can hope even to poke a chimney above the line of the ramparts, and none until recently has dared to venture outside the wall. To experience Aigues Mortes in the red sunset is to be carried back into the medieval days of siege and chivalry. And during daylight hours one may for a few francs walk round the town on the parapet of the walls, an experience not to be missed.

The circuit starts at the powerful Tour de Constance, still capped with the iron cage-work of the medieval lighthouse. This tower was built by Louis to defend his port but was later used as a prison for those who dared to hold beliefs contrary to the established order, and it is still a particularly holy place to all French protestants. In it was incarcerated at the age of eight the girl Marie Durand, and probably it was she who carved the inscription *Au Ciel – Résistez* in the place of confinement she shared with other protestants whom she sustained and comforted in their imprisonment. One day the governor of the Languedoc inspected the tower and had the cell opened. Out of the goodness of his heart, or from remorse, he released the maid and some of her companions. Marie Durand was then no longer a girl. She was a grown woman of forty-five and her memory was specially celebrated in 1985, three hundred years after Louis XIV infamously revoked the Edict of Nantes which for nearly a century had guaranteed a modest freedom of religion. Then the Huguenots had to flee for their lives or be murdered, robbed, and in many cases made to serve out their lives as slaves in the royal galleys. A very moving monument to these latter unwilling seamen is there at the entrance to the Tour de Constance, an appropriate reminder that for all the magnificence of Versailles – and the building of the Canal du Midi, for that matter – Le Roi Soleil behaved in an inexcusable fashion to those who believed differently from his influential catholic advisers, and thereby drove much of the best talent out of his dominions.

From the walls one can have a complete view of the compact little town with its central square and the streets laid out in an exact geometric pattern.

One can also peer down on whatever is happening below – which is likely to be a hen scratching in the refuse, a cat surreptitiously salvaging a fish head from a dustbin, or perhaps an old woman dozing before her doorway with the knitting lying on her lap. Looking northward one may see the Cevennes, blue as ever in the afternoon haze and to the right the narrowing azure ribbon of canal leading toward St Gilles. Across the waterlogged shallows on the seaward side several tall pyramids point up to the sky, pure white. They are large enough to be seen for several miles, and in fact they are made of salt. For salt is one product which can be culled from this desolate landscape. Another is wine, and the headquarters of the Listel vintages are visible to the left of the grau. Another co-operative is just outside the walls on the southern side. Once again, the wine is drinkable, but it is worth waiting another few days of voyage.

Aigues Mortes is much visited nowadays, and its former age-old quiet is replaced in the summer by all the trade of tourism. Nevertheless it is a place to be experienced. The market square contains a fine statue of the young King Louis, crown on head, ready to leave for the Middle East, and seeming to look out disdainfully over the rows of tables and chairs of the surrounding cafés. The 'Fête d'Aigues Mortes', takes place about the middle of October. This is an entirely local affair, with the town band often playing in the square. There are contests of pétanque, and bicycle racing, and outside the walls there is all the fun of the fair for a whole week. But the central core of the fête is the daily series of bull-games conducted in an arena consisting almost entirely of private family boxes or pews with three or four tiers of wooden seats. There is a small stand for visitors, and all the entertainment is free of charge.

It is impossible to travel far in the Languedoc without noticing the fascination that tauromachy, or the cult of the bull, has for the people of the area, so that all the way from the Rhone to Toulouse one is sure to come across posters tacked to trees or pasted on hoardings, advertising the next local event in which men match their skill against that of the bull.

Indeed, some sort of entertainment involving bulls is the favourite local sport throughout the Midi, and it has nothing at all in common with the cruelties and slaughterhouse scenes of Spanish bull fighting. The corrida, with its killing of a helpless bull after allowing it to eviscerate a few terrified horses, is not entirely confined to Spain itself and the one blot on the happy Languedoc is that this deliberate cruelty spills over occasionally into the arenas of Nimes and Arles, Beaucaire and other places. I have to admit that on the few occcasions when I have read in the newspaper that one of the over-dressed Spanish experts in this kind of cruelty has been the victim of a surprise move by a wounded bull and has been gored and trampled to death, I have not felt like shedding tears and have even found it difficult to repress a cheer of delight.

Any friend of animals or of the world we share with them must deplore this tradition of the corrida. Debased and inhuman as such blood-letting is, it is a direct descendant of the horrors of the Roman amphitheatres, and of course the arenas of both Arles and Nimes were indeed places where such bloodthirsty spectacles could be seen in Roman times. But the bull games such as those of Aigues Mortes are entirely different. They are derived from the ancient sport of the Grecian settlers of Marseille and other coastal settlements, and if a bull should lose a hair of its head, or be hurt in any way, the audience would be most distressed.

In this Grecian or Provencal form, youths match their skill against that of the animal. The exact form in which they do so varies considerably, but usually the festival begins with an abrivado such as I witnessed at Trinquetaille. The guardians or cowboys of the Camargue on their sturdy little half wild horses drive bulls along the street, sometimes from a cattle truck at one end to a similar one at the other, but often on their way to the arena. Side streets are generally barricaded off, but the population has to look after itself and dodges into doorways and behind trees, or climbs on to windowsills as I have done myself. Occasionally the cruelty latent in many men may show itself in that someone will try to kick a bull as it passes, but on the whole such activities are not approved and a spirit of gentleness marks the entire event.

The most frequent type of bull match is the *course de cocarde*. This event takes places in the arena, which even the smallest town possesses. The bulls are run for about a quarter of an hour each, during which time athletic young men try to get themselves chased at such close quarters that they can reach behind them with a sort of comb and snatch a tassel which is tied between the horns, or perhaps bound tight round the base. Whether successful or not, the *razeteur* then has to take a flying leap over a stout fence to escape. Occasionally the bull follows, an event which clears the adjacent rows of seats with magical speed. (The *razet* is not the comb, but the swooping semi-circular rush with which the competitor needs to approach the animal to stand a chance of success.)

Small cash prizes are offered, various shops or public spirited individuals continually adding a few francs until the last cocarde has gone or, which is more likely, the bull's time is up. The sport may be played by expert razeteurs, impeccably dressed in white, in which case the bull's horns are not tampered with. On other occasions the contest is a 'course libre', free for all who like to try it, and then the horn points are padded or covered with blunt knobs, so that a bruising and trampling is the worst one could suffer. In fact, it is very rare for a player to be injured, as none is likely to get himself deliberately chased by a bull unless he is quite sure he can get away and clear the fence. The amateur contests are notable for the number of youths who boisterously enter the arena to impress their girl

friends, but are out and over the fence the moment the bull even looks
casually in their direction. All the same it is not a good idea for a holiday
visitor to try to show off. The fence he will have to leap may be higher
than he thinks.

Nor should he be deceived by the fact that the animals may sometimes
be announced as *vaches* and then prove indeed to be not bulls but cows.
A domestic cow has been bred up for centuries for milk production and
is as placid as – a cow. Shouting and waving the arms will send a fat
Frisian fleeing to the furthest corner of the field. But not so the cow of
the black cattle of the Camargue. Released into the arena she will snort,
paw the ground, fling up the dust and rush like a rocket at anyone in the
arena who shouts or moves, just as the female of the wild Chillingham
cattle of northern England will immediately charge at an intruder.

Inevitably one wonders how the *razeteurs* learn their art without being
tossed or trampled to death. The same problem might worry a Provencal
watching Rugby football for the first time. However, I have seen some of
the first stages, as at Les Saintes Maries, where in the interval the arena
was open to the under twelves, one of whom had a pair of horns on his
head. It was really just a game of tig, but it had all the elements of chasing
and escaping. At Beaucaire I have also seen the arena thrown open to
young boys, and on that occasion there was an Alsatian dog which would
rush at any who might be running and nudge him in the leg, but with its
mouth shut. If a boy stood still, the dog did not go for him at all, which
is much the same with the bull.

A common and highly entertaining sport which I have often watched
on Friday nights at Aigues Mortes is *"tauropiscine"*, in which one can win
a few francs for getting the bull into the swimming pool, a shallow temporary one in the middle of the arena. Even though a player may fling himself
into the water under the bull's nose, the creature is most likely to stop
obstinately at the brink. This is a safer entertainment than the cocarde
for the volunteer visitor, and a fifteen year old English schoolboy friend
of mine who entered the ring at Aigues Mortes had the bull in the water
twice and was the only player to succeed. However, I have also seen a lad
fling himself into the pool, only to be followed by the bull, who promptly
sat on him. So perhaps discretion is still the better course.

The variety of games is endless. '*Tauroball*' is a scratch game of soccer
between two opposing teams, the only addition being a loose bull on the
pitch. To my mind it is a great improvement on professional football, and
I would like to see the same done with cricket, which then would be far
less soporific. Then there is mere clowning. Some tauroclowns are exceedingly expert. The tricks include such items as dressing up as a woman
and getting the corset stuck round ones ankles just as the animal charges.
I have seen the clown at Les Saintes Maries skiing behind the tail of a

bull which is rushing after his companion, and a dancing couple at Beaucaire who deftly let the bull rush between them at each sally. There is no end to the possibilities, and the event is a thoroughly good and harmless entertainment for children. But most astonishing of all is, I think, the 'long leap'. This, which is a direct import from the Greece of long ago, is one of the most expert tricks – and again, an inexperienced boatman should not be persuaded to volunteer. At one end of the area is a man who keeps making as if to run toward the other end, where there is a bull held on a few yards of rope. The man starts, the bull starts and is suddenly checked. The man goes back, and starts again. So does the bull, only to be checked once more. And so on. This seems to have the effect of winding the bull up like clockwork, for when at perhaps the twelfth or fifteenth sortie the rope is slipped the creature charges for all it is worth, head down, snorting, and dust flying. At the same instant the man races straight toward it, and with brilliant precision places his hands on top of its head and vaults right over the animal to turn a somersault in the air and land behind its tail. In another version, the man suddenly stops, erect and motionless. The bull seems baffled, for it will stop just short of him and turn aside. This too needs considerable nerve, and complete confidence in the bull behaving as it should and not being psychologically maladjusted.

All the way from St Gilles to Aigues Mortes the black cattle are to be seen, grazing the rough ground and the swampy marshes, or roaming over the wasteland in a semi-wild state, and inevitably one wonders where they came from. In fact, they are now more domesticated than wild, and they exist in *manades*, which correspond roughly to different stables. The term really means a group of cattle or horse which one Camargue guardian or cow-boy can 'hold in his hand' or look after. With their fine black coats and heavy shoulders the animals may be survivors of the original *Bos primigenius*, or they may be descendants of a line of cattle imported by the Greeks for very much the same purposes as now. From the moment of birth they are marked and under the care of a *guardien* until three years old. Then they are castrated, an operation simply performed in these days by slipping a stout rubber ring over the scrotum. This shuts off the blood supply, the testes degenerate and eventually drop off. Naturally, the tying is not a pleasant sensation, and a bull may very reasonably wish to turn upon the castrator and attack him. For this reason the *guardiens* sometimes provide scarecrow effigies stuffed with straw, upon which the young animal can vent his fury after the stricture.

Probably the first public appearance of the bullock will be running through the streets in an abrivado, after which he will gradually be put through his paces as a performer in the arena. He is known to the audience by name – I can recall one named Desiré being a great favourite at St Gilles – and he soon becomes used to the business. He knows that his time is up when a fanfare on the loud speakers announces the end of a bout, and he will usually at once stop chasing the *razeteurs* and trot meekly toward the exit where the lorry is parked to take him home. If he does not, an elderly cow with a bell round her neck is sent into the arena to call him home to mummy or a retired bull may be sent in to accompany out a reluctant cow. Some beasts become as well known by name as champion race horses in other countries, and are individually announced on the posters. The bronze bull on the Rhone wall at Beaucaire is one of the most famous of all, named Clairon.

I have known Aigues Mortes for more than twenty years, and have a special affection for it. In the early days it was a forgotten town, far from anywhere, and even if year by year it has become more and more popular and the price of a cup of coffee in the square has gone up in parallel, nothing can take away its charm. The old men, tanned and wrinkled, still sit on the seat beside the great bastion of the eastern gate, the Sunday market outside the long wall still has the profusion of cheese and meat, paté and bread and vegetables, and of course the sad ubiquitous African with his pitiful display of tawdry trinkets still hoping for a customer. I have even seen one of them stand all morning beside a pair of new grand-father clocks, perhaps unable to realise that such an object is not easily taken home in a shopping basket. Of course, the place has changed, but one can still draw in there for nothing, which one may well have to do if the swing bridge is closed for the passage in summertime only of the little red and white train to the seaside at Le Grau du Roi.

This is another place of considerable but quite different charm. A channel rich in mullet runs down from the railway bridge corner to the Mediterranean three miles away. Probably it follows the route by which Louis IX set out with his fleet, and it ends in the seaside resort of Le Grau, which is really the fishing port of Aigues Mortes and a very picturesque one too. It is cut clean in two by the waterway, and beyond the swing bridges which connect the two sides there are built out over the water shrimp saloons and shell fish saloons, oyster saloons and in fact saloons for every sort of invertebrate one can extract from the sea, and at the extreme end a line of hotels tries to find its feet on the sandbank which flanks the salt marsh on its seaward side. It is a small resort, unsophisticated and without any ambition of competing with the Cote d'Azur, and if the town itself is of no great beauty the waterway is lined with dozens of fishing boats, sunbaked and salty, their faded paint of sun-bleached blue and white or russet brown bringing gaiety to the pinkish tints of the houses.

Some time in mid-June there takes place at Le Grau du Roi the Fête de la Mer et des Pêcheurs. This includes bull games in the arena and no doubt a march of brass bands and majorettes, but there is also a fine contest of water jousting on the channel through the town. On the Sunday the entire fishing fleet puts out to sea, and visitors are invited to go on board free of charge for the ceremony of blessing the sea and casting overboard wreaths in memory of those fishermen who never returned. This is a very colourful and moving occasion, and one which is taken very seriously.

It is on the run down to Le Grau du Roi – which is totally devoid of quays or anything but rocks along the sides of the channel – that flamingoes can be seen, and seen properly. When first I went to Arles, flamingoes existed in the Camargue but they were something of a rarity. I had to apply to the office of the Nature Conservancy and buy a pass which was valid for four hours if I remember right. Somewhere down the right bank of the river we were allowed to drive in to the reserve and bump our way along a series of dykes and banks to the holy of holies, the vast Étang de Vaccarés, where we were assured we would see flamingoes. I think we probably did, but they were at such a great distance that I am still not sure that they might not have been minute specks of dust on the prisms of my field glasses.

Certainly, the birds existed in the Camargue at that time, but they seemed to have forgotten how to breed until ingenious conservationists built for them some little artificial mounds not much bigger than an up-turned waste paper basket. This seems to have been just what the birds were waiting for. They began to breed, if not like flies, then at least like flamingoes. More mounds were built, the birds adopted do-it-yourself habits, and during the quarter of a century that I have voyaged through the area west of the Rhone they have multiplied to such an extent that flocks of hundreds and even thousands can be seen in the meres and lagoons all the way from Aigues Mortes to Sète and down the branch canal which runs from Narbonne to La Nouvelle. On the way to Le Grau du Roi they are just over the canal bank, pale pink and awkward looking, snabbling at the algae with head inverted in the shallow water and seeing the world upside down. Maybe they will rise and fly in line, displaying the full glory of the intense rose and black that is only seen during their slow flight.

They are strange birds, these. They live in crowds with the young among them, each mummy knowing its chick purely by some slight difference in the plaintive cheeping sound. Black-headed gulls may stalk alongside a flock wading in the shallows, waiting for an opportunity to snatch a baby and tear it to pieces. But the adults seem completely unmoved. There is no screaming or flapping of wings, merely a momentary look of resignation before returning to the business of noisly snabbling the green algae.

The flamingo needs shallows, sunshine – and flamingoes. It is the temperature combined with the fertilising excrement that causes the algae to grow fast enough to cater for the daily needs of such quantities of feeders.

And variations in the water level may cause the flock to move. The water must be shallow but not dried up, and along the canal to Sète it is noticeable how their locations may change from one year to another. They no longer need the secret remoteness of the Étang de Vaccarés but from the train or the canal one can see them wandering through the shallow and rather dirty water by the refinery at Frontignan or the Sète gas works.

Some might find the waterway to Sète dull, but I do not. From Aigues Mortes the scenery soon changes, and the canal is dyked off from a series of wide and shallow meres with faded and forgotten little village ports in the hazy distance toward the hills to starboard. These lagoons are the haunts of duck and scoter, of flamingo, and of men who sit in little green boats armed with a gun or a rod, a net or a trident, for whatever kind of game comes closest. Between these wide waters and the sea there is only the low and narrow bar of sand which has been dropped by the current and flung up by the waves to seal them off, and this tenuous line of dry land supports at its eastern end the seaside resorts of Carnon Plage and Palavas-les-Flots. The last of these has all the fun of the seaside, from ice-cream and a roller-coaster to an arena for bull-games, but it has a curious sort of dignity of its own, too. Somewhat on the style of a Dutch town it has a number of canals with a row of houses down either side, these waterways leading off from the course of the River Lez, which stretches from the Canal du Rhone à Sète down to the sea, where a sizeable yacht port has been built. Unfortunately a low bridge prevents any but the smallest of craft from entering the Lez where it crosses the main canal, so the sea is inaccessible for a boat of any size, but Palavas is worth a visit just the same for there is a gay stateliness about the buildings which flank the Lez on either side, and near the yacht port one can cross from shore to shore by means of an aerial bridge, a sort of cable-car which soars above the mast of any fishing boat which may be coming in with a catch, or a trip-boat carrying a load of visitors for a promenade-en-mer.

Once when we walked into Palavas it happened to be on the day when, for some fishy reason or other, the Lez was teeming with *daurade*, that particularly bony and unattractive deep-bellied fish which the French like to regard as a delicacy. My wife's cookery book describes this creature, the "Gilt-head bream" as a prized fish, formerly sacred to Aphrodite, and reckons it superior to all other kinds of bream, but to me that is the faintest of recommendations. But of course the temptation as the hordes swam along the Lez on their way to or from the salty lagoons was one that the visitors and inhabitants of Palavas could not resist, and each bridge was lined on either side with so many fishermen that there was hardly a moment when at least one daurade was not flapping and twisting on a line being reeled in.

Beyond the area of the anglers we found crowds ranged along the river walls and stagings and jetties, for the all-Languedoc jousting finals were to begin, and as a spectator sport I have always found it one of the best. The battle is between successions of champions representing their respective teams, and they look very fine and grand in their curious craft, shaped like a ship's lifeboat and with seats for eight or ten oarsmen, the one in white, elegantly trimmed in scarlet, the other white and blue. Each has an elegant female figurehead, and the sides of the boat are painted with baroque curtains gathered into folds and tied with tasselled cords of gold. At the stern a long raised ramp projects far above the water to end in a tiny platform. The relays of jousters of the two teams sit near the stern, ready to be poised on their perches for the attack. Each craft has its musicians, and the two vessels are rowed furiously towards each other with oars straining, drum and oboe playing, and the people shouting deliriously from the wharves and balconies and the bridges. A moment of sudden silence, and the boats glide swiftly past each other with a powerful momentum. Each combatant levels his lance toward his rival's shield and tries to parry his thrust. A moment of unsteadiness, a splash, and the victor raises high his lance whilst his adversary swims ashore. The water is warm if not excessively clean and the sport is a good-humoured one which is not limited entirely to the Languedoc. I have watched it in Toulon, in Vienne and even as far north as Strasbourg, but it is on the littoral of the Languedoc that it reaches its most expert heights.

Beyond Palavas the seaside development stops, and the sand bar is almost entirely deserted except for a cluster of fishermen's huts or a caravan site clinging to the shelf where the grau breaks through to the sea. Though romantic the scene is one of extraordinary solitude, and the loneliness is made suddenly more acute when one realises that a simple cracked and buttressed building clustered about by pines on a knoll to the seaward side of the canal is all that remains of the cathedral of Maguelone, a see which has been extinct for centuries. The place was destroyed by Charles Martel when retreating from the invading Moors in the 8th century, and although it was rebuilt in the twelfth, the people left it for less swampy surroundings. The broken down cathedral has recently been restored, and is the setting for excellent concerts by leading chamber orchestras. It is reached by a little ferry, and is a curious place to visit, but the first time I did so was by anchoring offshore when chugging down the coast, and jumping overboard to swim to the sandy Mediterranean beach on the further side of the island and walk up to the ruins through the vines.

It is upon this strange and remote place that centres the story of Pierre of Provence, young and handsome and chivalrous, who, having heard of the astounding loveliness of the daughter of the King of Naples set off to that far-off destination to behold her for himself, and jousted before her in the tournament then taking place. It proved to be a case of mutual love at first sight, but unfortunately the King of Naples had promised the fair princess Maguelone to a prince, so there was nothing for the young couple but to elope, in the full certainty of an undying love. It can be noted here that this was not a case of betrothal with parental approval, so the story is a perfectly proper one for a romantic troubadour to relate.

In the noontide heat Maguelone became tired, so the couple sat in the shade of a tree and she fell asleep on his lap. Pierre noticed a little silken bag in her bosom, and filled with curiosity he quietly drew it out to peer inside. With joy he saw it contained three rings he had sent to her earlier through her nurse (he must have been quite young at the time) and not wishing to wake her he put down the little purse on a stone. Unfortunately a raven swooped, snatched the bag and flew off with it.

Pierre pushed his coat as a pillow under Maguelone's head, then rushed after the raven, which eventually perched on a rock in the sea. He flung a stone at the bird and gave it such a fright that it opened its beak and dropped the little bag into the water. At this, he hurried off to find a boat and rowed out to collect the purse, which fortunately was still floating. But the wind got up, and while still trying to retrieve the jewels, Pierre was blown out to sea and eventually reached land again at Alexandria, where the Sultan took him on as his private page.

Meanwhile, the poor girl awoke and found herself alone. After a fearful night in the forest she set out for Rome, and so that she would not be detected by her father's men she managed to exchange clothes with a female pilgrim, and disguised herself as an anchorite. Eventually she set out from Genoa on a ship bound for Aigues Mortes. Hearing of a small island which would serve her as a hermitage, she used her remaining jewellery to pay for the building of a church, and a hospital for the pilgrims and the poor. The one woman who became her close friend was the Countess of Melgueil (now Mauguio), who eventually unburdened herself to Maguelone of the great tragedy in her life. Her beloved son had gone off in a fit of romantic dreaming about some girl or other to Naples, and had never been heard of since.

One day a local fisherman netted a tunny, and brought it to the count as a present. When it was gutted, the stomach of the fish was found to contain a little bag with three rings. At once the countess recognised them as the ones she had given to her dear son, and, of course, she told her friend Maguelone about this extraordinary incident, and showed her the rings.

The story now moves to Alexandria, where Pierre had become such a favourite that the Sultan had come to regard him very much as his own son, and eventually allowed him to return to Provence to visit his home. Pierre had amassed a fortune, but to keep it hidden from the skipper and crew of the cargo vessel on which he was to travel he packed it in fourteen barrels topped up with salt. One day the vessel put in for water at an island off the coast of Corsica, and Pierre went ashore to stretch his legs. He walked some way into the interior, lay down in the sun and went sound asleep.

The crew searched for Pierre but were unable to find him, so eventually the captain assumed some awful fate had overtaken him and set sail without him. When the ship reached Provence, the honest skipper felt that he could not keep the belongings of a man lost on the voyage, and hearing of the energetic and saintly young woman who ministered to the sick he sailed along the shore to the small islet and presented her with the barrels of salt. When one day she needed some more salt and went to dig in one of the barrels she was amazed to find the store of treasure, with which she reconstructed and enlarged the church and hospital.

As for Pierre he became ill on his small island, and though sick and half-starved he was lucky enough to be rescued by some fishermen who put in there. Having also heard of Maguelone they delivered him to her care, but he was so transformed through his sufferings that she did not recognise him. And because she was wearing a veil he, of course, did not realise who she was. Then at last came the day when he told her of his life's great sorrow, the loss of his one true love. The rest of the tale can easily be imagined, and as the fair Maguelone was a free agent and had not taken the veil but was only disguised as one who might have done so, the happy ending was just as one could wish. After which the troubadour no doubt passed round the hat.

Another story makes a more obvious connection for the name of Maguelone. Simon the leper is said in this version to have been among the boatload of refugees from the Holy Land, and to have settled on the island where there was a temple served by Vestal virgins. He preached the gospel, which so upset them that the women murdered him and flung his body into the *étang*. His companion, Mary Magdalene, escaped and transferred herself to the cave of the Sainte Baume in Provence after sheltering for a short while in another cave close to the island, at what is now Villeneuve-les-Maguelone. It is her name that is recalled in that strangely romantic isle.

Of all the times I have run this canal past Maguelone, perhaps the most beautiful was on a summer's night late in August. The faintest crescent of moon lay ahead, the pines on the hillock by the cathedral moved ever so slightly in the warm breeze, and gulls sat silent on the posts on the dyke over which eel fishermen had draped their nets. But ahead and on both sides of *Thames Commodore* scores of unearthly arrows in palest blue accompanied her, this magic being the disturbance in the water as mullet or bream by the dozen flashed their way through the hosts of Noctiluca or other phosphorescent organisms. It was a fairy, unreal sight, as though a host of spirits were clearing the canal for us and helping us on our way. But even by day the course is beautiful, the dry hills slashed with a red gash where the autoroute has been sliced through the rocks, the tower and faded rooftops of Villeneuve, and somewhat more astern the tall, forbidding mass of the Pic du Loup, the final burst of the Cevennes beyond the shimmering blocks of bustling Montpellier.

Soon the tall refinery chimneys of Frontignan come into view, but however much the air may reek of hydrocarbons the cramped and ancient little town is still concerned, as it has been for centuries, with producing a wine with a flavour all of its own. Rabelais and Louis XIV both extolled the delights of Muscat de Frontignan, and so did Voltaire in a letter to a friend whom he implored to save his life by sending him a quart of it. It is pinkish brown, sweet and aromatic, pressed from the grapes which grow along the canal bank and beneath the equally aromatic clouds floating downwind of the refinery. It is said that Hercules himself arrived at Frontignan at vintage time. He was so taken with the wine that he filled his wine-skin in order to take the muscat up to Olympus to delight the chief of the gods. And Zeus, when he tasted the wine brought to him by the victorious hero and traveller, declared that it was better than ambrosia. From that day onward the proper drink of the deities would be the sweet muscat of Frontignan, the god declared. Anyone who shares the opinion of Zeus, or of Thomas Jefferson (who ordered one hundred and twenty bottles for President George Washington) can draw in at the blending establishment by the bridge and load the wine aboard. Others will have to draw in there in any case to await the lifting of the bridge.

Approaching Sète the canal becomes dirtier, its banks littered with rubbish. But there is compensation in the fact that this is the part of the route where one again comes very close to the flamingoes. Incongruously, they stand unconcerned in the shallows over the canal bank beyond the oil storage tanks, busily dredging up food with their inverted scoops. Beyond their marsh the route broadens out and at last opens to the long inland salt lake of the Bassin de Thau. The approach to the town itself, and the exit to the sea is to the left, through the channel crossed by two immense lifting bridges. At least, that is how things are now, but in 1962 things were different. On reaching the backstairs area of Sète we forked left into the Canal de la Peyrade which ran for a mile or two past warehouses and timber yards, wharves and heaps of rubbish to emerge into the dock basin and cross it right into the centre of the town. The mooring was a pleasant one, with baker and grocer within a stone's throw and the continual bustle of coming and going over the bridge beside which we moored. Beyond this bridge the waterway ran out into the main town canal, which crosses Sète from end to end and makes the place just as beautiful as it really is.

In those days it was my habit to try to discover in advance something about the places I hoped to visit during the summer's voyage. I knew nothing about Sète, or Cette as they sometimes spelled it, except that it was at the eastern end of the line of the Canal du Midi, and was where the waterway reached the sea and seagoing vessels unloaded into barges or vice-versa. Normally I would write to the mayor, who would instruct a minion to send me a lot of material about tennis courts and the municipal swimming bath, but on this occasion I wrote to the harbourmaster to ask what facilities there were. In reply he wrote to say that Sète was the mightiest French Mediterranean port after Marseille (Toulon being a naval base, apparently did not count) and that it had ferry traffic to North Africa. It was a great place for refineries, and tanker craft were continually on the move, I was given to understand. That was hardly surprising, I thought, for the chief of the port went on to say that there were eighteen pipe-lines. Then he explained that only one of these was for hydrocarbons; the rest carried wine. If the *Commodore* wished to stay and winter in the port of Sète she would be most welcome.

The picture of Sète that this conjured up was not very far from the truth. Traffic rumbled over the cobbled street and along the quaysides, much of it tanker lorries but not bearing the familiar house colours of Esso and Shell or BP. Instead they were Cinzano and Dubonnet or Martini and Rossi, or more often nameless carriers from which a tell-tale dripping of dark red into a bucket hung beneath the stop-cock at the rear indicated that this was the produce of the Languedoc on its way to be blended or bottled. A smell of wine born on the wings of the mistral pervaded the whole town, but when the mistral died and was replaced by a warm wind from the south then the odour changed too. It changed to fish, for the harbour master had omitted to mention that Sète was a major port for the sardine trade. Freezer lorries from as far away as Boulogne and Dunkirk would be loaded at the fish quay and drive for a day and a night to deliver fresh fish that had never swum in the North Sea or flopped over the Dogger Bank or the Varne.

It was this immense activity of fishing that gave Sète so much of its charm, the big drifters in their sun-faded paint of blue and green and red jostling for position at the unloading quay where the town canal ran toward its end behind the huge protecting mole. And this canal at that time was spanned by three or four swing bridges, and a strident ringing of bells preceded the clanging of barriers as each span in turn swung to let pass some craft on its way to or from the great salty lake of the Étang de Thau. Nowadays, in the interest of lessening the congestion of road traffic the bridges have been replaced by fixed ones just high enough to pass the one-man oyster boats from the ports or the Étang, but no more – though I myself have rowed round the town for my own amusement and to the astonishment of the Sètois. Large ships and *Thames Commodore* have had in recent years to proceed via the docks, and there a whole succession of big bridges will open without demur one after the other if one asks at the harbour office. It is satisfactory for the boatman, if somewhat frustrating for any family bound for the seaside and having to wait in a lengthy queue of traffic until one has graciously passed by.

The main reason for the undoubted charm of Sète, lying at the foot of the Mont St Clair which long ago was an offshore island, lies in its origin. Up until the year of the Great Fire of London there was no settlement there of any kind, but the French had long been concerned that there was no port along the whole of the Mediterranean coast west of Marseille, except for small creeks with a handful of fishing boats. Richelieu had tried to overcome this deficiency by building a naval base at the foot of the Cap d'Agde a little further west, but only one mole (now incorporated in the enormous development of the marina) was partly completed. It was the construction of the Canal du Midi that gave the impetus to the founding of a harbour. If sea ships were to transfer cargoes to barges there had of course to be a port where they could do so. The Canal du Midi was to end in the Étang de Thau, and in 1666 Colbert instructed Riquet, the builder of the canal, to construct a terminal port. Riquet very wisely chose the lee side of the Mont St Clair at the far end of the Étang, and he cut through the sandbank which separated it from the sea. A vast breakwater was built in the sea to protect the site from storm waves driven from the south, and the channel itself was laid out very much on the Dutch pattern, with half the street on either side and a number of bridges spanning the cut. Louis XIV was persuaded by Colbert to give tax concessions to anyone settling there, and quickly a polyglot collection of merchants arrived from all round the Mediterranean to settle in the houses and business premises stretching down either side of the canal. These houses were built all in the same period; the late sixteen hundreds. It was a time of fine style and good taste even in modest buildings, and it is this homogeneity – as opposed to the uniformity of a modern planning authority – which makes Sète so delightful a place to walk in and sniff the air, or to sit and paint the waterfront with its brightly coloured craft.

Sète considers itself to be the centre of the sport of water jousting, and those combatants knocked off their perches are fortunate in that the water of the town canal is astonishingly clean, and the jousters run no risks from pollution. Sea anemones of various exotic kinds wave their tentacles from the quay walls and bridge piers, and mussels grow on the piles. The cleanliness is due to the changes in wind and air pressure, for the fourteen mile length of the Étang de Thau is connected to the sea only through this canal and a couple of minor unnavigable creeks further west. An offshore wind will cause the sea to recede somewhat and the salty water streams through the town at a pace that can reach more than a knot or two. And it is the same outgoing current which can catch yachtsmen unawares as they come from apparently still water into the broad gulley leading up to the main railway and road bridges to wait for the opening time. Suddenly they find themselves being driven down on the bridges faster than their small engine can drive them in the opposite direction.

A year or two back we were lying at the pretty quayside on the Étang side of the bridges, just ahead of an empty barge which had delivered a cargo from central France. Outside it lay a cruiser yacht in charge of a young man who was delivering it from Germany to some Spanish marina. He was a pleasant fellow and might have looked even more attractive if he had brought his razor with him on such a long voyage. In the evening he wandered out, probably to the Café de la Marine, and presumably returned late, tired, and maybe overfilled with beer or wine. He had a dog as company and as guard for the boat, an unattractive cur with rather large teeth and a disposition not to regard strangers as anything but objects to be bitten.

About seven in the morning the barge skipper told us he was leaving. He knocked on the side of the cruiser and the dog came on deck, barking hysterically and gnashing its teeth. The skipper knocked again and again, but there was no sign of the young man. The bargemaster then started his engine, cast off, shoved out into the stream, and instead of giving one of the yacht's lines to us so that we could haul it alongside ourselves or against the quay he merely flung them in the water and steamed away toward the canal to Frontignan. The water was streaming swiftly through the bridges and it carried the cruiser rapidly toward them. In no time at all the boat had struck the massive railway span and tilted sharply sideways in the current. We could hear the crack as the mast broke in two. The German did not witness this accident, and I presumed he was ashore buying his provisions.

I was preparing to try the difficult task of rescuing the boat, savage dog and all, which would not have been easy because we also were too high for the span, when a fishing boat came by which was a foot or two lower and so was able to pass under the bridges. The skipper asked me how the boat had got there and I told him. I also had the name and registration number of the barge which I later telephoned to the canal office, suggesting that the ship could conveniently be stopped by not raising the bridge at Frontignan. The fisherman was quite as shocked as we were at the barge skipper's behaviour so he turned, ran down on the stream, swung round, and managed to extract the cruiser without more than a certain amount of splintering of the grip rails on the cabin roof. He then towed it up to the quay and we helped him make the boat fast. All the while the dog shrieked and slobbered but we avoided being mauled.

Some ten minutes later the young man appeared. But not from the boulangerie. His head came through the hatch and he sleepily rubbed his eyes, wondering how he had come to lie against the quay instead of the barge. I pointed to the wreckage on deck, the split tabernacle and broken mast.

"I must have slept soundly," he said mildly. And patting the vociferous dog he went below to dress. Or perhaps to turn in again.

An extra charm of Sète for myself lies in the fact that one can steam straight into the dock basin either from the sea or through the series of bridges from the Étang, select a convenient berth close to such shops as one needs, and simply stay there with no other accompaniment than perhaps a few hands from a trawler using the broad quay to lay out and darn one of their nets. No official comes round to chase one off the wall, none comes with a receipt book to demand the ridiculous charges levied by marinas (of which there is one just round the corner from the sardine berths). It is a friendly place from which one may come and go as one wishes. And (except in the yacht harbour) the water is everywhere clean.

I once left Sète late in the evening by sea, to head for Le Grau du Roi. I knew that the swing bridge giving access to the cut to Aigues Mortes opened at eight in the morning but not again until the afternoon, so I drew in just short of Le Grau at La Grande Motte, the first and perhaps the most famous of the new coastal developments. It is a vast place nowadays with restaurants and a casino and hotels and even with schools for local people who have taken the chance to move there from Montpellier. It was about two in the morning when I turned through the entrance, so I drew in on the first piece of vertical wall, ready to leave early in the morning.

Just as I was preparing to cast off the lines a man came stumbling down the steps from the capitainerie, calling to me to Stop, Stop, Stop!

"How long is your boat?"

"Thirteen metres," I replied.

"That will be thirty four francs for the night," he said, pulling out his receipt book.

"What! Thirty four francs for lying on that piece of wall for four and a half hours in the middle of the night – I wouldn't dream of it." I had the word *escroquerie* very near my tongue, but I thought it not polite to suggest it was a swindle, even if it was one.

The port official looked sad. "That is the charge," he said, as though he were going to burst into tears. "Thirty four francs. It may seem to you excessive..."

"It does."

Silence for a moment. Then, "What would you consider to be a just and reasonable charge?"

It was my turn to think. "Two francs fifty," I said pleasantly.

"Two francs fifty," he repeated. "Yes, two francs fifty."

I gave him the coins, which of course went into his pocket, as I did not get a receipt. We shook hands, great friends, and I cast off to make for Le Grau du Roi.

VI

Wintering in Sète – the President's authority — Mèze and
Marseillan – Riquet and the Canal du Midi – wreck of the
Marseillette – massacre of the Agde lock – Agde and Le Grau
– the Oeuvre du Libron.

I t was at Sète that I made my first acquaintance with what I consider an
excellent delicacy; the *violet des rochers*. Down near the trawlers and
drifters there are stalls and restaurants selling delicious sea food; and to
my mind the *violet* is one of the best. One can find it for sale all the way
from Port Vendres to Le Grau du Roi, and I cannot resist it. The creature
is a tunicate and I can best describe it as shapeless and looking like an
elongated cow pat with a few hairs and covered with warts. Its colour is
a blackish green, the consistency like that of perished rubber, it has a
slight grittiness, squirts one in the eye when squeezed, and nothing could
look more revolting. But the bright yellow interior flesh, soft and with a
strong flavour of iodine is never to be forgotten. Besides, it has a sort of
laboratory smell, which I find wonderfully nostalgic.

Leaving the boat at Sète for the winter proved to be the cheapest over-
wintering I ever had. The town seemed to be singularly devoid of facilities
for looking after boats, and even in the Étang de Thau there was nothing
resembling a shipyard which would take charge of a boat. By the time I
realised this it was too late to go elsewhere and as I had booked sleepers
on the Paris express later in the evening there was no choice but to find
a piece of unoccupied quayside outside the police station, turn off the
sea-cocks and the fuel and disconnect the battery, and walk in at the door
to announce to the officer on duty that I would be back in five months
and expect to find the boat still there. I emphasised this expectation with
the gift of a packet of nineteen cigarettes – there had originally been
twenty, but I had tried one to see if they were smokable – and then
departed for the station. Five months later *Commodore* was still there where
I had left her, waiting patiently to set out again to explore the Canal du
Midi, a fact which I thought merited a rather more generous hand-out of
cigarettes. The next task was to consider whether I had done everything
that official etiquette and regulations demanded.

In the modern days of international travel and ubiquitous yachting it is
not easy to conceive how different things were only a quarter of a century
ago. When I made this first voyage right across France to reach the Mediter-

ranean that great republic was not particularly used to foreign boats entering or leaving except by such usual places as Le Havre or Bordeaux. Even then, one had to be equipped in advance with a Carnet de Douane which needed stamping at entry and a Permis de Circulation which had to be stamped at such locks as were deemed to be important enough to have rubber stamps. This last procedure seemed unnecessary and usually was so, but it could be used by canal officials in an ingenious way. When I passed the lock at the northern end of the summit pound of the Canal de l'Est I noticed that the keeper looked at his watch and wrote in tiny figures below his stamp the time. One did not need to be a great detective to guess that this was to see how long one took to cover the length of the pound, which was more than six miles long and was of course subject to a speed limit.

I worked out that I was expected to take nearly two hours to reach the other end, but that was no problem. Half way along the pound we passed close to a village, so a shopping stop for half an hour took care of the margin. Once on the same pound I came upon two barges hiding in a wood to mop up the extra minutes, and on another voyage we had company in the entrance lock of a pleasant elderly German who was in a hurry, as German yachtsmen so often are. I told him about the speed trap but he pooh-poohed the idea. They could not do anything, he said, if you covered the ground faster than their ridiculous limit allowed. And so he set off at a fast rate of knots.

But he was mistaken. When (after the customary shopping stop) we arrived at the further end, his boat was still outside the lock. The divisional engineer had demanded fifteen hundred francs penalty from him (about one hundred and fifty pounds). He had not got it. Not in francs, and the keeper refused to take payment in German Marks or anything other than genuine Marianne Francs, paid right there over the counter. The owner then offered to descend the flight of fourteen locks and turn right to run into Épinal, where he would find a bank to change his money, but the keeper would have none of it. I thought this a little unreasonable, because he merely had to telephone to the fifteenth lock and tell them not to let the boat through until the money was handed over, but of course I realised we were in Alsace, an area with a century of unhappy memories where Germans were concerned. So I offered to pay the fine and accompany the offender down the fourteen locks to the port of Épinal, where we intended in any case to stop for an excursion into the Vosges. This was agreed. I had enough francs aboard to meet the bill and later that day I was able to walk into Épinal town with the unhappy but pleasant owner of the German yacht and find a bank to change his money.

In those days one never quite knew what requests or objections might be put forward by French frontier officials and I have told elsewhere how after two days of argument *Commodore* was only admitted into France at Givet by being certified as a coal barge travelling in ballast. At Sète we were in the Languedoc, in a land of smiles and sweet reasonableness, of easy going geniality rather than of strict nose-to-the-small-print officialdom, but I still wanted to be sure that I was not doing anything incorrectly, and as I might later wish to go out to sea and along the coast I reported to the Customs House and was received with courtesy, affability, smiles, bonhommie and everything one would expect of the south outside the tourist areas. All would be in order I was assured. They would furnish me with a *Passeport pour Bateau*, free of charge and with pleasure.

This certificate was not the green one in use in later years until discontinued as being an unnecessary nuisance, but a beautiful piece of paper printed in flowery and almost gothic script. A clerk was instructed to fill it out properly and stamp and sign it, but when it was all but complete he paused, pen in hand.

"I cannot sign it," he said sadly. "No, it is impossible." He appeared to be about to burst into tears. Then he turned towards his colleagues at their desks.

"It says 'Signed for and on behalf of the President of the French Republic'. How can I do that, I don't even know him. I have never met him. Not even seen him."

The President in question was General de Gaulle, whose portrait complete with medals, nose and pill-box cap was staring down at us from the wall at the back.

"There he is," exclaimed one of the other clerks, pointing. "That is the President. Now you have seen him."

"Yes, yes. But to sign on his behalf....Me, an official in the *Douanes Françaises*..." He held up the paper, and waved it. "No, it is too great a responsibility."

His fellow clerks all left their desks and came to the counter.

"Go on Jacques," said one. "Think how proud your wife will be when you go home tonight and tell her that you have signed a paper on behalf of the General!"

"But I cannot...."

"Be a devil, Jacques," said another. "Just sign it – the President will never know."

"But it is like forging his signature."

Everyone except the serious-minded clerk thought the matter a most hilarious one, and the laughter brought the chief bustling out of his office to discover what it was that was so entertaining.

The clerk showed him the paper. "You see, Sir, what it says. *For and on behalf of the President of the French Republic.* The responsibility is too great, too great certainly."

The chief patted him gently on the back, took the paper from him, signed it and handed it to me. I thanked him and the whole office, and amid a shower of good wishes I left, wondering whether the poor Jacques would be haunted by the feeling that the greatest moment of his life had come, unexpected, and if he regretted that his courage had failed him when it came to signing for the greatest of living Frenchmen. But at least he had used the rubber stamp.

A visit to the harbour office to arrange for the two huge spans to be lifted that separated us from the Étang de Thau, and soon we were chugging out into the great salt lake. Small one-man boats were plying over it and a number of wine barges were ploughing the water on their way from the vineyards of the Corbières and Minervois to be pumped out at the terminals of the seventeen pipe-lines which were not for hydrocarbons.

The Étang or Bassin de Thau is a vast expanse of extremely salt water famous for its oysters and mussels which grow suspended from the forests of wooden piles and sawn-up superannuated railway lines which bristle from its northern half. It is a lake of great beauty, but also of very heavy seas if the mistral is blowing along it from the east, or the tramontana from the west.

Of the three little towns on its northern side, Bouzigues has a marina, but more attractive to my mind and further from industrial smoke and dust, is Mèze, half way along the northern shore. The water tower and the church on the former ramparts are visible soon after leaving Sète and seem to beckon the voyager to visit its very picturesque harbour. Picturesque, that is, because it is so natural, with the rubbish-cluttered pile-driving barges of the shellfish trade, and the small green and blue fishing boats, the piles of nets and the rakes with enormously long handles for scratching on the bottom of the lake. Up behind, the old town is a maze of narrow streets where old men sit chatting in the evening sun, the women are tatting or busy with crochet, and cats peer round every corner as though engaged in some secret conspiracy. I like Mèze, and never tire of it. Besides, it has a little sandy beach, a wonderful spot for a bathe, as the water is clean, and salt enough to float upon even if rather sore on the eyes.

Mèze has a remarkable animal which appears on special occasions, of which 19th August is a regular one. Like the Tarasque, he is a creature of great antiquity, but he is not a dragon or monster. He is a great bull, and his motive power is provided by eight men inside his hide of cloth. He is led meekly enough by a drover armed with a goad, but he can roar you as gently as any sucking-dove, for he is equipped with a pitched or resined cord attached to a sort of drum made from a barrel over the end of which is stretched the skin of a donkey. When the cord is pulled through the hand, a most fearful and ominous bellowing is produced – enough to send any visitor running for his life. That Mèze should have this unusual creature woven into its life is not so very strange, for in the name of the Bassin de Thau itself we have an echo of *taurus*, the bull.

Marseillan, the most westerly port on the northern shore, was formerly a place from where wine barges continually ran down the lake to Sète. It has now been somewhat marinated, and is one of the bases of the innumerable hire cruisers which enterprising Britons have installed on the canals of the Midi. There is a hotel and restaurant at the edge of the harbour, but the town cannot compete with Mèze for charm. Its only claim to romance is in the tale of that lovely and innocent girl, Scribotte, who was seized upon the shore by Moorish pirates and sold as a slave to a caliph. Her young swain, Mas of Marseillan, nearly died of grief, but pulling himself together he determined to rescue her. Having suitably disguised himself he enlisted with the Moors and worked his way up the army of the Saracens until through sheer ability he speedily attained the rank of general. Now he had the opportunity to come more closely into the company of the Caliph, and having spied out the land, he entered the harem, swiftly snatched up his beloved and fled. Many were the fights and hair-breadth escapes which still lay in their path, but at last they reached their home port of Marseillan, where they married and lived happily ever after.

From Marseillan it is less than ten minutes to the lighthouse of Les Onglous, the mark without which it would be difficult to pick out the mouth of the Canal du Midi which leaves the Bassin de Thau at its foot. For more than a mile the cut runs straight ahead across marshes which are half land and half lake. The water is alive with fish, and along the edge of the canal locals stand up to their waists in the mud to grub up something edible. Eventually the canal swings sharply to the right before reaching the conical Pic St Loup behind which lies the enormous new port, nudist colony, and development of the Cap d'Agde, fortunately not visible from the canal. But soon enough the canal reaches the lock of Bagnas, the first of seventy-seven on the gradual and beautiful climb to the watershed more than a hundred miles distant and six hundred feet above the Bassin de Thau – though actually the number of locks is decreasing on account of new engineering works. But Bagnas lock, like most on the canal, has served for three hundred years and apart from a change in the paddle gear has not been much altered. Like all the original Midi locks, it is not rectangular, but built as an ellipse, a shape which may be wasteful of water but which is an excellent one for withstanding the push of the surrounding land. In fact, the entire canal is a masterpiece of engineering and a monument to the man who was not himself an engineer, but who constructed the canal just the same. He must be introduced more fully at this point, for without knowing the origin of the canal and the part played by this one man, one can miss many things of great interest during the voyage.

In the year 1604 a christening was held in the cathedral of Béziers, and it is said that the godmother prophesied that the child being baptized would be the means of securing a great highway of communication across the Languedoc. The lady was the Marquise Riquetti, the child Pierre-Paul Riquet, a relative whose Italian origins already lay far behind him, so that his own parents now used the name in its French form. Probably nobody paid much attention to the prophecy, and certainly the young Riquet left school with no attainments beyond reading, writing and arithmetic. As the professions were therefore closed to him, his father put him into the Inland Revenue, where he worked as a reasonably honest man with no very obvious future except that of enriching himself at the expense of others.

But now we must jump back further. Ninety years before the birth of Riquet, the French King Francis I had returned from his Duchy of Milan, bringing with him the decorator Leonardo da Vinci, who was also a notable engineer of canals. Together they planned cross-country routes in the centre and in the south, and a survey was actually made for a Canal des Deux Mers which would have joined the Aude at Carcassonne to the Garonne near Toulouse, but before anything could be undertaken the King's attention and money were fully occupied in wars, and the next step forward was taken by Henry IV, who charged the Archbishop of Narbonne to report upon the best course for such a canal. The good bishop selected roughly the same route as the surveyor of Francis I, and he reported to his royal patron that any canal would have to cross the pass of the Castelnaudary plain. He correctly identified the lowest point of the divide as the Pierres de Naurouze, a jumble of rocks some thirty miles east of Toulouse, but this point was more than some six hundred feet above sea level, and it had the unfortunate characteristic that it was comparatively dry. As no streams of any size could be found within several leagues in any direction, it would obviously be impossible to provide the canal with water, the archbishop reported.

So things remained until the day when Pierre-Paul Riquet the tax man, Baron of Bonrepos, was reposing in thought upon that same spot. He was fifty-five and undistinguished, and the prophecy of his godmother still lay utterly unfulfilled. He had made a heap of money and bought some farms, he was a baron, and in the eyes of the world a respectable and successful man. Yet his dream was that the canal which the kings of France had planned might actually be built, and this was the strange fancy which brought him to haunt the locality of the rough pile of rocks which stood like some monument placed by inexpert giants to mark the pass of Naurouze.

It happened one day that Riquet, lost in thought, strayed a short way from the rocks and noticed a little spring, the Fontaine de la Grave. Watching the trickle of water he observed that at one point it divided into two streams, and that the one trickle ran eastward, the other west. In a flash of genius Riquet saw the solution to the problem of a canal across the Languedoc. The water of the spring divided and eventually reached the two seas. If he could somehow convey to that point an infinitely greater supply of water, enough to float ships, then this supply could be split in the same way and the land spanned by a navigable waterway from coast to coast. The real question was how such a great and continual flow of water could be achieved.

Riquet's next step was to betake himself to the Montagne Noire some way north of Naurouze, where hills up to three thousand feet in height were covered in deep forests. The rainfall there was much higher than in the arid lands through which most of the canal would have to pass, and after tramping through the forest and riding over the hills the Baron of Bonrepos was convinced that there was water enough and to spare, provided the streams could somehow be diverted and their water made to flow all the way to Naurouze. Satisfied that it could be done, he shared his idea with a lad named Pierre, son of the well-borer and smith at Revel. Pierre became enthusiastic, and it was partly through his practical energy that the canal was eventually to be completed, but for the moment he and the Baron contented themselves with building a miniature canal in the park of Bonrepos, north of Toulouse, to study some of the practical problems.

At this stage, Riquet was advised by his friend the Bishop of Toulouse to take into his private service a young engineer named Francois Andreossy, who had seen canals in Italy and had some practical knowledge. The only person thoroughly opposed to the project was the Baroness, who was convinced that this mad scheme of canal building would sooner or later swallow up the whole of the family fortune and estates. Besides, she could not abide that young man Andreossy. In both these opinions she was right. Like all the great canal men, Riquet was to die impoverished. Andreossy was to introduce many ingenious ideas, but he turned against his employer and attempted to persuade the King, Louis XIV, to recognise him as the real genius behind the scheme.

With the explorations complete, Riquet very wisely wrote to the Premier Minister Colbert, outlining in some detail his conviction that the Canal des Deux Mers was a practical proposition. That energetic and imaginative man seized upon it as a truly great enterprise, and he realised that by its sheer scale and audacity it would appeal to 'Le Roi Soleil'. This it certainly did, and Louis XIV ordered commissioners to examine the scheme. Riquet himself took them to the Montagne Noire, explained just how and where he proposed to convey the water, and as they still seemed reluctant to believe that such a thing could really be done, he offered to have a trial feeder dug at his own expense, all the way to Naurouze. This offer was accepted, and in five months Riquet and the faithful Pierre had achieved the construction of a pilot channel fifty miles in length for his proposed Rigole de la Plaine, to bring water from the River Sor. The Commissioners were summoned, the sluice was opened, and the officials could see for themselves a copious flow of water arriving at the vital point of the divide between Mediterranean and Atlantic.

Louis XIV appointed Riquet contractor, and in 1666 the work was begun. Fifteen years later, the first ships passed down the canal – the Canal Royal as it was now called – and when Voltaire came to write of the era of the 'Roi Soleil' he had no hesitation in declaring that the most glorious of all the monuments of that era, by its usefulness as well as its grandeur, and by virtue of the difficulties that had to be overcome, was the canal in the Languedoc which joined the two seas. None would nowadays dispute that it was the greatest feat of civil engineering between Roman times and the nineteenth century.

The edict of Louis XIV proudly pointed out that not even the most ambitious and able princes or nations had been able to think actually of putting this great work in hand, and stressed that the waterway, a great work of peace, was to be constructed in a manner well worthy of the royal interest, and capable of perpetuating for centuries to come the grandeur, the abundance and the happiness of the reign of its royal patron. And this it most certainly does. It is impossible to pass over the aqueducts, sail through the first canal tunnel in all the world, mount the locks and see the means devised for supplying water to the canal without being enormously impressed, even if it is Riquet and Colbert rather than Louis XIV who will be remembered.

The letters patent also placed the charges of maintenance of the canal upon Riquet and his descendants in perpetuity, and in return they were to levy the navigation charges. Thus the crown obtained the credit without the risk. Twelve hundred men and five hundred women were soon on the job, most of them at the personal charge of the Baron himself.

The crown and the States of Languedoc eventually subscribed considerable sums, but, as usual, to cut a canal proved more expensive than had been foreseen. Although it was completed in only fifteen years, the project had actually cost nearly sixteen million pounds of gold, of which Riquet had personally provided almost one sixth. The source of his own money for the construction of the canal was largely from the tax on salt which he was empowered to collect, and when the level of taxation was raised to an extent that caused Catalan peasants to revolt he answered by burning down their villages. This in turn led to rioting and even to the death of some demonstrators. Even then, he so impoverished his estate that more than half a century was to pass before his descendants could work off the debt and see a profit on the costs of management.

In May 1681 the Royal Commissioners came to view the completed canal before it was filled. Then the water was admitted from the feeders at Naurouze, and within a few days the level was high enough for them to go aboard ship at Toulouse for a ceremonial voyage, their ship being followed by 23 laden barges bound for the fair at Beaucaire. Music, flags, acclamations of the crowds and blessings of the clergy accompanied them all the way, and poets vied with each other in their eulogy of commemorative odes and sonnets. Verses survive in Latin and Italian, in French, and of course in the Occitan tongue. Never had there been such delight, such unrestrained pride in an achievement of which the country and its people could justly be proud.

Yet there was a sad note, too. Only seven months earlier Pierre-Paul Riquet, Baron of Bonrepos, had died in poverty, his farms and estates mortgaged to the hilt to finance the canal. It was Pierre, the wellman's son from Revel, who had doggedly seen the work through the last few months of difficulty to its completion, and who accompanied the Royal Commissioners on their triumphal voyage through to the new port of Sète which his friend and master had designed.

After the first lock at Bagnas, the canal immediately takes on its typical character which it retains nearly all the way to Toulouse. Plane trees on either bank form a splendid avenue, and at their foot is an almost unbroken line of yellow water irises which here and there are replaced by orange lilies. While gliding through this scene of ombrageous beauty the boatman can glance at the plane trees and do a quick calculation that between himself and Toulouse some eighty to one hundred thousand plane trees line the banks and spread their branches far over the water. From this it should follow that he must not be too surprised if the filter becomes blocked by leaves, or if, from time to time, a heavy clunk on the propeller indicates a sunken and waterlogged limb dislodged by the winter gales. Soon the waterway breaks out into the River Hérault, to leave it again shortly on the further side and come to the round lock of Agde. This is not unique (there is another at Bruges) but with three pairs of gates all opening at different levels it corresponds to a triangle junction on the railway. The main line of canal is straight ahead, the gates to the left leading to a cut which joins the Hérault below the town weir, and so provides another exit to the Mediterranean.

In the lock cut there lay in 1963 a very ancient wooden barge with the name *Marseillette*. It had seen better days, but was more or less intact with its immense tiller, a sort of fo'c'sle ahead of the open hold, and a covered area near the stern which formed the living quarters. The ship had no motor, and I always suspected that it was moored at the place where the old horse died that had hauled it, for the craft obstructed nearly half of the narrow cut.

Aboard the *Marseillette* there lived an ancient mariner, a tall, thin man with a faded walrus moustache, and his only companions were a number of cats which crouched around on the superstructure and which the skipper presumably fed in a meagre way with the left-overs of his own meals. There was a diminutive vegetable patch on the bank where he supplemented his diet with a few carrots, a leek or two, and some parsley.

I had seen this sort of arrangement before, especially in the end of the Oise at Conflans-Ste Honorine where there were dozens of such decaying motorless, immobile craft slowly rotting to pieces but inhabited by people who had spent all of their working life on the boat and could not face leaving it for the strange, bustling, threatening life ashore. So I guessed that the old man aboard the barge outside Agde lock was such a one. And he was.

Altogether we must have passed through that lock-cut twenty or thirty times in the course of the next twenty years. And each time the boat was more decayed, rot had spread further, but the man still lived there. Toward the end of the 1970s the skipper had abandoned his efforts to keep her afloat. She had settled on the bottom, and yellow water-irises grew in the mud and debris of the hold. The roof of the living accommodation had collapsed, and a few fertiliser sacks salvaged from neighbouring fields formed a make-shift cover. One or two pots and pans were ranged on some of the transverse timbers still above water, and a rickety plank gave access to the bank for the lone skipper and an ever increasing family of cats; ginger, black, brindled and grey. We wondered that the old man could survive under such conditions with the water slowly creeping, month by month, up toward the boards upon which he slept. My wife asked at the lock whether anything was being done for the man, and received the expected answer: the local authority had offered him a flat in an old people's home, but he would have none of it. The *Marseillette* was his home, and always would be.

Early in the 1980s the ship had canted over somewhat, and on the one side what was left of the gunwale was awash. There was not so much as a cat to be seen, and it was clear that the ship was uninhabited. Again, we enquired at the lock. What had become of the captain of the *Marseillette*?

The answer was as one might suspect. With only a plank or two left below him and the rotted roof above to serve as a perch for the cats, the local health authority had acted. They had found the old man shrunken and not in the best of health, so they had taken him away to a snug little flat with heating and a proper bed, and probably meals on wheels too. His new quarters were idyllic, such a cosy place as any would be glad to have in their old age. Any, except the skipper. In only two weeks it had killed him.

During the next year or two the *Marseillette* sank lower, and once I saw a water rat swim out from the reeds sprouting through her planking. But the cats had gone. None of those passing the old wreck in the smart blue hire-cruisers would ever guess that it had once been the only place on earth where that one particular individual could live in comfort. Comfort of the spirit, beside which rheumatism, arthritis, and all the other ills to which he must have been subject were as nothing.

It was shortly before the old man was taken off his boat that we happened to come up to Agde lock from the direction of Bagnas, intending to use the side gate and pass out into Agde town and thence to the sea as we had often done before. We had to wait awhile as an aged gravel barge had come up from Agde and was being raised in the lock. We made fast to the staging outside and went up to the lockside to chat as was our custom. The lock filled, the barge lumbered out and pursued its shaky, shuddering way along the cut, past the *Marseillette* and out to the river. We moved in and made fast, when something happened which I have never really understood. The keeper was winding shut one of the gates when a sudden surge came down the cut, caused perhaps in some way or other by the drawing off of water by the heavily laden barge and the sudden rushing in of river water when the craft had cleared the entrance. But whatever the explanation, a surge of great violence hit the half closed gate and the windlass handle was wrenched round by the rack and pinion mechanism as the gate started to slam. The lock-keeper grabbed the handle, but such was the power in the surge that he was pulled off his feet and flung right over the bullnose outside the gate. This, to guard against winter floods in the Hérault, was some fifteen feet high, and the lock-keeper was simply hurled over it to land in the canal and disappear from sight.

My wife scrambled down the bank, I looked from above. There was not a sign of the man. But the splash had been heard by a young man who had brought a bucket of food for the *Marseillette's* cats, and running up to the bullnose he promptly dived in, to surface a moment later dragging with him the inert form of the keeper whose face was blue and lips a deep purple. We thought he was dead but Ingrid helped turn him so that his head was down the bank and his feet up, and as the canal water ran out of his lungs he gave vent to the most awful moanings like a cow in pain.

"You see, he has a pacemaker," the heroic young man explained casually.

A pacemaker! Here was a man with a heart that could only be kept going mechanically, and he was put to work the one lock between the Mediterranean and the Atlantic which had four pairs of gates and not just two, every one of them cranked by hand – as were all the paddles too. Why on earth, I wondered, had they not installed him at one of the locks such as Béziers where there was nothing to be done but stroll out of the house, murmur a *bonjour* and press a button to set all the relays in motion. I expressed this opinion to the young man and again to the knot of people who had now collected, drawn by the scent of a possible tragedy.

But no, they assured us. The divisional engineer had offered him other locks; and the good man's wife, who had just now gone into the town to do some shopping, had repeatedly told him he should retire, or take one of the easier jobs on offer to him. But he would have none of it. He wanted to be in Agde, he liked lock-keeping, and he liked that particular lock. Everyone told him he was being absurd, but that only made him the more obstinate, it seemed.

We were relieved to see the first traces of colour appear in his lips, and soon the poor man stopped moaning. His eyes, which had appeared as those of a man with no vision, cleared, and he looked about him. We helped him up, and he shook himself like a wet dog. He had better go home to the lock-house and get dried and lie down, we suggested. Yes, he would do that, he said. And off he went.

Not only were we now without a lock-keeper – not a very serious matter for anyone who had worked some five thousand locks in his time – but the mysterious surge of water had slammed the gate with such a crash that the whole opening mechanism had come adrift. The rack and pinion was disengaged, the windlass that the unfortunate man had tried to hold had come out of its bearings. However, I always had enough heavy tools aboard to cope with the unexpected, so I fetched them up and began to dismantle the machinery. After I had been working for a quarter of an hour or so, the skipper of a hire cruiser waiting on the further side of the lock came up.

"I hope you won't be much longer," he said in a reprimanding tone. "I want to get through Bagnas before they close for lunch."

I resisted the temptation to push him into the lock, and just as I was finishing the job another man came up wearing a rather smart suit. "Thank you," he said. "You can leave it to me now."

I looked at him. It was the lock-keeper, hale and apparently hearty and dressed in his Sunday best while his other clothes dried in the sun. He did not need to lie down, he said. He felt fine. And in spite of all Ingrid's gentle remonstrances, he insisted on winding the reconstituted gate machinery. It was a year before we passed Agde lock again. In the meantime the keeper had died.

When Riquet designed the so-called *écluse ronde* at Agde it was in fact not circular but more uterus-shaped. It was necessary for boats coming from either east or west to be able to turn out of the south gate toward the town and sea, whereas the northern wall was just curved like that of the other locks. From pictures, and from personal acquaintance with it before it was 'massacred' I have no hesitation in saying that the round lock of Agde was one of the most elegant and beautifully shaped engineering works of the seventeenth century.

The word 'massacred' is not mine. I agree with the sentiment, but not the use of that particular word, as I have always thought a fair number of people (or locks) had to be slaughtered to make a massacre. But perhaps that is just being pedantic. The term was used by the speaker who addressed a public

protest meeting at Agde about the alterations to the Canal du Midi which
were then being begun. And one thing that I learned from his speech was
that the two incomplete stone structures on either side of the cut where it
ran out into the river in the middle of the town were not the remains of
bridge abutments demolished during the second world war (which in fact
did not touch Agde) but were the unfinished bases erected by Riquet for
two monumental pieces of statuary, probably of Louis XIV and the Spirit
of Commerce or some such creature, which were never commissioned for
lack of funds.

But to return to the protest meeting – as ineffective as all such meetings
are doomed to be – or more correctly to the subject of it; the Canal du Midi
was built to take ships up to thirty metres long and five and a half broad.
Riquet, of course, did not work in metres but in *toises*, which were about
6.4 feet apiece, or very roughly two metres, but he built his canal a century
or more ahead of most other French waterways, and these others gradually
came to conform to the "Freycinet standard", allowing a ship of thirty-eight
metres length and just over five metres beam to pass the locks. The result of
this was that the standard péniches of the north could reach Sète but could
not enter the Canal du Midi, for which they were too long. Nor could the
Midi barges penetrate into the northern canals (even if they could be hauled
up the Rhone by tugs) because they were just too broad to pass through
Freycinet lock-gates. So, as regards canal traffic, France was cut into three
zones: Brittany (with locks smaller than those of the Midi); the main industrial area of the north stretching from the Channel ports to the Rhine
and down to the Saône; and the Midi, together with its extension from
Toulouse to Bordeaux (the Canal latéral à la Garonne) which was added
nearly two centuries later to the same dimensions.

This meant, of course, that there could be no through traffic from one
zone to another. It was like having the different railway regions with dis-
similar gauges of track. With the growth of industry in Toulouse especially,
the need to adapt the Midi to the Freycinet standard was obvious. In the
nineteen sixties, work was put in hand on the single locks first, and at one
end or the other an extra nine metres of pen were added, with new gates. In
doing this, the fine curve of the lockside was inevitably destroyed, but that
was unavoidable. Where a double-step lock existed (as at Salléles d'Aude) it
was possible to deepen one half and add higher gates at the bottom. Triple
and quadruple locks had by 1986 not been tackled, but at least the route
was theoretically open for Freycinet craft to penetrate to the Port of La
Nouvelle.

The problem of the Agde lock was obviously a knotty one. It had to be
Freycinetted in two different directions, and the solution taken was to demolish all but the one relatively small piece of it between the southern and
western gates, and rebuild the remainder further out and in concrete with

trees and flower beds to soften the blow. Perhaps the engineers did the best they could under the circumstances, but that Riquet's masterpiece was indeed slaughtered there can be no doubt. The only alternative would have been to preserve it as an 'industrial monument', lovely but unused, and reroute the canal by means perhaps of a new lock in the river weir at Agde and a bypass cut, but that would have been a vastly expensive operation. So the 'massacre' was authorised, and, personally, I have to admit that the extended three-way lock is a pleasant and interesting place for anyone who never saw Riquet's original masterpiece of gently sloping walls and delicate curves.

So now it is time to enter the lock, turn sideways and lie along a straight wall at the edge of the deeper part of the pen which points to the southern exit. Soon we are passing at dead slow along a very narrow cut beneath the trees and out between the stumps of the commemorative monuments to join the Hérault again just by the town bridge. And across the river is what, without doubt, is one of the prettiest waterfronts in the whole of France, the broad stone quay backed by cramped and faded houses extending down river to where the heavy craft come up the stream to unload sardines, and cats help to clean the quays of debris. It is a peaceful and natural scene dominated by the enormous black mass of the cathedral of St Étienne, built eight centuries ago of lava from the nearby hill and so tough and unweathered that it looks as though consecrated only a year or two ago and made of some new and resistant breeze block.

It is abundantly clear that the Bishop of Agde, back in the days when infidels were on the prowl by sea, was going to have no nonsense, and the cathedral was constructed to make an impregnable fort. There is not so much as an arrow slit or embrasure to let a chink of light penetrate its astonishing blank facade. Instead there are machicolations, battlements, and all manner of handy places from which to pour boiling water or shoot down attackers with arrows. The tower is a fortified keep with turrets commanding a view of the walls, and there is even a means of hauling up supplies from ground level. Naturally, the nave is as dark as a dungeon, and nothing could be more eloquent of the state of affairs in twelfth century Agde and along the littoral if the church had thus to be protected.

Agde was another Phocean foundation and was established at what was then the mouth of the Hérault by the energetic traders who were installed at Marseille. Gradually, it became removed a little from the sea and its trade declined in competition with Aigues Mortes, but Richelieu hoped to make it the premier port of the Mediterranean and began to fit it out by the construction of his vast mole a little to the east and near the cape. Whilst he was still alive the States of the Languedoc had to accept the idea and foot the bill, but as soon as he died they stopped the work, and the mole is now merely a part of the works of the Cap d'Agde marina complex.

Agde is an excellent specimen of the kind of French town which seems to survive the centuries with little change. Tucked away behind the main shopping street is a most picturesque and natural maze of twisting alleys and narrow streets with the washing hung out high overhead. Tidy and obviously prosperous inhabitants emerge from rickety doors which have not seen paint for a century, or lean to chat across the street from windows in houses which look as though they could crumble at any moment. But the same houses, built mainly of lava, are rich in curious detail of carving and masonry, and have escaped the artificiality of becoming a tourist attraction. Through these streets one comes to the bustling market area, and in the Rue de Fraternité stands a fine patrician house now transformed into the local museum. The work of local enthusiasts who have shown excellent taste as well as ingenuity, it contains not only many exhibits from the Greek period but ranges of rooms showing domestic scenes of various ages, set out with great skill and charm. Another local curiosity near the waterfront is a commemorative fountain or mock gateway from the year X. However, the date refers to the year ten of the Revolution, not of the Christian era.

Below the town the river sweeps away broad and serene, and sometimes ploughed by a drifter homeward bound and trailing a vast length of net in the fresh water to wash it. In less than half an hour the sea is in sight, beyond the double town of Le Grau d'Agde spilled along both sides of the Hérault without any connecting bridge – though there are ferries for foot-passengers only. It is a popular little resort without quite the scruffy charm of Le Grau du Roi, and like that other grau it has no facilities whatsoever for a visiting boat to stop, so one either has to turn round, or anchor in midstream, or run out between the long moles of piled-up rocks and past the innumerable statuesque anglers who always frequent such places, and feel the swell of the Gulf of Lions lift the boat gently and playfully. Far to the right one can then just make out in clear weather the bulk of the Montagne de la Clape, a little short of La Nouvelle, and sometimes I have seen much further out to sea than seems proper the vast shining range of the mighty snow-capped Pyrenees.

Westward from the round lock of Agde the canal crosses a marshy landscape and runs only a few feet above sea level. There are fields of vines, and ranches advertising pony-trekking trips for the summer visitors, and wherever they have bushes to sit in there are nightingales shouting their heads off in the delicious early days of summer. It is not a notable landscape and perhaps not typical of the Canal du Midi because for several miles there is a gap in the line of plane trees which otherwise follow the banks so characteristically. Maybe the water is too brackish for their roots, for near the next lock at the village of Portiragnes they begin again. But four miles before that the canal passes through a structure which was added after Riquet's time and is, so far as I am aware, unique.

I have often admired the Oeuvre du Libron, and when on one of our voyages we had a Swedish engineer aboard who was very well acquainted with almost every aspect of engineering I stopped at the *Oeuvre*, conducted him over the top of the structure, let him examine it in the greatest detail and then tell me what it was for. And there, to my great delight, he completely and utterly failed. He could think of no possible purpose for such an extraordinary affair, and if I happened to know better that was merely because the thing had puzzled me so greatly that on an earlier voyage I had stopped and asked the genial *guardien* who lived in a house beside it to explain it for me. Which he willingly did.

Aboard a boat one passes through a structure which has a lattice-work of girders overhead, carrying dozens of short pieces of railway line on which are mounted trolleys bearing windlasses, chains and hooks. The sides of the structure are only solid in certain parts, but elsewhere there are heavy boards in slots, or one may see through to a little trickling stream decked out with flowering water weeds. This stream is the River Libron in its customary humble state.

The Libron does not run in at one side of the canal and out at the other as do the Vidourle and the Lez between Aigues Mortes and Sète. That canal being at sea-level the rivers are neither higher nor lower than the waterway and merely have in each case a watery crossroads with it. But as they drain the foothills of the area around Lunel and Montpellier they may rise in flood, in which case a set of huge steel gates is dropped into the canal on either side of the river to prevent the flood from running along the waterways. Navigation is of course halted until the flood is run off. But the Libron is a few feet lower than the canal and so it flows underneath the canal in a culvert. All is well until heavy rain in the Cevennes runs swiftly off the hard rocky land and swells the Libron to such an extent that the culvert could never cope with it.

As the Libron can actually rise after heavy rain by as much as six or eight feet, and that in a matter of no more than an hour, the canal bank would of course act as a dam, the countryside would be inundated, the canal itself overfilled, and navigation interrupted. It is the task of the *guardien* to put the device into operation as soon as he is warned by telephone from some minor oracle of the Échelle de Chasse species that a flood is on its way.

The *Oeuvre* is really a lock, but the gates at either end are normally drawn back. They do not swing, but can be moved in and out by some of the vast assemblage of cranks, trolleys, levers, chains and ratchets overhead. And each gate is not a flat affair but a massive steel tunnel large enough to take all the water of the Libron in flood. If a boat is coming from the direction of Agde, all the sluices are set to send the whole flood through the further gate. The boat passes the first gate, which is withdrawn to the side, enters the centre section, comes to a halt, the first tunnel-gate is put into position behind it, and the sluices are then changed over to discharge the Libron through it. The gate ahead is then moved out of the way, and the boat can proceed. This extraordinary device enables a river to cross the canal at a speed of several knots and with its surface several feet higher than the waterway, without any effect on the Canal du Midi itself. It was installed because heavy rain in the Cevennes could sometimes hold up traffic for days on end at this crossing. And that rain storms can be heavy there is no doubt at all. Many of the roads crossing the plain between the mountains and the coast are obviously well provided with ditches and are sometimes raised higher than the countryside around, yet there are notices of *risque d'inondation*, and occasionally a board with a scale on it to indicate that the inundation can credibly be expected to put the road, fields, vines and everything under several feet of water.

I have always wished to be within range of the stretch of canal between Agde and Portiragnes when the fateful message comes to interrupt the placid life of the *guardien*, and the Libron begins its inexorable rise. In more than twenty years acquaintance with the Midi that has never been my good fortune, but one year at least I came near to it. We happened to have passed out of the round lock to take the sea route to the Cap d'Agde, where I intended to leave *Thames Commodore* for a few weeks. When we reached the pierheads of Le Grau there was such a sea running that we had to turn back and come up to Agde again, to lie at a pleasant berth opposite the cathedral. The newspaper talked of a tremendous storm sweeping the Languedoc, and of houses swept away in Toulouse.

When we turned in that evening the Hérault had risen only a little, but its colour was changed from greenish to a sort of purplish red, a sure sign that floods upstream were washing away part of the countryside. Next morning the weir, normally no more than a trickle ankle-deep, was thundering its red-stained torrent, and over the top came entire pine trees, roots and all, and sometimes a few unhappy vines and the stakes to which they had been trained. Any doubts I might have had about *risque d'inondation* were dispelled.

Top: Autumn at Aigues Mortes
Bottom: The Hérault at Agde

Top: The Oeuvre du Libron
Bottom: Capestang bridge

VII

Béziers and Riquet – carnival of animals – destruction of the city – water slope of Fonseranes – Riquet's tunnel – Enserune and Hannibal – Capestang's troubadour – wars of religion – the canal and the Huguenots – down to Narbonne – *Phylloxera* the devastator.

T he approach to Béziers by water is dirty. It is not only in France that town dwellers seem to think that a canal is there to be used as a public rubbish receptacle, but somehow one wonders how such a quantity of hunks of polystyrene packing and the general mess of chewed-up plastic flavoured occasionally with the blown-up body of a dead cat or dog comes to be there. But we can avert our eyes, and pursue our way to the lengthened two-into-one lock which gives access to the port basin of Béziers. For that city is worth any amount of rubbish on the way.

The port has changed over the years. In the nineteen sixties the long stone quay was still lined with wine barges loading or discharging to the wine warehouses and blending establishments across the road. As at St Gilles, the ground was stained a purplish red and the rain splashed the colour up the walls of the buildings. Now the same quayside is a halt only for hire boats, charter barges, and a few of those old craft bought by some hopeful young couple who find that to put the vessel into serviceable condition demands much more cash and much more time and work than they had imagined. Too much, in fact – and the dream slowly becomes run-down and finally an abandoned wreck.

The port is in a very backstairs area of Béziers, but from its upper end one could formerly scramble down a bank, exchange pleasantries with a few tramps frying *friture* from the canal over a wood fire in the wasteland, pick ones way through the accumulated rubbish of years and up some steps over a derelict commercial building, and so reach the foot of the town and climb doggedly up to the wide allée in the centre. It hardly needs to be said that this fine street is the Allées Paul Riquet, half way along which is an extremely handsome statue of the Baron de Bonrepos himself. For the Bitterois or inhabitants of Béziers are rightly proud of their great canal man. Besides, he was not only a native of the place but he was so determined to take his canal to his native town, and thus enhance its trade, that he became involved in serious difficulties.

The city happens to be perched on one side of a deep valley with the canal approaching from the other. The Baron de Bonrepos decided to lead the waterway on a contour to the very edge of the valley and then drop down a flight of eight locks to the Orb, pass down the river itself for half a mile or more, and then strike out through the left bank toward Agde. To do this he had to find some means of leaving the valley of the Aude and taking his waterway over the ridge of the Orb basin. The whole success of the canal depended upon his original vision that water could be made to flow from Naurouze all the way to the sea, and naturally this meant that the canal had to fall somewhat along the whole of its course. There could be no question of suddenly climbing again, as this would make it impossible to supply the hump with water.

So it seemed impossible to take the waterway out of the one river valley and into another. Although the ridge between them was not very high, even a single lock rising the wrong way was something which could not be contemplated. But Riquet was not to be beaten, and he decided to pierce the ridge with a tunnel, the first canal tunnel in the world. In this way he brought the Canal Royal to the valley edge, straight across from his native town, but to take his canal down into the course of the Orb and out again below the town was one of the few mistakes he made. The rest of the way from the summit the route had deliberately been kept out of the bottoms of river valleys, so that navigation would not be interrupted by sudden floods or prolonged droughts, but here this wise principle was thrown over, with unfortunate results.

The Orb does not have to cope with thawing snows from the Pyrenees, but the hills along its upper reaches are more than three thousand feet high and they can deliver great quantities of water. Riquet found the Orb at Béziers to be a river which for much of the year was so shallow that it could not float a laden barge, whereas at other times violent floods could raise new shoals and race past the city with a current too formidable for boats of any kind. First, he raised the water level by a weir, but this made the river deposit more of its mud, and it did not prevent the serious interruptions caused by floods.

Riquet could have thrown an aqueduct over the river, but this would have been an undertaking even greater than other river crossings he had dealt with in that way. Perhaps he considered it and decided against it, or it may be that he was confident that the floods and shallows of the Orb could be tamed. Nevertheless, the passage of the Orb proved so unsatisfactory that the aqueduct had eventually to be built, and in 1857 a new piece of canal was cut from part-way down the great flight of locks opposite the city, and the waterway was made to fly over the river. This is its present route.

Béziers is the capital of the wine trade, and it is this and the canal which form the main subjects of the excellent local museum. The city really consists of the spacious nineteenth century town around the Allées, and the attached and much older part clustered on the edge of the hill and around the astonishing cathedral which can be seen for miles out to sea and is a useful landmark for sailors. It is also a place where, on the first Sunday in July, one may have the good fortune to discover a get-together of most of the fabulous animals which inhabit the Languedoc. They do not always meet at Béziers; it may be the turn of Pézenas or some other small town, but wherever they may happen to meet one may see marching through the streets the roaring bull of Mèze and such curious animals as the wolf of Loupian, the hedgehog of Roujan, the horse of Florensac, the goat of Montagnac and the pig of St André-de-Sangonis, each of which has its own strange origin.

The foal of Pézenas dates back to Louis VIII, who had a favourite mare which fell sick during the festivities which attended his visit to the town. Upon leaving he decided to part from his beloved steed and he left it in the care of the local magistrates, asking them to look after it well. But when he returned, he found not only the mare alive and kicking but a foal also, which was proudly led before him decorated with garlands. So delighted was the king that he asked the town to commemorate the event by constructing a foal of wood, which was to be present at all local festivities. Today's successor to the original is not easily recognised as a foal, being much larger than an elephant and having at least a dozen legs. But a foal it is, by royal command.

The ass of Gignac resembles in its origin the geese which saved the Roman Capitol, and is the recollection of a donkey which roused the inhabitants in the nick of time when the town was about to be attacked at dead of night by Moorish invaders. Another ass comes from Bessan. Formerly there was a donkey fair in that town and after an assinine beauty competition the winner was paraded through the streets, decorated with garlands of flowers. Eventually the fair died out, but the donkey survived in wooden form.

The camel of Béziers goes back to the earliest Christian legends of the area. It is said that the first missionary to Béziers was St Aphrodise, an aged Egyptian who earlier in his life had given shelter to Joseph and Mary and the infant Jesus during their flight into Egypt to escape Herod's massacre of children. When already an old man he decided to set out as an evangelist, and riding upon his camel he eventually reached Béziers, where he was murdered. A local knight took charge of his faithful beast, and nowadays an effigy of the camel is carried every year in procession to the church of its patron in Béziers, besides being allowed to join the other beasts for the annual congress.

In spite of this pleasant tomfoolery of legendary quadrupeds and in spite also of the busy supermarkets and the heavy traffic thundering through the lower area of the town, Béziers has never been able to forget or forgive the frightful fate that it suffered when the army of the crusade against the Albigensians arrived outside its walls. Looking across from the canal aqueduct to the old town and the majestic cathedral high on the hill above the Orb, it is a terrible thought amid so much beauty that there, on the feast of St Mary Magdalene in the year 1209, an event occurred which was to seal the destruction of as high and fine a civilization as Europe then knew. For on the very day after the murder of Pierre de Castelnau as he left St Gilles, the signal was given for the war against the heretics, a crusade against those who did not accept the authority of the Church of Rome, and in particular against the Count of Toulouse and his young nephew Raymond-Roger de Trencavel, Viscount of Béziers and Carcassonne, in whose territories the heretics were firmly established and tolerated.

Pope Innocent III announced an all-out attack upon Béziers. He wrote to all bishops, archbishops, counts and barons and knights of France and the North, summoning them to root out the heretics. Great forces of knights from France and Germany and Brabant gradually gathered at Lyon for the crusade, some no doubt in pious obedience and many stimulated by the smell of loot. Their numbers were swelled by many thousands of mercenaries, outlaws and brigands and cut-throats who were prepared to fight anybody, and by a horde of pilgrims who hoped to be in at the death and earn the wholesale indulgence granted by Innocent III in advance to any who might strike down and murder a heretic. In the same month that Count Raymond made his second journey to St Gilles to be flayed by the legates, an armada of lighters began to float down from Lyon. Within a short space of time the largest army Europe had ever seen was encamped outside the walls of Béziers.

Every member of the vast beleaguering force had a reason for enthusiasm. The nobles could have the credit of doing their forty day crusade military service without the dangerous voyage to the Holy Land and the menace of Saracen hordes. The heretics, abhorring bloodshed, were complete pacifists and – at least in the early stages of the war – would be cleft asunder rather than raised a hand in self-defence. They were hardly a dangerous enemy, and there was freedom to seize their goods and lands. The mercenaries were after the loot by which alone they lived. The pilgrims, thousands of them led by a kind of wild mass hysteria, had the chance (according to the Pope) of winning salvation and forgiveness by the mere act of murdering.

Yet in spite of such attractions the seige of Béziers promised to be a long one, for the city was well placed and ably defended.

The crusading forces issued an ultimatum. Béziers could hand over some two hundred known heretics and their families, and the rest of the population would go free. Otherwise the city would be attacked.

This choice was put to the townspeople by their Catholic bishop, and though the burghers must certainly have been predominantly Catholic, they burned with indignation at the suggestion that they should hand over their fellow citizens. They would rather be drowned, they said, than submit to such terms.

The details of what happened next have never been fully known, but it seems that the defenders made a rash sally and the attackers managed to wrest from them the control of one of the gates. Almost at once the fortified city itself was open to the full fury of the mercenaries, and of the frenzied pilgrims following at their heels in the hope of achieving salvation through slaughter. Behind them came the knights in armour, furious that the mercenaries and mob were smashing and wrecking so much of value that might have become their own.

It was not only the heretics who were thus cut down, but the whole population, much of it loyal and Catholic. The difficulty of distinguishing heretics, other than the ministers in their black robes, had already occurred to some of the nobles, and according to the testimony of a German monk who took part in the assault, they posed the question to Arnaldus Amalricus, the leader of the troops and Abbot of Cîteaux.

'Kill the lot', he replied. 'God will recognise his own'. This may be apocryphal (though few in Béziers would doubt its authenticity), yet so it was to be. House after house was broken open, every man, woman and child was clubbed to death or cut down and trampled upon. As the insane fury spread down the streets, the citizens fled in panic to the sanctuary of the great cathedral and the other churches of the town. Priests and monks tolled the bells to summon them, and beyond the clanging and pealing the din of destruction and the screams of the victims filled the air.

But the crusaders had no intention of respecting sanctuary. The prize was too rich for them to be robbed of it so simply, and battering in the doors of the churches they slaughtered the people where they prayed and slew the priests at the altar. Seven thousand were said by a contemporary report to have been murdered in the church of the Madeleine alone, and the Abbot of Cîteaux was able to write to Innocent III to report on his success. 'Some twenty thousand citizens were killed by the sword, without regard to age or sex,' he wrote.

The wholesale destruction in the city infuriated the French knights. They cared little for the citizens, but they could not abide seeing the rough mercenaries plundering the wealth of so fine a city. So, among the score of thousand corpses, they turned on the unarmoured mercenaries and stripped them of their ill-gotten gains. Furious, these men were steeled to destroy everything in sight, and rather than let the riches of Béziers fall into the hands of the lords and barons they fired the houses. Quickly the city was swept by the flames, and the cathedral itself cracked, trembled, and crashed to the ground to bury the dead and dying under a heap of rubble and hot masonry.

For three days the crusaders then rested from their exertions, taking their ease in the meadows beside the Orb in the good conscience of a worthy deed well done. Then they moved on, and ahead of them travelled the news of their ruthlessness with such effect that the people of the country fled from their path and many of them took to the forests, or the mountain fastnesses of the Pyrenees.

There always seems to be something going on in Béziers, even if it is regrettably an occasional Spanish-style bullfight, as though so much blood was spilled in the thirteenth century that a little more in the twentieth does not matter. But it may also be something more appealing, such as the inter-town majorette competitions of the whole area.

The first time I ever saw majorettes was in Agde. I fumbled my way in to the dark nave of the cathedral, where a service was in progress, and as my eyes grew accustomed to the dimness, I saw, sitting in the seats ahead of me, rows of uniformed individuals wearing the kind of dressy hats one would have expected at the Battle of Waterloo. I wondered that they wore them in church, for I had not yet discovered that they were females, but when they marched out in their blue uniforms with white boots and mini-skirts I thought they looked extremely elegant. Later that day they marched ahead of the competing champions down to the river for the opening of the water jousting.

Majorettes seem to be present on every festive occasion. I like their performances and it is noticeable how good it is for girls to be made to stand up and move with freedom instead of sitting on the school steps like so many abandoned sacks of potatoes. On this occasion at Béziers there was a riot of different coloured uniforms, and everything from very professional performances to less expert efforts. But the girls enjoyed it and so did we. Then in the evening came the time for the competition for individuals. Most of these were the captains (or should it be colonels?) of the bands which had competed in the afternoon, and among them were a few whose choreography was so perfect and so complex that we were sure they were at least the more accomplished students of ballet schools, or whole-time professional dancers. It needs expertise and a good eye as well as good feet to dance a complicated measure and at the same time keep not just one, or two, but three silver-knobbed batons twirling in the air above one's head.

I like to see people enjoying themselves by having a holiday on a hired boat, but it is at Béziers that irritation sometimes appears, and pushing and shoving to get into a lock can occur. One does not need to be a great mathematician to work out that if the locks on the way from Agde will fill in five minutes and those at Béziers in twelve or fifteen, boats will begin to accumulate there during the day. Indeed, it was in part the discovery of twenty-eight hired cruisers waiting ahead of us at the great staircase lock that made us decide that maybe the Midi was becoming too crowded for our liking.

However, once through the port of Béziers the canal crosses the Orb on a magnificent aqueduct from which one can look over the river and the medieval bridge to the old city which saw such terrible slaughter. Then follows a long and stately curve between two tall continuous lines of cypresses which were not in fact put there for aesthetic reasons but because the approach to the aqueduct involved the construction of a very high embankment. Ships towed by horses were at the mercy of the mistral, and without the massive windbreak of trees they would simply have been blown into the shore.

Then comes the famous staircase of seven locks, which presented such problems when the lengthening process was begun on the canal that they were fortunately spared from a massacre and are to be preserved as a monument to the engineering of bygone ages. To bypass them for larger craft than Midi-sized barges, a *pente d'eau* was built in the nineteen eighties, the second one of its kind in the world. The first is further ahead, by the turn to Montauban, many miles and locks beyond Toulouse on the Canal Latéral à la Garonne.

One problem of a long flight of locks is that a lot of water is used on the upward run. Another is the staffing of the installations. Finally, there is the time involved, which can be a costly matter for the boatman. All these can be overcome by some sort of vertical lift like the one at St Louis d'Arzviller in the Vosges, which cuts out seventeen locks and saves one and a half days for a barge, but such a device and the even larger ones in Belgium and Germany are enormously expensive to build. The problem of how to build a boat lift which would be simple but relatively cheap was solved by the canal engineer Jean Aubert of the Ponts et Chaussées in an entirely original fashion and tried experimentally at the short flight of locks at Montech near the Montauban turn. His water-slope was opened in 1974.

The principal is really very simple, thought brilliant. The canal passes up the hill as a concrete trough at a slope of three per cent. The actual slope is of course dry, but at its lower end it runs out into the level and water-filled canal. The barge comes to a stop and is pushed up the trough, floating in a wedge-shaped puddle of water, by two locomotives on tracks on either side, which shove a plunger with the same shape as the cross section of the canal. At the top level there is a water-tight gate sealing off the canal, and this drops when the barge arrives in its own puddle. The one at Béziers is basically the same, and differs mainly in the arrangement of the locomotive, which is a single one straddling the whole slope.

From the top of Fonseranes lock the Canal du Midi winds away westward in one of the longest stretches of level in the world. In spite of the fact that the country is quite hilly, the distance to the next lock at Argens is more than thirty-three miles. It is a beautiful cruising ground with many surprises, the canal wandering hither and thither to keep to the one contour.

Sometimes its gentle and erratic course is spun through pastures or vineyards, or it may pass along a twisting avenue of cypresses or the more usual
huge plane trees. Now and again it curves round the edge of a hill as though
anxious to give a conducted tour of the landscape, and one can look over its
bank toward a wide expanse of arid semi-desert, dry and stony and cracked
with the heat, a waste of limestone blocks eroded by wind and interspersed
with prickly pear and other plants which flourish on the poor ground.
Bright yellow brooms smother the banks, helianthemums and orange-
centred cystus lay their flowers wide open to the brilliant heat of a sun so intense that to stop outside the shadow patches of the tall trees at midday can
be roasting. But that is why the trees are there. The good Baron of Bonrepos overlooked nothing and knew the desirability of shade. Some of the
gigantic planes which stretch along the banks are alleged to be his original
ones, but this seems improbable.

From the point of view of canal-building the long pound is ingenious. A
boat ascending the locks of Fonseranes needs a lockful of water for each
step, though a descending boat takes its own single lockful with it. If this
flight were at the end of a short canal section, the bed would be drained, and
there would also be a considerable flow toward the locks. But the same effect spread out over thirty miles is negligible, so in fact the long pound
serves as a great reservoir.

The country through which Riquet laid his canal was usually dry but it
could be subject to heavy rains, and for this reason he wisely kept the course
well above the level of adjacent rivers. But the canal itself received the waters of various brooks in addition to the feeders cut from the Black Mountain, and weirs and spillways and sluices were provided in great numbers so
that surplus water could be got rid of. Even then, flooding was such a
menace that the great military engineer Vauban diverted more than fifty
brooks in 1688, providing culverts or siphons for the water to pass under
the canal instead of through it. As a result, it was sometimes short of water
in drought periods, but an exceptionally violent storm could still flood the
canal, and in 1766 a tremendous cloudburst raised the water level in the
long pound by several feet. Where the canal lay in a dip this merely caused a
flood, but at Capestang the course ran round the edge of a hill, and there the
water pouring over the bank and into the town washed away the side of the
canal itself, and more than ten thousand labourers had to work for two
months to plug the breach and restore navigation. This was always one of
the dangers of the long pound. If it slid, the water could cause a huge flood,
so the pound was eventually fitted with two siphons. At Capestang and
Ventenac siphons built of stone were inserted in the canal, their bends a
foot or more above the normal water level. A flood would start the siphons,
and the entire contents of the canal would then be discharged into spillways
until there was only two feet of water left. At that level, air pipes would be

exposed, the siphons would be interrupted, and the canal could refill again, and by this very ingenious means further diastrous floods were avoided.

Three miles from Fonseranes the route passes under a fine stone bridge at Colombiers, and another few minutes brings in sight the short cutting leading to the mouth of the high vault of the Percée de Malpas, the tunnel which Riquet cut through the barrier of the Enserune ridge. This tunnel is very short by French standards, a mere 160 yards or so, but it is another milestone in waterway engineering because it represents the first attempt to take ships through a hill, in a tunnel.

The ridge separates the Aude and Orb valleys, and three tunnels pierce it at different levels. The Bordeaux-Sète railway takes the same opportunity to change valleys and the track actually passes through the hill far beneath the canal, entering on the starboard hand and emerging to port, so that the boatman may be passing diagonally over an express at the same moment that a car on the winding road on the top is somewhere above him. But beneath these is an even older tunnel, dug in medieval times to drain the Étang de Montady.

It may well have been the existence of this subterranean aqueduct which gave Riquet the idea of tunnelling instead of making a very deep cutting in the soft rock, but in so doing he was trying something never before attempted. When his force of labourers arrived at the Enserune ridge they found the rock to be an extremely soft tufa stone which, though easy to excavate, was not very firm. The engineers hesitated, refusing to cut a passage lest the roof should fall in. Word that the works had run into difficulty reach Colbert, who appointed M. d'Aguesseau, Governor of the Languedoc, to investigate the matter with a commission. The governor immediately ordered the works to be suspended until the commissioners could arrive, view the obstacle, and make their report to the chief minister on the bad passage or 'mal pas'. Riquet's enemies were delighted and brought every possible intrigue to bear with Colbert to have the canal stopped altogether. The Premier Minister was content to await the report of the commission, but the reaction of the Baron de Bonrepos was typical. Having brought his canal thus far, he was not to be beaten, and summoning his workmen he harangued them.

Did they know, he asked, what the people of Toulouse were saying? No? The folk of Toulouse were laughing at their cowardice, and saying that these men could not drill through the mountain if they tried! The works, they taunted, would have to be stopped. Did anyone want that to happen? Would they rather go home and be scoffed at for their timidity?

The labourers were roused and swore that nothing could stop them. They would show the world what could be done.

They had exactly six days, Riquet told them, until the commissioners would be coming, intent on closing the works, so within six days they must be through the ridge and out the other side.

Six days later Governor d'Aguesseau and the commission arrived. The Baron bowed a welcome and offered to conduct them on a tour of the works. By the light of torches he led them through the tunnel, carefully evading their questions about the purpose of the great vault in which they found themselves. At length they reached the further end, and the governor somewhat impatiently asked to be taken to the 'mal pas', the difficult passage which was holding up progress.

'You have just passed through it,' replied Riquet. And as the object of the investigation was no longer there, the officials could report that the work was progressing without hindrance.

In fact, it seems that the locality was known as Malpas before Riquet's day, but that does not detract from his achievement. The tunnel of Malpas had been cut without difficulty and without accident, but Riquet wisely accepted that the rock was too soft for permanent safety and so decided to line the vault throughout. A wooden ceiling was erected inside, but after ten years it had to be replaced. A masonry vaulting was then built into part of the tunnel, and the roof has held ever since. But just how soft the stone is (and how easy to cut in the first place) is very clear at the western end, where, in the course of three hundred years, the blasting of the mistral has eroded it into fantastic shapes of the kind that a modern art gallery might offer for sale at several hundred pounds a square foot.

The tunnel burrows under the lower part of the ridge of Enserune (Anseduna to the Romans), and the road which crosses overhead passes by a curious unnamed monument which in fact is a Merovingian tombstone, a hint that we are heading for the dark ages. Actually, the road climbs to something much earlier than that, for among the pines where the cicadas sit and perform their electronic music love songs, and extending half a mile beyond the copse to the west, the whole ridge of the hill is the site of the oppidum of Enserune, an 'Iberian' town of the sixth century BC onwards. An excellent museum shows some of the finds, and far from exhibiting a mass of shards such as Job might have scraped himself with on the dunghill it is filled with very fine objects from the various towns which succeeded each other on the site. Plenty of houses and silos and cisterns have been excavated too.

But who were the Iberians? Nobody seems to be sure. They presumably chose this site not so much for its defensive possibilities – it was centuries before it had so much as a wall – but because it overlooked the narrow neck of land over which passed all the traffic between east and west, and between Africa and Spain on the one hand and France and Italy (to use modern terminology) on the other. Enserune was not the only oppidum but it was one of the largest, and one may assume that its early inhabitants, who lived in simple wattle houses without any plan, were not warlike but made a living by trading with and supplying the caravans on their way through, caravans which were easily seen approaching. It may well have been the arrival of the business-minded Phoceans in Marseille and Agde that drew these less developed people down from the Cevennes to *profiter* as the French so simply put it. If so, it was an ideal place to settle; the valleys of the Aude, Orb and Hérault were not far away, and down below the hill on the north eastern side was the great Étang de Montady, a marshy area good for crops and maybe for wildlife too. On the southern side the Domitian Way was later to be constructed.

Whoever these people may have been, the sixth century rude village of the Iberians was replaced about 425 BC by a well laid out town of stone houses which lasted for some two hundred years. There is no need for us to examine here the methods of burial, or the objects dug up – all this can be discovered in the museum by the enthusiast, who will find there articles of use or beauty imported from the most surprising places. But it is certain that this second township was destroyed about the year 220 BC, although it was then well fortified.

Against whom was it fortified? The Celts, one might think, who were on one of their periodic rampages. But it appears very probable that the Celts were there already, living in some sort of harmony and mixture with the Iberians. And three other oppida along the littoral were sacked at the same time, presumably by the same attacker.

This is where the schoolboy should scratch his head and ask who else might have been there around that time. The answer is – Hannibal, who passed up through Spain to the Rhone in 218, along with his vast army and his elephants. Livy depicts the local tribes as reasonably pacific, but there can be no doubt that Hannibal's soldiery passed along the line of the oppida, and very probably the army provisioned itself at the expense of the inhabitants. The fact that Hannibal was well received along the same road in the year 207 BC might merely indicate that the inhabitants of the newly built 'Enserune 3' did not wish to share the fate of their predecessors by fighting him.

When first I passed by Enserune in 1963 there was not much to be seen, but a quarter of a century of skilled and patient excavation has done wonders, and more than five hundred tombs have been carefully opened up. Even now it is clear that the town extended far along the ridge to the west, and there is enough buried there to last archaeologists for another hundred years to come.

Below the ridge is the one part of France immediately identifiable by a lost aircraft pilot who happens to see it through a gap in the clouds. It is the site of the former Étang de Montady, a circular area more than a mile across and laid out with spokes like a bicycle wheel. The spokes are in fact the dykes and drainage channels which for hundreds of years have conducted the water of the former bog to the centre, whence it disappears to flow underground through the watershed ridge in its own medieval tunnel. Land tenure and division of the sectors between sons has produced the extraordinary lay out of the fields, which may have rows of a score or more of vines or other crops across the wider edge near the circumference and dwindle regularly until the last row nearest the centre is a single vine or little more. From the ground the Étang de Montady does not show itself off to advantage and is merely a place which it is inadvisable to cross in order to buy bread in Montady itself, because the whole thing is a maze of deep and waterlogged ditches. But from the air, or from the site of Enserune, the view over this extraordinary area is one never to be forgotten.

Soon the canal passes in a cutting through the village of Poilhes, where there is a Roman (or Iberian?) storage silo excavated in the soft rock right beside the canal. Whether others disappeared in the diggings I do not know, but the seventeenth century was not a period when contractors stopped work just because they happened upon something antique. Poilhes is the first village to be set squarely upon the canal, which passes through it below the level of the houses, which seem to peer down at the boats in quiet curiosity. The older part of the village is on the left or lower side and is in no way remarkable, and yet its rusty dusty houses with their shutters closed to keep out the heat of the midday sun have that curious peace about them which belongs to a village of the French South. Vines straggle over the doorways and down the walls, and the short and stocky men with weather-tanned faces sit silent and content under the great tree held together with iron bands, or on a reversed chair outside their own doorways. There is a single village store where there may be more gossip than trade, and a post office just identifiable in the flaked and faded lettering over the door. And of course there is a vintners' co-operative, for this is an area of vin de table rather than of splendid chateaux and splendid prices as in Burgundy.

At the foot of the opposite bank of the canal cutting the village wash-house still exists, though I doubt if it is still in use as it was when I first drew in at Poilhes a quarter of a century ago. In those days the canal authority provided the laundry facilities for those without domestic plumbing, and women in straw hats would come and launder their lingerie, standing or kneeling in a shallow stone pit with the edge of the stone rubbing-slab a mere two or three inches above the level of the water, so that wine tanker-barges and my own *Commodore* would politely ease off to avoid filling the pit with their wash or sweeping away the laundered garments. Then in the evening the young ladies of Poilhes would come down to the washery and use it for diving, swimming happily in the clean water. In those days I dropped a rope ladder over the side and joined them, but nowadays when five hundred hire craft with direct-venting toilets are using the canal I would not do so. And nor would the newer generation of young ladies of Poilhes.

The hire trade may have brought prosperity to the épicerie, but it has brought a polluting effluent too.

We are not a quarter of the way along the long pound yet, so we can follow it as it winds its leisurely way along the contour beyond the Enserune ridge and comes in sight of the massive bulk of the church of Capestang first to port, then astern, or almost dead ahead – which is some indication of how the canal wriggles. It is only three quarters of an hour distant and that village has long been one of my favourite stops.

The name of the place means Carp Mere, but the lake was drained in the 19th century. In 1209 a deputation from Narbonne came to Capestang led by an archbishop of whom even Pope Innocent III could declare that he knew no other God but money. They had come to meet the crusaders, and to promise the obedience of their own city. Rather than suffer the fate of Béziers, they would themselves hand over their heretics. With that single cowardly episode, which was no fault of the people of Capestang, the town disappeared from history.

I used erroneously to believe Capestang to be the home of that remarkable character among troubadours, Guillaume de Cabestang. Even if I was wrong, the tale of the end of his life of serenading is entertaining, though perhaps best not told at dinner. Guillaume paid court to the Countess of Roussillon, a lady no doubt of fascinating charm who was probably greatly flattered to have the troubadour seek her out and sing to her of love and chivalry, and tell tales of secret romances. But her husband, the Count, was not so pleased. Whether it was that he did not believe that the art of the troubadour was the only activity that took place during Guillaume's frequent visits, or merely that he was thoroughly sick of having the man mooning about his domain, he had had enough. He lay in wait, rushed out upon the troubadour and killed him.

His next act was to do a bit of post mortem work. The Count carved out Guillaume's heart, took it to the kitchens and had it cooked – though I am not sure of the recipe used – and served up to her ladyship for dinner. During the course of the meal he asked her if she liked the pig's heart he had acquired for her as a special delicacy. She replied, yes indeed, it was delicious.

"Ha, ha!" quoth the Count, leering no doubt with villainous satisfaction. And he gloatingly revealed to her what it was that she had been eating with such relish. But the effect of his pleasantry was disastrous. The Countess dropped her knife and fork and flung herself out of the window of the great hall. And the result of that was that the families of the two victims, Guillaume and the Countess, joined together and swore enmity toward the Count and his family in a feud which was never to be resolved.

Capestang is not a particularly beautiful village, but for years we had friends there. One was a barbary ape who would climb to the top of the courtyard wall of his home and if I was carrying a baguette he would hold out a little pink hand for a piece. Another was the fat little dog that lived in the house of the guardien by the quay, and if she scented that we were off for a walk into the country to pick a bunch of the deep purple wild iris, or just to wander through the vineyards, she would trot along the whole way as though anxious that we should not get lost. Yet another was the driver of the morning bus to distant Castres who would slow down by the canal bridge if he saw *Thames Commodore* lying there, as he knew there was a chance that we might want to go with him to the top of the pass near St Pons de Thomières, where the long distance path GR77 crossed the road. We could follow the track to Prémian in another valley over the hills, just in time to catch another bus four hours later and set out on our way home to the quay. Otherwise Capestang is a place with a chateau so ruined as hardly to be identifiable, a sufficient space to play boules, a vintner's co-operative, and the huge church so utterly out of proportion to the size of the village that one is not surprised that the builders gave up when they had only achieved the eastern end of what might have been intended as a great cathedral. Even then, they had to slice away the bottom few feet of one of the buttresses so that carts could pass round the corner. But never mind; beauty is not the most important thing in a church, and it was in Capestang that we joined the people for their enthusiastic and joyful mass on Easter morning. There was, of course, no protestant church in such a village, though in the days of Riquet there might possibly have been one, although I doubt it. Certainly, there would have been protestants, but they might conceivably have met in a house, or travelled to another village, or even to Narbonne.

In the Languedoc the protestant revolt, crushed in its infancy at the time of the Albigensians, was reborn aboout 1560. At first the protestants worked at their trades as noisily as possible, beating pans or engaging in joinery during the hours of mass, at the end of which the catholics would dance in the streets to drum and tabor, encited by their priests to retaliate. But this naughty-boy behaviour did not last long. Within months priests were being murdered, altars overturned, relics and statues torn down. In reply, the catholics massacred their enemies in towns such as Carcassonne and Castelnaudary. The wars of religion swept to and fro, towns becoming alternately protestant or catholic in name until, at the end of the century the Edict of Nantes put an end for a while to the worst of the cruelties.

The excesses to which the parties could go were remarkable. The Huguenot Claude of Narbonne, Baron de Faugères (a place which is the name of a good wine these days), attacked Lodève in 1573 by entering the town at night through a sewer and emerging from a grating of which the bars had been sawn through by a locksmith in a fortnight of consecutive night-time working. Once in the town with his band of confederates, the baron seized the body of St Fulcran who had died in the tenth century and was venerated in Lodève, and dragged the remains round the town. Unable to burn the shrivelled corpse, which seemed to be incombustible, he discharged a few pistol shots into it, pulled it apart and had the remains sold by the local butcher in order that the catholics would find themselves eating the relic. Naturally, there is a suitable legend that one hand of St Fulcran which was being boiled up for soup raised the lid of the pot and bestowed a blessing on the cooks. While all this was going on, priests and catholic worthies were murdered, the women raped. But some years later it was the baron's own turn. Murdered by his own mother who had remained staunchly catholic, he was eventually beheaded and the local people – who always enjoyed a little macabre fun – played boules with his head down the streets of Lodève.

Strangely, these animosities and struggles between catholic and protestant involved also the building of the canal du Midi, for that project was undertaken during the years when the Edict of Nantes guaranteed freedom of worship. Not that the guarantee guaranteed very much except that major massacres were avoided. The Huguenots were subjected to one restriction after another, and the catholic authorities hated them. Sometimes this may have been an anger that any should try to argue with orthodoxy, at others it was perhaps a fear of the liberating spirit of protestantism, which threatened the ecclesiastical hierarchy itself.

Many interests were opposed to Riquet's scheme to link the seas with a canal, especially the great landowners. They realised that the rich harvests of the Aquitaine would be loaded aboard ship and easily exported to the Languedoc and Provence, and that this would cause a collapse in the price of grain, a most important source of their income. Besides, the cost of the waterway would be enormous, and they feared the imposition of higher taxes to pay for the canal, their own enemy. Riquet was well aware of the anti-canal feeling in high circles, but he had an ally in Colbert, who had visions of the naval vessels of the French crown being able to pass from sea to sea instead of rounding Gibraltar – a dream that was never to come true.

The landowners supported the catholic cause; indeed, the church was a considerable landowner too. So the twenty-two bishops of the Languedoc were mainly if not altogether opponents of Riquet. But their greatest enemy was the growth of protestantism, and they were prepared to do a deal. If Colbert would obtain for them permission further to restrict the rights of the protestants and even to demolish their churches, they would see to it that the States of the Languedoc would provide financial support for the canal. Through this simple and infamous piece of horse-trading, the business was completed. Even if he lost his own relative wealth in the canal construction, Riquet's waterway was duly completed. And the protestant churches were burned. One hundred and thirty *temples* (non-conformist churches or chapels in the English sense of the words) were destroyed in the

Languedoc, where it was also not unknown to abduct the children of Huguenots into convents and monasteries because an edict laid down that in the event of a protestant child becoming catholic, the parents had to pay for his 're-education'.

It is sad to recall that the construction of the canal was involved in this suppression of thought and worship, but so it was. And without in any way diminishing my admiration for Riquet, it is only right that one brought up like myself in the non-conformist tradition should remember that the beauty of the canal along which one is voyaging in such happy content was founded in part upon the persecution of one's fellows. Of course, we must forgive those who persecute *us*, but we have no warrant to forgive those who persecute others. Nor, on the other hand, can I transfer on to catholics in the twentieth century the wickedness of cardinals in the seventeenth or of popes in the thirteenth. And it is reasonable to assume that if the twenty-two Languedoc bishops had not been able to buy demolition permits for the churches of the dissidents by a grant of money for the canal they would have traded something else instead.

So we can only sigh over the sadness of this blot on the loveliest of water-ways, return aboard, and cast off to negotiate the lowest and most awkward bridge on the whole length of the canal. Its sides and arch bear the marks of many an impact with the wheelhouses of barges, but we have nearly two inches over the corners of the windshield provided we manoeuvre the boat absolutely accurately into the centre of the arch and also late in the morning – when the one-way downward locking at Fonseranes will have used enough water to drop the level by perhaps as much as two inches. A friend of mine with a considerably larger yacht took aboard thirty of the Capestang population to drop the ship a few inches, and he told me that he only took the women. They were happy to sit chatting and knitting he said, and did not interfere, whereas men always wanted to tell him how to do it.

Away to the south and at the further side of the vanished mere in which the carp once lived is the village of Ouveillan. We first discovered it because of the need for a ladies' hairdresser but it was not long before we were introduced to the turbulent past of the village in the violent days of the wars of religion through a most enterprising pageant put on after dark on a stage which made use of part of the surviving castle walls to which other structures were ingeniously added. Ouveillan is no large place, but it could muster a force of something like a hundred and fifty actors of all ages, every one of them faultlessly dressed in the way of the period, whether they were Inquisitors at Carcassonne or humble serfs, or the village idiot. The following year an even more ambitious pageant was put on by the villagers amid the ruins of the nearby abbey of Fontcalvy, lost in the vineyards, and here again the people were going about their proper medieval occupations with implements, utensils and everything re-constructed with complete accuracy. The players included a dog, and a pig, and when the abbey was finally attacked it was a force of ten horsemen who thundered across the stage in darkness, firing the buildings and assaulting the place with a barrage of thunder-flashes. And the horses never reared or neighed or did anything out of order.

Perhaps most of those who have hired a boat at a price which is not cheap are unlikely to explore far to the side of the waterway, but keeping an open eye for the notices posted on trees or in the village *alimentation* one can discover an astonishing selection of entertainments which are put on more for the delight of the local people than for visitors and holiday-makers. I have already indicated that I can enjoy water-jousting, appreciate the regimented elegance of majorettes and jump to a windowsill to avoid the rush of bulls in an abrivado, but there are other and more sober entertainments to be had within striking distance of the canal, and as they rarely start until half past nine or later there is no need to forgo cruising time, for the locks are already shut and navigation stopped. We both happen to love music, and in one single summer season we were able to hear a baroque concert by the Neuchatel Chamber Orchestra, a masterly evening of the highest quality by the Symphony Orchestra of Lyon, an evening of Vivaldi and Albinoni in the moonlit cloisters of St Nazaire on the cliff edge of Béziers, the Montpellier Chamber Orchestra in a programme of three trumpet concertos and works by Bartok and Grieg, and finally a majestic performance by the London Symphony Orchestra which included Mahler's "Titan" symphony, a work that is not one of my particular favourites but is very rarely heard because of the expense of hiring all the extra players to satisfy Mahler's requirements. A friend of mine in the LSO told me ten years before this concert that to include this item on a programme cost not less than £2,000 in extra pay, and as that had to be recovered by bumping up the price of the tickets it was a risky undertaking that orchestras preferred to avoid. I can well understand them. On this occasion there were ninety-five players in action.

All these entertainments were sell-outs, and it was not a snooty audience that sat there in their shirt-sleeves under the lingering dusk of the soft Languedoc evenings. But I was bound to wonder where, other than in great centres of music such as London or Vienna, one could find such an abundance of good concerts within a single summer month.

About one and a half hours ahead the canal passes under a very elegant *dos-d'âne* or hump-backed bridge beside the remains of a handsome two storeyed stone house built in the Riquet period for some purpose connected with the canal. We had long admired it, and on one of our voyages we stayed at the 'port' of Argeliers, a stone wall just beyond the bridge, and we actually measured the whole building in detail because we wrongly thought that the Ponts et Chaussées might be willing to sell it. I must admit

that I am glad they were not, because the work of laying on water and electricity and some form of drainage would have been daunting, but I shall always be grateful to that ruin because it gave us the urge to find an alternative.

It was just before Christmas in the coldest winter for a hundred years –
the palm trees were killed all along the Riviera – when our attempt to secure
the canal house failed; but already we loved the area so much that in the first
week of the New Year we sat on a frozen bank outside Argeliers to eat a pic-
nic of baguette and paté and wait for two o'clock. Because at that hour, the
lady in the charcuterie assured us, just around the corner we would find M.
Le Grix, who would return earlier than that from his office in Narbonne
but would of course need some time for lunch. If anyone would know of a
house for sale in the area it would be M. Le Grix, she said.

This was good news, as we had already spent two days inspecting ruined
farms and unsaleable pigsties. And it proved correct. We shared a glass of
red wine with the Le Grix family in the warmth and odour of a fire of vine
stalks, and within an hour we felt much as Brigham Young must have done
as he looked down from the mountain side above where Salt Lake City now
stands, and exclaimed in delight and conviction, "This is the place!" Of
course, we were not looking out across a great waste of salt flats, but over
miles of vines, and rough garrigue with huge banks of broom and copses of
Aleppo pines toward the hills of the Corbières and in the far distance the
bluff of the arid La Clape massif beyond Narbonne. Next day we signed the
contract, and after the customary French legal delays we were able to start
converting a small villa to our own liking. And a very happy place it was to
prove, yet even before we had completed the works the first disastrous fire
swept across our territory, to be followed before many months had passed
by another, which destroyed most of our foreground view. There is a limit
to the charm of a prospect of ashes, and so we began again – and even
better.

Glancing northward from the canal by the hump-back bridge at Argeliers
one can see about two miles away a little village cramped on the lower slope
of a range of hills. Three tall arches and a tower behind them indicate some
sort of chateau, though in fact the tower belongs to the church behind it.
The village is Montouliers (which means Mount of Olives), a wine-produc-
ing locality of the Minervois, and to my mind as charming as any, and it was
there that by a stroke of luck we came upon our ideal second home. Not that
we were the first people to live there, for the caves on what was soon to become our own property had been inhabited about 150,000 years earlier. I
am sure those dim human shapes must sometimes have looked out in the
evening sun and felt the enchantment of much the same view that we have
today, except that they could not as yet see in the plain below the curious
snaking line of plane trees which mark the trace of the long pound of

Riquet's Canal des Deux Mers.

At Argeliers the canal decides to turn back on itself, as though to have a final view of the church at Capestang, then wriggles a bit before entering a mile of straight cut, an excellent place for blackberrying from on board at the side away from the towpath, as the bushes flourish with their feet in the water and the fruit is large and juicy. We shall give one long and two short blasts just before the railway bridge at the end of the long straight, and hope that any hired cruiser crew who hear it will know what it means, which is that at the junction of waterways we are turning sharp left under the roving bridge of the towpath to aim for Narbonne.

This is a corner which was to become very familiar to us, for it was to be during several years the final base of our *Thames Commodore*. She would lie patiently against the grassy bank under the great umbrella pines with their colonies of cicadas, awaiting our next visit and carefully tended by Mike and Jane Ripper who had been her nurses for years at Aigues Mortes until they moved to their cottage at the canal junction, a small building – a ruin when it came into their possession – which once had served as stabling for the horses which drew the fly-boats down to Narbonne. And it was from that same corner that we saw her finally disappear down the long pound one summer's day in 1986 on her way to England and a new owner.

Five locks in quick succession lead down the side-branch to Salléles d'Aude with its tanker-terminal for wine to be carried by water to Bordeaux for blending, and it was there that in 1986 we sat on the quayside under the village plane trees to see a mini-son-et-lumière of the most extraordinary ship ever to be seen on the canal, the *Pount*.

The idea of the *Pount* expedition was the brain-child of André Gil-Artagnan, an archaeologist whose enthusiasm for Egypt and things nautical led him to spend several years building on the bank of the Canal Latéral à la Garonne a full-size replica of an Egyptian ship of the second millenium BC, constructed according to all such details as could be meticulously gleaned from contemporary representations in the paintings and carvings of ancient Egypt. She was to cross France to Sète, undergo her sea-trials, and then load a suitable cargo for a voyage to "the land of Pount", down the coast of East Africa. Thence she was to sail the Incense Route along the African coast, round the Cape, and return to the Mediterranean and Egypt by Gibraltar, a bold undertaking indeed. And there she was at Salléles whilst her constructor explained for twenty francs a seat how the Pharaoh Queen Hatshepsut (c. 1500 BC) sent at the request of the god Amon Ra a trading mission to the land of Pount, generally believed to be Somalia. As the lights came on, the familiar figure of the great queen was to be seen seated on the deck, and however genuinely feminine she might be she was portrayed with a massive black beard trimly cut, and a loin-cloth. Being a Pharaoh she had of course to have these royal accessories, and I found myself wondering whether in real life she had had a hook-on-beard which she took off in bed at night. In fact, I believe it was the Phoenicians who first sailed round Africa, and that – according to Herodotus – was about one thousand years later, in the seventh century BC. But we must not split hairs in Salléles.

Two more locks through Salléles, and the canal reaches the River Aude itself. Then comes a dog-leg crossing of the stream to behind the shelter of the weir, two more locks along five miles of narrow cut between banks high enough to shut out floods of the Aude but also the view. The first of the locks is the Écluse de Raonel, and just above it the water of the canal streams swiftly and mysteriously away as though bent upon some special purpose. And that is indeed the case.

One day in the summer of 1878 Monsieur Dreuilhe, a vintner with fields of vines close to the village of Ouveillan, noticed two patches of withered and drooping vines in the vineyard of his neighbour, Colonel Barille of the Chateau Chambard – a very good wine which we often took aboard at Capestang. Realising the cause and the disaster about to overtake the only form of livlihood in the area, he quickly wrote to the local paper to announce that *Phylloxera* was on the march. By the following year the pest was reported over a wide area stretching almost from the Canal du Midi to the coast.

The wine-louse, or *Phylloxera vastatrix*, has a complicated life-cycle. It passes the winter as a wingless parthenogenetic female on the rootlets of the vine, and for the benefit of the non-biologists I should perhaps explain that parthenogenetic means that the female reproduces without any assistance from a male. It is also monophagous – eating only one kind of plant, in this case the vine. A highly specialised creature, it has no enemies. Except for the unfortunate vintner.

The sucking of these little creatures produces galls on the root, and from their eggs a winged form hatches, parthenogenetic as was the mother. This winged insect emerges in spring from the ground and flies to the leaves of the vine where it lay two sorts of eggs; larger ones which hatch into wingless females, and smaller ones which turn into wingless males. These then copulate on the bark of the stem, and each female then lays a single large winter egg, which in the following spring becomes a wingless female, which in turn produces galls by stinging the leaves and shoots and depositing in them an egg which becomes a parthenogenetic female, climbs down to the roots to spend the winter there and begins the cycle all over again. We can leave the further details to the entomologist, but this summary is enough to show that all parts of the vine are affected. Yet it also makes it clear that *Phylloxera* is vulnerable if one can interrupt the cycle, and this is most easily done by drowning the root-living stage.

Nowadays immune root-stocks are available, but a century ago the only means to hand was to put the vineyards under water, and the government authorised the use of the Canal du Midi, the Canal de la Robine and the River Aude for the purpose. Eventually more than eighty kilometres of artificial watercourses were dug by syndicates of wine-growers, an expensive task for which they were eventually reimbursed by the state. One of the main networks is the complex of the Canal de Raonel, which is why above the lock one can see the water flowing away so swiftly to disappear round the bend behind the trees. Already some of the vineyards may be standing in water too, for even if *Phylloxera* may not be the plague that once it was the flat land stretching away toward the hills of La Clape and the coast was of course salty from its origins, and the Canal de Raonel provides the chance through its sluices and dykes and syphons not only of watering the vineyards in the intense sumer heat and drought but of leaching out the residual salt. In this way the louse, having bid fair to ruin vineyards by the hundred, has eventually benefited the vintners by providing them with a perfect system of irrigation.

One more lock, charmingly set beside a park with a backwater and weeping willows, and one is chugging into the centre of a city so ancient that it once had Mark Anthony as the distinguished governor of Narbo Martius. Before I went there first in 1963 I had sent the usual letter to the city to solicit information about it and was surprised to receive a brochure in English with the title "Visit Narbonne, the glorious pasted!" As we approached the city I was continually turning over in my mind the problem of who had pasted it. The Germans? No. The Americans or the RAF, aiming at another bridge, of which Narbonne had eleven over the canal? It seemed unlikely. Could they be referring to Hannibal? He was suspected of having pasted Enserune. Finding no clue in the green Michelin guide, I wondered whether the Syndicate of Initiative would perhaps have a French leaflet with more information, so I went to ask them.

They were very obliging, but the French leaflet was the same in content. Yet the title gave me the information I wanted: *"Visitez Narbonne au passé glorieux!"* It was not pasted at all. Just past-ed.

However great it was in Roman times, as it undoubtedly was, Narbonne has no great buildings from those days such as exist at Vienne and Orange, Arles and Nimes. Here and there an odd column has been brought to light, and one of the churches has been converted into a museum where Roman sculptures survive by the hundred. One of them even shows a pleasant representation of a Roman fishing boat with a lateral rudder in the form of a broad oar – the much more efficient stern rudder was not invented until the 13th century. But there is no amphitheatre, no temple or triumphal gate, only the Horreum, a warehouse for market goods. Narbonne was, if not pasted, too often sacked for its glories to have survived. Yet in a way this is an illusion, for Narbonne could reasonably boast of the bridge just below the lock, a bridge which carries a pedestrian street and a double row of tall, characterful houses which, where they face each other across the paving, contain smart shops. For the roadway where people wander to look in at the shop windows is none other than the Domitian Way, the highway built in the second century BC to serve all the ports and coastal towns from the Rhone delta to Gibraltar, and the bridge upon which the whole lot stand is indeed one of Roman origin, and was known as the Pons Vetus. It was in fact the Romans who dug the canal from the nearby port to the étangs and the sea. A notice on the bridge says that mariners damaging it will have to pay, but as a collision with its low and rather awkward arch might involve demolishing two row of shops and houses, to say nothing of a classified monument of antiquity, I suspect that even Lloyds underwriters might hesitate to pay out in full.

I have a special reason for feeling affectionate toward Narbonne lock, automated and electrified for many years now. In 1963 it was worked in the ordinary way by hand, and when we passed down it was in late June, and already some of the lock-keepers in the south were away on their annual holidays, being replaced by students who could be assumed to understand the workings of a lock. When we drew in to the pen, a young man of about twenty-one came out of the doorway of the lock house, read the name *Commodore* on the bow, and walked straight up to our steersman son Hugh, who had just completed his third year at King's, Cambridge.

"You have got a double first," he said in perfect English, shaking him by the hand. "My congratulations!"

IIX

Narbonne Market – down through the lagoons – Port de la Nouvelle – magnificent mussels – the empty canal – forcing the Aude – the flyboats – an ode to Riquet.

There are few pleasanter places to lie aboard a boat than the centre of Narbonne, especially for those who do not want to pay mooring charges and at the same time are not too squeamish about being outside a public lavatory. Up above, in the long space beneath the plane trees, a market takes place every day, with boots and shoes, tin-openers, straw hats, and surplus stocks of ladies' clothing; and the ubiquitous African will be there too, with his plastic elephant tusks and bangles. Sometimes the stalls extend for another few hundred yards along the main road toward Spain, and there may be real saffron and a few score other spices, shopping baskets, honey, video cassettes and second-hand pop records. There may also be American cloth, Provençal cotton prints in great variety, and the bolt ends of fabrics from factories. Two of Ingrid's most admired dresses have been made of material picked up in street markets.

Beside the crowded coming and going of the open stalls beneath the trees the covered market is the place where we do our shopping whether on a boat or at Montouliers – except on Wednesdays, when the entire main street of Lézignan-Corbières is cordonned off to allow the stalls and travelling shops to range themselves along road and pavement alike. Then there will be a lorry with a tank of live trout, a stall with twenty different varieties of olives, and our favourite wagons of cheese and of jambon de montagne. But the Narbonne market is an excellent one, and living in Jersey it fascinates me to see that pollack (which we only use for fish pudding) costs very much more than golden mullet and other excellent table fish. There are also those poor little greenish crabs crawling about in a tray, which the French seem able to chew just as they are. Still, I enjoy the *violet des rochers*, so why should others not appreciate raw crab, pincers and all?

Across from the moorings is the splendid Archbishop's Palace, now the City Hall, with four defending turrets. Through the main gate one enters the trap of a battlemented and fortified street leading to the buildings of the palace itself, with two rounded guard towers topped with coolie hats. These strong-points sustained and protected the whole range of buildings from attack at the rear, and the Archbishop must have felt secure. No Archbishop now lives in this splendid place but one can easily imagine his eminence of earlier times seated in the audience chamber with an important emissary from the Vatican, discussing over a bottle of Corbières or Fitou the next move in the fight against reformation.

At the back of the palace is the cathedral of St Just, or what little of it exists. Not that it was bombed or burned, but owing to oversight on the part of the architect or an overweening confidence on the part of the Archbishop in the decay of things secular, the edifice was unfortunately begun so close to the fortified city walls that when the choir was completed it already reached to the ramparts and no further growth was possible. The pillars and vaulting remain incomplete, all tailored for the moment when the city should crumble into dust and leave space for the cathedral to grow a nave, but for the last seven hundred years Narbonne has obstinately refused to crumble and the poor cathedral has been thwarted.

The waterway from Mandirac lock below Narbonne to the sea at La Nouvelle is utterly different from any other. The trees are left behind, and the track of the canal wanders about between abandoned lavender fields and one-time evaporation basins of ruined salines on one side, and the startling beauty of the wide Étang de Sigéan on the other. Flamingoes stalk sedately through the shallows, and over the deeper water terns dive for small fish. Rows of stakes mark the eel nets, and here and there a solitary man in a narrow wooden boat may be following the trap to its narrow end to see what the luck of the night may have brought him. I have myself caught an eel for breakfast in the canal, with a drop-net hauled over one of the davits on the stern.

At the further shore, the sun bleached town of Sigéan basks in the light reflected from the water, and further to the left one may be surprised with the aid of good binoculars to make out a lion or two, somnolent under an umbrella tree, and even a few pelicans on the water, the area being part of the African Reserve or wild-life park. Then, for a while, the canal has open water beyond the bank on either side as it threads its way past the Étang de Gruissan, a sheet of water which is only separated from the sea by a long sand bar on which a few bungalows perch precariously in the distance. It is a landscape of extraordinary desolation and solitude, the only sign of human life near the canal being the lonely farmhouse on the one-time island of Ste Lucie, set at the foot of the solitary pine-clad bluff which rises so improbably from the watery wasteland.

The known history of the isle goes back to the first century AD, when it was a real island in a bay which extended much of the way to Narbonne. It was a seaport, having connections with various harbours of the Phoceans who had previously founded not only Marseille but Agde and other colonies along the coast. Later it became the site of a monastery, and in more recent times the vines which covered the high plateau were replaced by cattle, but maybe the cows and pigs, and even the sheep could not contend with its dry climate, for in the mid-twentieth century Ste Lucie became for some years a hunting reserve for trigger-happy chasseurs. If these in turn gave up, the birds must have been thankful indeed. And I have always been on the side of the birds.

There are plenty of curiosities. One is a broad bed of oyster shells half way up to the top of the island, not a sign that the island as such was once under the sea but a demonstration that the buckling of the surface as the plates collided could not only force up irresistibly the major fold of the Pyrenees but could also produce a local and minor crinkle such as was in fact the origin of Ste Lucie and of the other strange but now deserted island in the same one-time bay of the sea, the Isle de Lot with its wedge-shaped mountain. Another oddity is the ingenious method of transporting the grapes to the wine-press, the machinery of which still survives in the undergrowth of the almost tropical jungle.

A vast pipe in sections of pottery was fixed to the face of the vertical cliff, and when harvesting on the high plateau the workers in the vineyard had merely to tip their loads into the orifice, and the raw material for Ste Lucie rouge would arrive directly into the stone basin of the press.

From the dry plateau with its own different but unusual vegetation there are wide views over the sea, the salt flats of La Nouvelle, and the mysterious étangs to either side of the embanked canal. On the north one can look down upon egrets and herons poking about among the reeds and weeds between the masonry banks of the canal once built by the Romans to lead from the Port of Ste Lucie direct to the shore of the Corbières, a fore-runner of the present canal which connects with the Robine, the creek which once served the Roman quays at Narbo Martius, Narbonne. On the western side the main railway track from Marseille and Narbonne to Spain curves round the noses of the cliffs, cutting off the bay at one point so that the water there is hardly replenished and the brilliant sun of the Midi has made its own salt factory and given this corner of the island a beach with drifts of what appears at first sight to be snow.

It is odd that the railway makes this detour instead of taking the shorter route by way of the western shore of the wide expanse of the Étang de Bages,but when in 1860 the line was constructed the people in the village of Bages were as scared of the pollution by the smoke of locomotives as others may be today at the presence within twenty miles of them of a nuclear power station. They refused permission for the railway to cross their territory, so the proprietors of the Midi line were obliged to use the sand-bar wending from near the lock at Mandirac to the Ile de Ste Lucie. The owner of the island readily agreed to the use of his foreshore provided he was given a mini-station of his own, a halt at which trains would stop on request. This gave him convenient transport to Perpignan and Narbonne, even if he had to drive half way round the island to reach the halt, which still survives and can be seen far below from the edge of the pine-scented plateau.

Soon the final lock drops the level slightly to the salt water of the straight which leads into the port of La Nouvelle. But this last mile is fascinating too, for over each bank are the wide flat salt-pans which yield the immense pyramids of salt upon which bulldozers crawl like flies on a sugar cone. The banks are brilliant with the reds and yellows of all those strange flowers which love a high concentration of salt – and droop and die at once if picked and put in a vase of fresh water. Fish, many of them mullet of some size, shoot past the boat as the drawing off disturbs them, and the air carries the slightly chemical and laboratory odour that the brackish cut exhales.

I have always thought the town of La Nouvelle to be the dullest in the whole of France. It has nothing of beauty or interest of any kind what-soever, but is just a collection of rather scruffy streets set out at right angles all the way to the wind-blown sea-front where a few hotels and blocks of apartments try to look as though they are cousins of those of Nice or Can-nes. But they are poor relations. Even the customs house looks run down, and it shares the generally depressed atmosphere of the rest of the town. I have been there many times, and found it one of the finest surviving exam-ples of the French obstructiveness.

When the Republic decided to discontinue the *Passeport pour Bateau* a system had to be devised which would allow foreigners reasonable use of a boat without the threat of being stung by a demand to pay Value Added Tax for importing the boat into the country. The scheme thought up was in theory simple; one could use the boat – stay aboard, that is – for up to six months in the year, provided one did not hire it or lend it to others outside the immediate family. When aboard, the boatman had to have the ships papers on board too, and when he left for home he had merely to hand them in to the nearest customs office, which stamped a form of receipt and logged the relevant date in their diary.

For some years we kept *Thames Commodore* at Aigues Mortes. The cus-toms office there was rarely open, but that did not matter; there was a letter box in the door for no other purpose than the sensible one of allowing yachtsmen to dump their papers. If the official was there he was genial, helpful, and expressed the opinion that it would be a real delight for him to see you the following year. A smile, a handshake, and that was that. But when we moved to keeping her at the canal junction near Salléles d'Aude we had to deal with La Nouvelle. It was about thirty miles distant and in-volved getting a lift to Narbonne and then catching one of the rare trains that condescended to stop at La Nouvelle and gave one time to reach the customs house by half past eleven, otherwise one risked being told in surly fashion round the end of a long treasured cigarette stub that one was too late because it took a long time to issue a receipt and the office shut at twelve.

The first time I trailed to La Nouvelle, the man refused the papers because I could not prove who I was. I returned to Salléles, and sent them by registered post. I enclosed a letter of receipt and even a stamped envelope, but this was still in the office when I called next spring, to be met with a statement that it was forbidden to send papers by post. One must present them in person. I asked to see the paragraph which decreed this, which only nettled the man more. But I got the papers.

In spite of its being a port of some modest size with a handful of sea-going ships along the quays, the La Nouvelle customs was shut on Saturdays, Sundays, Ascension Day, the Feast of the Bodily Assumption of the Blessed Virgin Mary, Liberation Day and I know not what besides. One had to consult the calendar carefully before setting out. It so happened that we usually returned home at the weekend, and as we often passed through La Nouvelle by boat on our way from Spain to Salléles it occurred to me that nothing could be easier than to show myself and the boat on Thursday, hand in the papers – which could be dated two days later to give plenty of time for us to reach Salléles – and that would be that. But no, that was out of the question. When I said that at Aigues Mortes one had only to pop the papers in a box the douane's blood pressure rose dangerously, so I said no more.

This La Nouvelle business was of course absurd in every way, and I always tried to humour the official there somehow. A jaunty 'Good morning' and a hand extended over the counter would be met with a scowl, although the hand would be taken. (I believe the French shake hands with even their sworn enemies.) Then I would be ignored for a while as the official stared at a table of import duties, or maybe saints' days. Once when he was performing his customary disregarding of Pilkington he began to whistle, rather well I thought. I put on my most charming smile and ventured a question.

"Do you play the violin?"

He looked up. "No." He looked down again, but I could see he was curious to know why this English idiot has asked such an irrelevant question. "The violin?"

"Yes. Do you play it?"

"Why should I?"

"Well, you were whistling..."

"What if I was? Can I not whistle without asking you?" He shoved his papers to one side.

"Of course, of course." I put on my gentle, calm-the-mad-dog-before-it-bites voice. "But it was Boccherini's Minuet, and I thought ..."

"Was it?"

"Yes. And you whistled it so very well I thought perhaps you had played it on the violin. It is a violin piece, you see. So I thought perhaps you must be an amateur musician."

He was a little flattered by this. Sufficiently to get out the file of deposited ships' papers and search for mine. As I left the building, Boccherini floated through the open window into the street. And I had the papers.

It would be wrong to give the impression that there was nothing to commend La Nouvelle in any way. There was indeed one thing, and I never ran in or out of the pierheads without taking advantage of it. There were no quays at all along the main channel but there was almost certain to be a muck-boat or a dredger or some other species of work boat on which to draw in for a quarter of an hour, or else I could double back outside the mole, drop anchor, put down a ladder and swim over. For the rocks on the inner side of the mole were thick with mussels of enormous size. *Moules marinière* has long been one of my favourites, but never have I had such *moules* as are to be had in the harbour of La Nouvelle for the picking. A jump overboard with a bucket on one's belt, and a quarter of an hour would yield kilo upon kilo of the delicious bivalves, and it was partly the looking forward to the splendid supper they would make that enabled us to regard La Nouvelle as having something to be said for it after all.

Once, when we were heading inland from La Nouvelle, we had passed the bend above Ste Lucie lock when I was a little disconcerted by what I saw protruding from the weed we were just passing. I went astern, and Ingrid came up from preparing the *marinière* in the galley to see what was happening.

I pointed as we backed down. A pair of feet, fresh-looking and pink were sticking up from the greenery. On several occasions as I have related elsewhere (*Small Boat Down the Years*) I had come across corpses in France and had towed them in or done whatever was necessary, and so I knew that corpses did not float head down and with their feet sticking up above the surface. Besides, these little pink feet were only about two inches from heel to toe. With a bucket on a rope and the help of a boathook we raised the body and brought her on board. She was wearing only a very cheap and scanty pair of pants and her lovely hair was completely matted with *Spirogyra*, but she was a beautiful doll and must have been treasured by some little girl who had unfortunately dropped her overboard. And dropped her weeks or even months earlier, to judge by the algal coating on the remainder of her body.

We quickly decided that with a little treatment and a good scrub and the shredding of the matted weed in her hair when it had dried in the sun, she would be an admirable extra member of the crew. In Béziers we found a frock for her, but her finest outfit of all was to be the handsome sailor suit with ship's name below the collar, specially made for her by a friend who was on board at the time of her retrieval. After the location where we found her the little girl was given the name Lucie and for two years she looked out of the saloon windows to delight passing children, before retiring to sit on top of a cupboard at Montouliers.

The same friend who designed Lucie's outfit later made a fine set of trousers and a padded waistcoat with everything down to boots and shoes for Anne. This newcomer's full name was Anne de Fonseranes, because she came to light in a heap of cut reeds and other rubbish raked out at the top gates of the Fonseranes flight of locks. She, too, was a beautiful doll, one of those expensive ones the size of a real child. That was one of the problems in clothing her. She, too, has joined Lucie and so has little Willie.

One occasionally meets a *péniche* in France or Belgium which has a little sailor up near the bow, a signalman holding two flags in such a way that his arms whirl round and he twists this way and that with the wind. Little Willie had been in the family – on *Thames Commodore's* bow, that is, when she was under way – for more than fifteen years. It happened that I had drawn in on a fuelling barge in Namur to fill up with diesel, and the man took me to the store below decks to find some small item I needed. Right in the front of the space was a heap of rubbish, and in it I could see a rather dilapidated sailor of the windspiel variety. I asked if I could have him.

"That's only rubbish," the man said. "I made it years ago to amuse the kids, that's all. You don't want that ... but of course if you do ..."

We had just then a friend on board who was exceedingly neat in his home maintenance, and for nearly a week he worked away in secret in *Thames Commodore's* forward toilet, cleaning, painting a sailor suit, delineating Little Willie's features, and making the flags, one for each hand. We later made these flags detachable so that we could always mount the right one in courtesy to whatever land we happened to be in, and when Willie retired from a life afloat he had his pedestal on the terrace where he could whirl away delightedly under the inspiration of the tramontana, with Ingrid's blue and gold of Sweden in one hand and the Jersey ensign in the other.

One of our journeys up from La Nouvelle was in May of 1981, because we wished to take part in some very special celebrations, the three hundredth anniversary of the opening to shipping of the Canal Royal des Deux Mers en Languedoc, in other words, the Canal du Midi. We hoped that *Thames Commodore* would take her station in the line of ships commemorating the first flotilla of boats, and even if we did not have our private musicians as had Cardinal Bonzy on that earlier occasion we thought it would be entertaining. Besides, I had already taken to the canal office in Carcassonne a very fine bronze plaque cast for the Inland Waterways Association by one of its members, and this was to be unveiled at the point where the feeder stream from the Montagne Noire poured its water into the summit pound. It was with some surprise that I noticed a few weeks in advance of this event that the Ponts et Chaussées had selected the precise period of the tercentenary to drain the canal of water for the usual annual maintenance work. It was a typical example of one French hand not knowing what the other hand was doing. More than that, it was a great pity, because – as an Irishman might put it – tercentenary celebrations only occur once in three hundred years. The best we could do – meaning the nearest we could get to the summit – was to take the sea route from Aigues Mortes to La Nouvelle and steam up to Narbonne, for that branch of the canal was not drained south of the crossing of the River Aude. We would lie in the centre of Narbonne, hire a car, and on the day before the festivities be "At Home" to the IWA party and those of the American Canal Society who were joining them for the trip and junkettings.

The ludicrous aspect of the affair was that the celebration was to be on the Friday if I remember rightly, and the canal was to be opened again for shipping at seven o'clock on the following Monday morning. With the help of the little Renault we had hired for a week we joined the IWA party to inspect the Fonseranes locks and the Malpas tunnel, and in the course of travelling through the countryside between there and Carcassonne I could note that – as expected – the thirty-three mile pound had not been drained, but otherwise there was hardly enough water in the canal sections for a duck to get its knees wet, and I was surprised to see how small the waterway looked, considering that laden barges could use it.

The celebrations were delightful, because they were unsophisticated, rural and natural. The government was not represented, a few mayors from neighbouring localities were there with their ladies – and for the benefit of those unfamiliar with French arrangements I should perhaps mention that one does not have to be a borough in the English sense to have a mayor; every village seems to have one to marry off the inhabitants on Saturday mornings. A number of canal officials and staff were present too, and probably outnumbering all the rest the parties from the IWA and the Friends of P. P. Riquet, a local society formed to promote the tercentenary. These all gathered among the trees on either bank of the *rigole* or feeder where its water gurgled over the sill into a small bay at the side of the canal, a place which had often been one of our own selected mooring spots. The leader of the IWA party made a brief speech and invited Mademoiselle Eveline Riquet de Caraman, perhaps the sole remaining descendant of the great builder, to unveil the bronze plaque, and then with great charm and elegance she made an address of thanks in faultless English (she had had, as she explained to Ingrid, an English nanny when she was a child) and the teacher from the hamlet of Montferrand across from the Pierres de Naurouze conducted her young pupils as they sang a song in honour of Riquet. We all adjourned for a dinner at the nearest town to this remote spot that could muster a restaurant. And that was that.

It was sad, if not sheer ridiculous, that no boats could be present, but now I was haunted by the belief that we should be stuck for another week or so in Narbonne. Between our berth and the summit at Naurouze lay some eighty miles of canal, and except for the few remaining miles of the long pound the whole stretch was either empty or only partly filled. Earlier on the Friday I had called at Carcassonne to see M. Gardon, the canal manager for the area, and asked him how it were conceivable that within two and a half days the necessary vast amount of water could possibly be forthcoming to fill all those miles of waterway.

"Do not break your head about it," he said gently. "On Sunday we shall be letting the water in."

"Sunday! But the whole canal is supposed to be open to navigation early on Monday morning!" I exclaimed.

M. Gardon smiled pleasantly. "It will be. You will see for yourself."

The canal being in any event filled with water as far as the lock of Gailhousti, immediately beyond the crossing of the Aude, we decided to leave Narbonne on the Sunday afternoon and steam slowly up to that point so that we could start from there on the Monday morning in the very unlikely event of there being water in the canal. The passage up through Narbonne is one I have always liked, and even those few years ago the new port with its pleasant flower beds and trees and excellent quayside did not exist. And these things have added to the attraction of what formerly was a rather Dutch type of waterway with a road on each side flanked by pleasant houses and vintners' establishments.

We had left all this behind us and were chugging peacefully along the cut without ill will to anyone when I noticed a man on the bank some way ahead, dancing and gesticulating as though stung by a hornet. Except that the gestures and shouting seemed to be directed towards ourselves. Although it was then the close season and coarse fishing was prohibited I realised that he was an angler. Coarse fishermen are more noted for glum silence than excitability, at least in Britain – and who might not feel a trifle dispirited when sitting for hours on a sodden bank staring at a float and knowing full well that if the improbable should happen and a fish take the bait it will be both small and of an inedible species and will have to be carefully unhooked and thrown back as soon as it has been weighed and properly recorded by the club secretary? In the Midi on the other hand they were less inclined to be misanthropic. The dry ground, the sunshine, the ambient scent of herbs and a bottle of strong Corbières red, all these things have a mellowing effect which result in a good bonhommie, a friendly attitude to the world in general, boats included. It was clear to me that the man on the bank ahead of us might be an exception, so I was ready to adopt my usual disarming tactic, which is simply to appear to interpret all shouting and yelling as a well-intended attempt to draw my attention to the blue sky, the beauty of the early colour in the vines, the stately grandeur of the plane trees and so forth. And if the fisherman should point at the float perilously close to our course and shout something not easily understood I usually found that to agree that the yellow irises cast fascinating reflections in the water would cut off the shouting and perhaps bring even a smile and a friendly nod. So, when I was knocked clean off the steering stool on to the deck by a heavy missile flung by this excited angler I was decidedly surprised. Had it hit me on the head I would not be writing this book about the delights of the Languedoc.

When we saw the man collecting cobblestones and half-bricks from the side of the service track we changed our minds about landing to chat to him or even to try to take a close-up photograph. However, the mere production of a camera caused him to drive off at great speed, with the tail of his Renault Four up in the air so we could not read the number. My arm not being broken as Ingrid at first thought, we used the camera to take some colour photographs of the injuries, and carried on with our enjoyable voyage. The photographs and a detailed description of the assailant were sent to the Narbonne police, and fifteen months later I attended a preliminary hearing before a magistrate, which was a hilarious affair which I have described elsewhere (*Small Boat Down the Years*) and resulted, I am glad to say, in the suspect – who bore no resemblance in age, stature, colour or any other respect to the man I had described – being allowed to go home without being arraigned on a charge of *Assault grave et criminel*.

Apart from being nearly killed by a psychopathic angler, we had no problems and took up our position for the night at the foot of the Gailhousti lock gates. Our evening stroll to listen to the nightingales was along the tow-path ahead of us and we could see right up the dry canal bed as far as the village of Salléles d'Aude. There was now only twelve hours to go, and it was obviously impossible that the canal could be filled in that time. The idea was ridiculous.

Ridiculous. About six o'clock next morning we were awakened by an intermittent slopping sound. I got out of my bunk and went on deck in the crisp, clear morning air. Water, yellowish   grey from sweeping over the muddy bottom of the canal was pouring over the top of the lockgates in a series of waves. M. Gardon was right. There was no need to break my head. What the *Ponts et Chaussées* decreed would indeed happen, whether that were refilling the whole canal in a day, or deciding to empty it at the time of Riquet's tercentenary.

It was two years later that we passed again under the Pons Vetus on our way inland from La Nouvelle, and when we reached Gua lock at the end of the city the woman in charge of it refused to let us in. We must wait two hours, she said, because there was no more than eighty centimetres of water in the canal beyond the lock. When I pointed out that the water was pouring over the top of the gates like a young Niagara Falls, and that therefore it could not conceivably be in short supply, she merely became angry. But I stuck to the obvious point, continually returning to it between bouts of remarks about *quel chaleur, ma foi*, and what a beautiful lock-house she had,

Top: Le Somail
Bottom: Montauban branch

Top: Garonne lateral canal
Bottom: The Dordogne at Bourg

and how about the children, and offering a lump of sugar to the lock dog
without having my hand bitten off, with the result that she softened enough
to reduce the waiting to one hour and a quarter, during the whole of which
time the lock waterfall continued, glinting and sparkling in the sunlight.
Meanwhile, we sat on deck drinking coffee and beaming whenever she
emerged from the lock house to look up the reach like one expecting her
husband to return from the crusades.

It was at the next lock that the shortage of water began. A foot or two of
muddy shore and a tangle of tufty plane tree roots flanked one bank beyond
it, and on the other side of the canal the reeds had a stripped-to-the-waist
appearance, combined with a tendency to collapse now that their support-
ing element had been withdrawn. This pound ran out after two or three
miles into the Aude, so obviously the river must be somewhat on the dry
side, I thought.

The keeper explained that the river was indeed very low, and that this
was due to the fact that in such a time of drought thirty miles or more
of vineyards on either side pumped water out to spray their vines and swell
the grapes. It was literally a case of water into wine. But the pumping
stopped at night and by morning there was always more water. There
would be no trouble for a boat drawing as much as five feet; or at least apart
from a few bumps that sort of depth could be expected. But now –
he clicked his tongue – the engineer said that to cross the Aude was only
permissible for craft drawing eight-five centimetres. How much did
we draw?

I said eighty. Not that I am a liar by nature, but when dealing with things
marine or aquatic I find that dimensions are best kept elastic. Indeed, I had
wisely faced over with plywood the tell-tale registered tonnage of twenty-
nine incised on the main beam, as I preferred to vary the tonnage according
to circumstances. Whenever an official asked *Thames Commodore's* tonnage
I casually enquired why he wanted to know. Was it perhaps for some kind
of national statistics? On the Rhine I knew the reason very well. It was that
ships of fifteen tons and over were obliged to take a pilot. So, on the Rhine,
she banted her figure to thirteen point four tons and everyone was happy.
Especially myself, who thereby saved several hundred solid German marks,
to say nothing of having to pay a couple of inspectors to travel two hundred
miles to inspect us. And so that our draught could also be varied, I had carefully also removed the marks put on the transome by the builders.

On this occasion, eighty seemed to me a nice round figure. I did not imagine that we could actually pursue a course across the Aude if really there
were no more than eighty-five centimetres of water in the river, but I usually found officials to be Jeremiahs – with the exception of course of the
Échelle de Chasse, who was omniscient and accurate.

So we duly passed Raonel lock and began our slow voyage along the cut, watching as a surprised water vole clambered up to his hole now exposed on dry land. The channel was, of course, narrow, and occasional clunks and clonks on the propellers told of rotten branches which had fallen from the plane trees overhanging the water. It was a slow journey but without difficulty, and after nearly an hour for three miles we came in sight of the stop lock of Moussoulens, where the canal ran out into the river behind a training wall just above the weir. We passed very slowly through the open lock and it was not hard to imagine why. Our keel was sliding along the bottom of the pen.

As for the River Aude, it looked remarkably dry. Far from having water pouring over the weir, there was a group of workmen with a digger in the river bed – or rather, on the dry land where the water normally lay – and they had removed some of the stones at the top of the spillway and were resetting them in cement. Elsewhere there was a jungle of tree trunks exposed, victims of former floods, looking like a film set for some fearful drama of prehistory. Yet all this was beyond the training wall, and when we turned to chug up about five yards from the shore I was pleased to find there was plenty of water.

Why five yards? Because this cross-over was originally designed for horse-hauled barges, and a combination of economics, hydraulics, and whatever other -ics experts use leads one to the conclusion that where L is the length of the towline, W the weight of the ship, C the coefficient of uncertainty, VDQS the quality of wine drunk by the skipper for lunch and H the square root of the age of the horse, the equation comes out at 15 feet. That is where the channel is, and always will be.

Obviously, if horses were hauling a vessel from one side of the river to the other, there must needs be some way of transferring the faithful steed and family pet from bank to bank. Here at Moussoulens it was some sort of platform held by a line from drifting away, this line being attached to a pulley which ran on a cable stretched between two handsome stone pylons, one on either bank. Equally obviously, the horse-drawn craft would have drifted across the stream somewhere close to the pylons but on the downstream side, and the channel would at least at one time have been on that line. So, carefully taking things slowly we sailed gently across the river, turned the nose down toward the entrance of the curving cut leading to Gailhousti lock, ran straight into a bank of particularly sticky mud, and stuck fast. Nor did our ship seem to wish to back out, however hard we urged her.

Of course, we had only to wait until the small hours of the following morning when the wine growers of the Corbières would be sleeping from their exertions and their pumps had long fallen silent so that the water pouring down from what scraps of snow were left in the Pyrenees would not be all extracted and sprayed over the countryside for conversion to more VDQS but would reach the weir, back up, and float us off, probably washing us gently down into the chaos of the primeval jungle without our even awakening. But it seemed to me that this was the occasion for seeing what our engines could do. I had purposely had the water cooling intakes moved well aft of amidships, because boat builders habitually placed them at the lowest point of the hull, so that at the first touch on a mudbank the pipes and pumps would be blocked solid and a rather grubby and smelly hour had to be spent taking them apart and cleaning them. Boatbuilders are monuments to unthinking traditionalism, perhaps because they do not actually own boats but merely build them, and my change, introduced after many days spent head downward in the bilge, had worked wonders. We could even moor as I had done at Arles, by driving hard up a mudbank without the slightest risk of pumpstipation.

The mud was very sticky indeed, but by twisting the wheel to and fro and blasting the stinking deposit away with our two teams of one hundred and forty horsepower apiece we went on our way rejoicing. Not rapidly, but making a foot or so in a minute until we had cut right through the bank and were in the end of the curving lock cut, which only had a few inches more of water but enough to let us move cautiously up the centre pushing through the silt. As we came up to the open gates, encouraged by the lock-keeper who had come to the river bank to watch, there was a bump. Not a hard one, but just a firm, restricting thump. It was the threshold of the lock, which evidently did not contain quite enough water to float us. But a final burst of full power shoved *Thames Commodore* up over the sill. A slight tilt forward as the lowest part of her anatomy crossed the line, and she slid nicely forward into the pen and we could climb up to close the gates.

I thought it would be interesting to look at the depth scale, a baby *échelle* on the outside of the lock. It stood at ninety five centimetres. I have always found the metric system annoying, stupid and confusing, and why on earth things should be described in umpteenth parts of an imaginary line drawn round the earth through Paris, and wrongly measured into the bargain, is something I have never been able to understand. But I knew our draught was nearly fifteen centimetres more than the indicated depth of water in the lock, so we had not done badly.

Back through Salléles d'Aude and up the six locks to the junction, a left turn past the unsightly and noisy mill factory which rests not, neither by day nor by night but sends a cloud of light pulverised cereal husk across the countryside, and within a minute we were crossing over the River Cesse, a splendid three arched bridge of stone bearing all the marks of the grandeur and determination of the great engineer Sebastien Vauban, who designed it after Riquet's death. One mile further ahead we came to Le Somail, a very picturesque hamlet built at the same time as the canal to serve as a loading place for the produce of the area around, and later coming into its own as a passenger depot.

Before the birth of the Sète-Bordeaux railway, which quickly took over the passenger traffic between Marseille and the Atlantic coast, the management of the Canal du Midi operated an excellent service of horse-drawn fly-boats which connected at the Sète end of the line with ships to Mediteranean ports, and with the trains to Marseille. At the western end the traveller could change at the canal basin of Toulouse to a fly-boat of the Garonne lateral canal, which in turn connected with a river steamer at Agen, on board which the journey to Bordeaux was completed. What with this, and the voyage down the Basin de Thau behind the steamer *Colbert* or the *Riquet*, or the *Vauban*, it must have been a splendid journey. The boats were divided into three classes, somewhat after the fashion of the American canal boats, and they were literally packet-boats, for they carried the mail. At the quay of Le Somail they would draw in for a moment to hand over the passengers and mail for Narbonne.

When the post boats were first introduced, thirty-six vessels were needed. The canal authorities decided that time would be saved if the boats did not pass through any of the flights of two or more locks, and of these there were twenty-two. A passenger from Toulouse to Agde would certainly have a speedy journey behind the horse-teams, but during the course of it he would have to change ships more than a score of times, jumping ashore at the top of every lock flight, stumbling down the towpath with his bags, and boarding the next vessel below the bottom gates. It was healthy exercise and an ingenious mode of travel.

The thirty-six ships with their relays of horse teams and their postillions brought plenty of life and bustle to the canal, but there was not much profit to be had from the business. Later a smaller number of craft achieved the journey at a slightly lesser speed but more conveniently, passing through the locks like any other boat. The only exception was at Béziers, where the long staircase and the awkward traverse of the Orb were not worth the effort.

Every morning a boat would leave Toulouse, stopping for midday dinner or for an overnight halt at pre-arranged places which had suitable inns, and arriving at the top of the Fonseranes locks about noon on the fourth day. The passengers then drove in to Béziers for lunch and afterwards embarked on another packet on the further side of the Orb, to reach Agde by evening. So the whole journey which the train nowadays knocks back in a little over two hours was one of several days. But people were not in a hurry, not by modern standards. There was much to see, much to admire, companions with whom to discuss the countryside around the canal over a bottle of Minervois. And surely most of all their admiration would have been for the sheer fact that one could now voyage from sea to sea.

"*Quand per lé premier cop*", one of the passengers might say, quoting an ode in Occitan (or the Langue d'Oc) by the poet Daveau, "'*las dos mars se juntéroun, dins l'Europo pertout lés poplés s'estouneron d'un miracle tant bèl."*

And his companion might have replied, *"Oc, tant qué lé moundé durara, toun noum, Riquet, brounzinara,"* a good demonstration of the fact that one does not need to know the language to understand it. And I agree. Riquet's name will always resound, *brounzinara*.

IX

The Vintners' Revolt – reforming a bargee – the siege of Minerve – rivers underground – Alaric and Clovis – pollution and the President – from Argens to Carcassonne – the Cité and its legends – the fate of Raymond-Roger – Lastours defiant.

L e Somail is in the Minervois, and so are Argeliers, Bize, Mailhac, and a score of other fascinating little towns perched at the edge of the dry, vine-covered slopes which fringe the garrigue or arid wasteland to the north of the Canal du Midi along the long pound and for a score of locks to the west. But south of the canal is Corbières country, with its wine capitals of Lézignan-Corbières and Narbonne. Very roughly the River Aude is the boundary between these two immensely productive vineyard areas, and the Corbières hills contain two sizeable enclaves of another Appellation Controllée, the Fitou. Altogether these wine fields and those that join them on their eastern side form the largest continuous mat of vineyards in Europe, a concentration of vines which stretches in geometrically laid out rows for more than 120 miles and produces wine which can be mediocre and undistinguished (and very cheap) but also has chateaux which produce vintages which to my mind are in every way the equal of the famous names of Burgundy and Bordeaux, the difference being that one does not need to pay pounds extra per bottle for a name which even then may not be genuine.

The earliest vintners of the Corbières, tough Gauls, were already marketing their wine before the Romans descended upon the region, and no doubt many a legionary enjoyed his draught of the local product, which was probably very poor stuff compared with the sophisticated wines which can nowadays be produced by blending Carignan and Grenache with a dash or two of Cinsaut and Syrah and Mourvedre, Terret Noir or Piquepoul. But quite apart from the sheer hard work that goes to making the filling of a single EEC-approved St Gobain glass bottle, the prosperity of the vintner has been menaced from time to time by hail and starlings, cheap Algerian plonk, phylloxera, the admission of Spain to the EEC, and the dubious practice of merchants and wholesalers. In the 1980s the more fiery hotheads entered a supermarket at Carcassonne smashed all the bottles of Spanish wine against the floor, and even turned an astonished English family off a hired cruiser on the canal and burned it. Just what these hysterical acts were expected to achieve is not obvious, but they are indicative of an anger and frustration smouldering beneath the surface. My own close friends among the vintners assure me that a good wine of the area has nothing to fear from competition with Spanish vintages.

Yet these troubles are nothing compared with the crisis at the beginning of the present century. In 1880 the wine was selling at 32.50 francs per litre. Twenty years later the price was little more than one sixth of that figure. Over-production and unrestricted import of Algerian wine were partly to blame, but government subsidies for sugar-beet growers led to the practice of adding sugar to bad wine and then topping down the density with water – admittedly a less lethal treatment than that of some Austrian and German vintners in the mid 1980s who spun out the wine with anti-freeze and water, but serious enough to enrage the good producers.

The first revolt by vintners was against the sugaring and adulteration encouraged by the wholesalers, and it was from Argeliers that a hero emerged to lead the campaign. Marcellin Albert was a vintner and wine merchant but also something of a comic, and he had the talent of leadership even if he may not always have been certain which way he was leading and why. He formed around himself an action committee and with demonstrations and marches he and his men roused the area until they marched upon Narbonne, where the socialist mayor was sufficiently frightened to give them his support, thinking no doubt that it was safer to go along with a popular uprising which he was unable to calm or restrain. The army of demonstrators grew continually. Nearly three quarters of a million marched upon Montpellier, the main railway line was blocked, and the City Hall in Béziers sacked – for now the leaders themselves could no longer hold their own forces in check.

Inevitably, the government had eventually to act, and Clemenceau ordered the army to move in. Narbonne was the scene of serious fighting, the renegade mayor and some of the Action Committee were captured and imprisoned. A territorial regiment was sent to the city to keep order, but it happened to be one in which many sons of vintners were enlisted and the result was that it mutinied and marched on Béziers before it was eventually disarmed and shipped over to Tunisia to cool off in an oasis. As for Marcellin Albert, so recently hailed as "The Redeemer", he was easily outwitted by Clemenceau and was quickly disowned by his fellows, villified, and sent in exile to Algeria. Nevertheless, the battle was to some extent won. The government brought in legislation to prohibit sugaring and adulteration of wine, and as a result the price began to recover. Calm was restored, and with the advent of World War I the wine industry benefited greatly from the rule that every soldier – and of course there were many millions – was to be issued with a quarter litre of wine every day. This 'pinard' took its name from the pinot, one of the species of vine which is a particular favourite in Alsace.

So the vintners' job has not always been a happy one, however gay and smiling the workers may appear between the rows of vines. Motorway bridges are sometimes daubed with anti-Spanish slogans, and bus shelters and vineyard buildings painted with *"CEE Ruine"*, or *"PS Traître"* – because it was the Parti Socialiste which agreed to the Spanish entry into the EEC (or CEE).

All the same, the better producers seem to have no trouble in selling abroad as well as at home, and even if the lesser breeds are likely to feel competition from Spain there is a demand for undistinguished wine for blending into proprietary vins de table, or into aperitifs. Not only St Gilles far to the east, but Béziers and Homps and Carcassonne had quays stained purple when first I past them in 1963, and the scent of wine drifted from the tanker barges lying alongside. In those days such craft were common, but now they are almost extinct, their place being taken by bowser lorries. Indeed, in 1985 there were only two barges making the eleven day round trip from Salléles to Bordeaux with a load of wine for the blenders.

It was with one of these craft that I had an unusual experience. Their progress was always announced ahead by lock telephone, and hired or private craft would very properly be cleared out of the way as each lock had to be made ready and waiting to speed the commercial craft on its journey. Such a barge had a crew of two, a man and wife, and between them they had to manoeuvre the boat, make fast, look to the warps, and shut or open the gates on one side while the keeper worked the others. There would probably be plenty of holiday boatmen standing around with their hands in their pockets, somewhat annoyed at having to wait for a mere working couple to do their job, but they never seemed inclined to help. Knowing what hard work it could be, especially in a staircase lock, Ingrid or I myself would always lend a hand without being invited to do so, and on this particular occasion I was standing on the gates of the triple lock at Trèbes, ready to wind the paddles as soon as the bottom gates had been closed.

The barge skipper was young, and had not yet learned to take things easily. He was also sullen and rather dirty, and the strong odour of wine did not come entirely from the cargo. He shut his gate, came racing up the steps and began to wind furiously, stopping only to shout curses and orders to his wife, a pale and frightened-looking creature who had to manage the motor, the wheel and the aft warp, and whom I could see to be about two thirds advanced in pregnancy. Roughly he yelled at her as she just stood there looking crushed, miserable and resigned, and not answering. After another bout or two of his cursing and swearing I could hold back no longer.

"Is that your wife?"

"Of course," he snarled.

Reprimanding bargemen for their behaviour is not one of my regular habits, but I thought I would risk it.

"You must not speak to her like that," I said decidedly. "Especially now when she is having a baby she needs to have kindness, gentleness, love and everything to make her life easier. It is hard enough work for a woman on a péniche, even if she is not six or seven months pregnant. You are not to behave like that toward her. Never. Never."

The bargee turned toward me, but he did not attempt either to punch me in the face or push me into the lock. He simply stared at me for a second or two in utter amazement that an elderly stranger, and a foreigner too, could reprimand him in such a way, calmly but firmly. Then with a shrug he resumed working his paddle.

"It is the wine," he muttered by way of an excuse. But he had stopped his shouting and when the barge went on its way he gave me a nod of his head and the vestige of a smile.

A few months later we were lying at the bank near another lock when the wine barge came in sight, running light from Bordeaux. The skipper saw us and eased off.

"It's a girl! You must come aboard and see," he exclaimed as he drew alongside.

I had never seen a man so transformed. He was washed and tidy, and as I jumped aboard to the open steering position – the wheelhouse being dismantled because of the low bridges – he called to his wife in a gentle voice to let us see the baby. I duly expressed my admiration, though in truth I find small babies less than attractive, but what I particularly noticed was the change in the girl. The hunted, terrified look had vanished, and everything about her showed that his treatment of her was completely altered from what I had seen before in the locks at Trèbes.

Until we retired from the canal we met this couple on several occasions. Once the skipper insisted that we should precede him and that he would work the lock for us. Another time a loud blast on his hooter announced that he was coming by, and as the ship came gliding past he leaned far out, holding on to the rail with one hand while he passed over a bottle of Brut with the other and went on his way as cheerily as anyone (and especially his wife) could wish.

Like so many good things, the long pound of the Canal du Midi has to come to an end, but before doing so it passes through three villages of the Minervois which live entirely on the production of wine, as one can see from the collection of mighty tanks behind their vintners' co-operatives. Ventenac, Paraza and Roubia may nowadays also sell baguettes and groceries to the hire craft parties, but wine is the business and a very active one too. Only at Paraza is there a genuine chateau in the sense of a castle of the count and not just a wine farm, and the wine from the Chateau de Paraza is one that I have sometimes carried home by car to Jersey where it has been reckoned a good one. All the same, there is an emotional or recollective quality in a bottle of wine that is inevitably lacking in one bought at the supermarket or wine shop back home, or the state liquor monopoly in Sweden. The bottle of Brut handed over by the barge-man was unmatured crude and probably more like purple dye than wine, but it tasted better than restaurant Moulin-à-Vent because of the kindness that came with it, and the earlier incident at Trèbes. So too, the Chateau de Paraza, a good wine in its own right, always held for us the extra private flavour of the time when the hard working young count invited us in to see the magnificent tapestries in the hall, and we could glance out over his terrace where the lunch was laid with impeccable taste and the finest in silver and porcelain for himself and the countess when the striking of Paraza's church clock would announce the holy hour of midday, when everything in the Languedoc stops and only resumes again, with a bit of luck, three or four hours later.

The fifty-three kilometre pound ends at the lock of Argens, just short of the extraordinary village of Argens-Minervois, certainly the most curious place to be seen from the canal until the huge fortified Cité of Carcassonne comes into view a day's voyage ahead. Argens stands on a hill, clustered around the edges of a tall, gaunt, twin-towered chateau which like so many in the Minervois is inhabited here and there in a casual sort of way whilst in some of the walls the window holes gape wide or are boarded up, and a few of the surrounding buildings have become tired of life and have consented to fall down the hillside or just collapse where they are.

On the canal bridge and the electricity post to one side the little red and white marks show that this is on the route of a GR, or Sentier de Grande Randonnée, one of the long distance paths which cross France from side to side and end to end and are such a delight to those who enjoy walking. This one is the GR 77, a familiar one to me because if I were to follow it up past the chateau of Argens and trace its course through pines and vines and over the hills for three hours, as I have often done, I would arrive in Pouzols, just one of those sleepy little places where nothing seems to happen beyond exchange of gossip on the seats set by the entrance to the chateau.

Pouzols is in the main clustered so tightly on its private hill that it is easier to take a car into the tapering streets than to drive it out again. It has a single shop, and a run-down and faded castle-fort overshadowing the plainer dwellings, yet outside the line of the original walls is this splendid mansion, mellow in its private copse of umbrella pines. The first time we passed that way I rang the bell, and Count Charles Fournas de Fabrezan came out to see who was there, his hands dripping red and his shirt and shorts as stained as those of the second murderer in Macbeth. But it was not a crime from which I had distracted him. It was merely the urgent work of dealing with the pressing of the autumn vintage, which promised to be exceptional.

I had a reason for ringing the bell. We were acquainted with a member of the family who lived nearly two thousand miles distant from Pouzols, in Sweden, for this chateau had been the ancestral home of the de la Gardies. An earlier de la Gardie, Pontus by name, had gone up to Denmark as a soldier of fortune to help fight the Swedes. When peace was restored de la Gardie transferred his allegiance to Sweden and became its brilliant commander in attacks upon the Russians. After the capture of Narva, many thousands of men, women and children were slaughtered "according to custom", as he noted. His son later succeeded in entering Moscow, and in the next generation Magnus Gabriel de la Gardie (Clark Gable) was the brilliant and trusted Chancellor to Queen Christina (Greta Garbo). And all this from the retiring, homely if elegant Chateau de Pouzols.

Once when we walked up from Pouzols to the top of the ridge, we startled Europe's largest species of owl, *Bubo bubo*, the eagle owl, standing more than two feet high without shoes and very properly known to the French as the Grand Duc. I thought he was lucky still to be alive at a time when the French were out in their thousands blazing away at anything that moved. Less surprising was a hoopoe, for such are common in the area and along the canal. I suspect it was Linnaeus who decided to name the bird *Upupa epops*, an attempt to copy its call. And just as my bird book told me that the hoopoe said "Hoop hoop" so it assured me that the eagle owl said "Boo boo". Neither of them spoke on that occasion, however, perhaps for fear of attracting the attention of hunters.

Another three or four hours and the path leads to Minerve, former capital of the Minervois – a role it has now surrendered to Olonzac. It is not often that one comes upon a siege catapult standing ready loaded with a rock held in its sling, ready for the besiegers to wind the windlass and haul back the tall pole to let go and watch as the massive counterweight of a stone-filled crate swings it up again and lets fly. But there is one at Minerve; or rather opposite the village, perched on the edge of the sheer cliff above the gorge of the Briant. But just in case exuberant youth should try to discover whether this engine of medieval warfare could really hurl rocks into Minerve, the weight is rather wisely padlocked.

It was in the year 1210 that Simon de Montfort appeared before Minerve and set up his siege. The site was virtually impregnable, for the village (or town as it probably was at that time) was set on the tip of the promontory or bullnose of land between the rivers Cesse and Briant, each of which was in a deep gorge but beneath it, for both streams disappear from sight several miles above Minerve and only emerge again as the united Cesse far beyond the site. Subterranean they still are, their beds lush with vegetable patches and little orchards of fruit trees, and quite apart from sinking below ground the Cesse has cut off the two wriggles in the gorge by piercing the rock and wearing it away to form two "ponts naturels" – a very modest name for the two huge natural tunnels which are more than one hundred and two hundred yards long respectively and reach a height of over one hundred feet. Indeed, Minerve is so protected that it is reached by a high bridge from beyond the Cesse.

There must have been many more inhabitants in 1210 than there are nowadays, when the total only just tops one hundred. For when after seven weeks de Montfort's siege catapult had smashed the well and breached the walls the town surrendered, and one hundred and eighty unrepentant Cathars were rounded up and burned alive in the tiny open space in front of the church. There must have been many others there who were not "heretics", but whatever their numbers they could only watch in mute terror as their fellows were burned to death without a murmur. As to why they were burned alive, this was not in any way meant to pre-empt their presumed journey to hell. Whatever the carnage at Béziers, the church forbade in theory the shedding of human blood, but flames got round that little difficulty in a way that no doubt satisfied de Montfort and Arnaldus Amalricus too. Outside the little church of St. Étienne (St Stephen) a simple memorial bearing a Cathar cross reminds the visitor of the frightful happening of long ago.

After climbing the steps to that sombre spot it is a relief to walk farther ahead between the village houses to where a track is cut in the side of the gorge of the Briant below the castle ruins and leads down to the confluence of river-beds and the tunnels cut by the Cesse. Once when we visited them, it was early in January and the tramontana falling off the snows of the Pyrenees was coming down the gorge. Concentrated by the narrower space of the tunnels, the wind reached such a speed that it was almost impossible to walk through in the teeth of the freezing gale, but on a hot summer's day the same caverns can be deliciously refreshing.

In the opposite direction from Minerve the same GR 77 leaves Argens by crossing the canal and then the Aude to lead through vines and pines for yet another sleepy village, Montbrun. There, they say, the lord of the manor was followed one day by a bedraggled pilgrim who continually tried to catch his attention. Disliking this importunate soliciting and finding that the man still followed him, the seigneur launched his hunting dogs which promptly and obediently made short work of the beggar and tore him in pieces. But then he noticed something strange. Doves began to flutter around the remains, and when he went to investigate the cause of such a phenomenon, his lordship was horrified to recognise in the victim of his anger none other than his own father, whom he had believed to have died when on a pilgrimage to the Holy Land. Mortified, he raised a votive chapel in expiation of his hot-headed crime, and it is still known as Nôtre-Dame-de-Colombier.

From Montbrun the track heads for the Mediterranean at Banyuls, by way of the Montagne d'Alaric. Not the mountain of the famous Visigothic

Alaric who sacked Rome but of a later successor, Alaric the Second, whose realm extended from the Loire across most of Spain and who was slain in 507 by the mighty Clovis in a battle near Poitiers. Clovis was orthodox, Alaric heterodox – that is, he subscribed to the Arian heresy which had been "anathematized" by the Council of Nicea in 325 but which in fact is not extinct sixteen and a half centuries later. So Clovis had theological approval for slaying Alaric, even if reasons of politics were probably paramount.

I have always been an admirer of Clovis, King of the Franks, since I saw the memorial at Soissons which commemorates the incident of the Soissons chalice. Clovis (or Chlodwig) had been converted by his Christian wife Clothilde, and Remigius the Bishop of Reims had to arrange a special piscine to cope with the baptism by total immersion of thousands of Clovis's troops.

The Frankish warriors had a way of robbing monasteries, and now the monks saw their chance. They told Clovis that some particularly fine communion vessels had been taken from them, and they asked him to be so kind as to recover them if he could. Clovis told them not to worry. It was the custom at the end of a campaign for the booty to be set out on view and for each warrior to take his share. He would keep his eyes open, and having the first choice he would select as his share the items the monks described to him, and hand them back.

When the day of distribution arrived, Clovis was as good as his word and picked out the various items on display at Soissons, including a particularly fine chalice the monks were desirous to recover. That was all he would take, he said modestly. It was now the turn of the others. But this did not please a rough and tough Frankish warrior, who stepped forward and demanded to know by what right young Clovis should be allowed to help himself to whatever he wished. And without waiting for a reply he raised his mighty twoedged sword above his head and brought it down with such force upon the chalice that he sliced it in two.

Clovis apparently said nothing. He had not sufficient power to risk being involved in a trial of strength with the Frank, so he appeared to disregard the matter. But he was only biding his time. He had his chance on the occasion when the victorious warriors were drawn up for his inspection, and like a modern general he walked along the line, making a remark here and there until he came to the tough who had worsted him.

Disgraceful, he said. Dirty equipment, lack of polish on the sword and buckler. And as for the shield, filthy was hardly the word for it. He thereupon snatched it and flung it on the ground in front of the infuriated warrior, who with an oath bent down to pick it up.

And that was his mistake, for as he did so Clovis swiftly drew his own mighty blade, raised it above his head, and brought it down so violently that – according to the Merovingian records – he cleft the man neatly in two from the crown of his head to the groin. Then he replaced his sword in its sheath.

"That's what he did to the chalice," he remarked as he moved on down the line.

From Argens the canal begins to climb rapidly, with every kilometre and every lock the country becomes richer, always with a sight of distant hills across the endless sea of vines. The next village beyond Argens is Homps, for many years a favourite with barges, for it has a long and broad stone quay against which several could lie for the night, and a glass or two of Minervois could be taken in the evening sunshine outside the simple inn at the end of the row of quayside houses. With its wine barges lying at the wall and the families taking their dinner under awnings on deck, Homps was a place of slow motion activity until the first barge got under way at six o'clock in the morning in order to be at the next lock by half past. When the barge traffic decreased the sleepiness of the village became even greater, but not for long. Modern Homps is a flourishing base for hire cruisers.

Just short of Homps the canal passes the Écluse de l'Ognon, the onion in question not being one poisoned in some dark medieval drama but merely a stream of that name which here passes under the canal in a culvert. The bay below the double lock is a particularly pleasant place to lie overnight, but on one occasion we found the stench from the stream so insufferable that to remain anywhere near it was impossible. Our friend Monsieur Busque, the rather studious lock-keeper of the Ognon, could not explain the fearful odour which came from the stream. It had not long been like that, he said.

Having moved out of nose reach of the offending stream, I decided to tackle the President of the French Republic. Monsieur Mitterand had recently stated on French television that he was all in favour of canals, and in a letter I reminded him of that fact, though I suspected that he had expressed his liking more in the hope of catching a few extra votes from boating cranks than from any abiding passion for waterways as such. I wrote and suggested respectfully that his interest in waterways might move him to discover why the Ognon stank to high heaven where it passed under the Canal du Midi, and also why the ditch near Aigues Mortes which once had been the Canal de Lunel was delivering a stream of fish bottom up and defunct into the Canal du Rhone à Sète. I gave him in proper French fashion the assurance of my most distinguished sentiments, and sent off the letter.

Some weeks later I was surprised to receive a letter from the President's secretary thanking me for my interest and informing me that his Excellency had had the letter forwarded to the Minister of Transport. A month or more later I had a letter from the secretary of the Minister of Transport thanking me for the interest expressed in my letter to his Excellency the President and informing me that the Minister had had the letter forwarded to the

Minister of the Environment and the Better Life. Buck-passing, I though was as highly developed in French as in British circles.

But no. Nine months passed, and then I had a letter from the Minister of the Better Life thanking me for my interest and so forth, and then going on to say that the pollution of the Ognon had been traced by his inspectors to a distillery somewhere in the back of beyond, and further that the death of fish in the defunct Canal de Lunel had been found to be caused by an effluent from a factory near Nimes. In either case steps had been taken to prevent continued contamination, and I could rest assured that both these nuisances were terminated.

I was amazed. Here I was, a typical Anglo-Saxon crank, sticking my nose into French ditches and turning it up in superior disgust, and the great machinery of the French Republic ground into action, and acted. I wondered what would happen if some insufferable Frenchman told Mrs Thatcher that he did not like all the duck excrement in St James' Park and wondered what she was going to do about it. Emboldened by this experience, I wrote to the mayor of Carcassonne and said that dozens of craft moored in the town port every day and the only provision for rubbish was two sawn-off oildrums which were full by midday, so that other refuse was piled around them to the huge delight of the rats which swarmed over the quayside at night. Why could they not provide those large and useful refuse bins on wheels? By return of post I had a letter thanking me for my observations and telling me that the bins had been installed that same day. France is renowned for its bureaucracy, but its officials can sometimes produce results with surprising efficiency.

The long pound is idyllic, but the locked section from Argens up to Carcassonne is one that I have always liked just as much. There are twenty-seven lock pens to be passed, only one trio having electrical operation, so there was plenty of time to look over the home produce of eggs and lettuces and leeks, and the wines from the local co-operative – often cheap and indifferent but occasionally (such as a good year of Lauran Cabaret) excellent. We always tended to buy as much at the locks as was possible, for two reasons. Firstly, the pay of the keepers was not high, and any little extra they could make by retailing made a difference. More important however, was the entry it gave into the life of the area. There was the opportunity to talk, admire the children, give a lump of sugar to the dog, inspect the garden, and generally to bridge the social gap between yachtsmen or hirer and lock-keeper or keeper's wife in the most easy and natural way. The value of these exchanges for both sides was far greater than that of the produce.

Four kilometres short of Carcassonne the canal rises steeply up the trio of electric locks to leap the River Fresquel and turn sharply away into a course different from the one originally dug by the crowd of soldiers and labourers under the order of Riquet. The fact is that the Baron of Bonrepos had left the city out of the itinerary. Considering that Carcassonne is much the largest and most important place between Béziers and Toulouse it may seem curious that Riquet decided to lay his canal near the city but just out of its reach. In fact he had his own reasons. By the time the canal was well under way the Baron was finding himself increasingly short of money, for Colbert always demanded a full and immediate return of the taxes Riquet collected for the Revenue and often pressed him very hard financially whilst encouraging him over the canal project. In need of funds, Riquet approached the Carcassonne council for subsidies; but as they could see that the canal was likely soon to reach their door without their having to spend a copper coin, they prevaricated and then graciously declined. This drove Riquet to re-route the canal on the other side of the hill to the north of the town, along an easier course. He even remained deaf to the entreaties of the Bishop of Carcassonne, who was most active in trying to have the line laid through the town.

Hardly had the canal been opened when Carcassonne found itself out on a limb. Bargemasters, merchants, the council and the bishop and dean and chapter all wanted something done about it. But it took one hundred and four years of discussion before the works were begun, an aqueduct was built to carry the canal over the Fresquel, and a deep cutting was excavated to bring the waterway in and out of the city. A good port was also dug. This immense amount of navvying would have been very expensive, but by good fortune there was a plentiful supply of Prussians captured at the battle of Jena. They were set to work on the canal, and the rock and soil they excavated was used to fill the city moats and build up the roads.

This newer section of canal provides a breathtaking view across the valley of the Aude to the astonishing medieval fortress of Carcassonne set on a hill of its own. It seems quite unreal, a coloured illustration from a children's book about princesses and wicked barons. Even from a distance one can distinguish the two outer rings of walls and within them the final redoubt, the Castle of the Counts, standing within its own separate moat. Scores of towers peep over each other's shoulders to see who the attacker may be, and the little cathedral stands at attention, its battlements ready to shield the defenders. One can well believe that in the days before artillery Carcassonne was impregnable.

The port is nowadays a rather smart affair with seats and ornamental trees, decorous street lamps and the special rubbish bins installed to pacify myself. Yet I regret the change, the vanishing of what once was there. For in 1963 the wine barges and commercial craft lay doubled along the length of the quay and a dockside crane on rails swung the bales and barrels in and out of their holds. Soon after, the barges began to disappear, but the splendid iron-age crane remained there, forlorn but stately and slightly rusty. In the early nineteen eighties drop-outs would sleep under its protective base but before long it was scrapped, the rails taken up, and none would know it had ever been there.

Carcassonne is not just a double town but a triple. There is the new one stretching from the canal port to the Aude, a place of streets laid out geometrically, a bustling centre of business and boutiques, a favourite overnight stop for buses heading for distant Lourdes. Then there is the rather scruffy area across the river, a jumble of town built after the destruction wrought by the Black Prince, and finally the ancient walled Cité, founded in Gallo-Roman days, developed into a mighty fortress which was only taken by treachery and eventually restored by that prince of expert architects Viollet le Duc.

This walled town is still lived in much as in the old days except that there is no count in the castle and the shops sell the rubbishy sort of souvenirs one would expect. It is undoubtedly one of the most visited sights in France, and in high summer its streets are thronged with coach-loads from all over Western Europe. For this reason it is difficult to see the place in its full austerity of might, but late in the evening the crowds miraculously vanish and that is the time to take the flight of steps near the castle and pass under an arch in the inner ring wall to the wide grassy expanse of the lists. One can walk most of the way round the fortress in this space and climb up steps or ramps to the outer walls too. It is quite likely that the area will be absolutely deserted, and one can think oneself back without difficulty into the medieval centuries of love and chivalry, of siege and starvation, of gallant knights jousting for the smile of their favoured ladies, and of a troubadour in the great hall of the castle of the counts bowing graciously before striking up to tell the story of some great deed of longer ago, perhaps even that of the brave woman who, in legend, held at bay the formidable forces of the mighty Charlemagne.

That the Cité is ancient one cannot fail to notice. There are indeed Gallo-Roman sections in the walls, and there are towers from the era of the Visigoths, those dark age characters who flit in and out of history books, broadsword in hand. There was a fortress on the hill in the days of Charlemagne, and one of the troubadour tales explains how the city came by its name. The great monarch invested the citadel, which was in the hands of the Infidel, and when the Saracen king fell into his hands and refused to become a Christian, Charlemagne very properly had him strangled. The Emperor imagined that this removal of their leader would be a deadly blow to the defenders, but the Saracen Queen Carcas took her husband's place and stirred the men to withstand the onslaught of the forces of Charlemagne.

Five long years the army encircled the beleaguered city, and five long years the defenders held out against spear and arrow, famine and lack of water. Or so it appeared, but in fact by this time only the Queen was alive.

She had made dummies of straw, and dressing them in the clothes of the dead defenders she propped them in the embrasures. She herself ran round the walls from one position to another, hurling darts and spears in the guise of a soldier, but changing hats between appearances. The soldiers of Charlemagne – simple fellows no doubt – were thus deceived into believing that the citadel was still held by a formidable force of Saracens, and had it not been for their belief that the provisions would run out they would have packed up and gone home. In fact, the brave and no doubt beautiful queen had almost come to the end of the rations, but not of her stratagems. The very last bucket of grain she gave to a surviving piglet, and when she had made it gorge itself to the gullet she tipped it over the battlements so that the poor creature burst asunder before the very eyes of the Emperor's troops. Again the poor fellows believed what they saw, and when it was reported to Charlemagne that the garrison was so well supplied that good grain could be used for rearing pigs, he ordered the siege to be raised. Soon the army was ready to start back toward Paris. This same tale of a corn-fed piglet of course occurs in connection with many medieval sieges, but that we have to overlook. Perhaps it was standard practice.

Carcas was no doubt relieved to see the enemy go. And then, all of a sudden, she felt terribly, frighteningly alone. Everyone else in Carcassonne had long been dead, and the Emperor's men were the only people she knew. Running out from the fortress she called after the troops, blowing a trumpet or perhaps (as some say) ringing a bell. One of the officers heard the call and hurried to tell Charlemagne.

'Your Majesty', he said, 'Carcas is calling'. That is, in the original, *'Carcas sonne'*.

With his customary generosity Charlemagne forgave her for tying down his forces so long and in vain, and as Carcas was willing to surrender the fortress and be baptized he turned back and entered the dead city. Then, as a mark of his esteem, and so that she might for ever be mistress of the city she had held so bravely, immediately after her christening he presented her with one of his most chivalrous officers as a new husband, to become the first Count of Carcassonne.

Thus the troubadours would tell the story of the naming of the city, with minstrel's licence that conveniently ignored the earlier name of Carcaso which the citadel bore long before Charlemagne. But we must not be too particular for truth, especially in a place which so easily conjures up the days of chivalry and romance.

I have already mentioned the troubadour Geoffrey Rudel, who fell in love with a lady of Carcassonne whom he had never so much as glimpsed, but accounts of whose beauty and grace had reached his ears in a far country, so that the love-lorn minstrel had no other desire than to come to her, and after terrible journeyings he reached the city and fell at her feet. So great was his love for her that he could not even frame a single word of speech or song to tell her, and gazing up at her he died, of sheer adoration. That was romance at its highest. But there was also Peirre Vidal, another troubadour, whose love-sickness took a different form. His lady love was named Louve, the she-wolf, a strange name for such a beautiful creature. To her he wrote his songs of adoration, ballads which dealt with her virtues and grace, yet in spite of his lyrical attentions the fair Louve gave herself to another. In a final demonstration of his eternal devotion to the only lady he could ever love, Vidal became a wolf. Dressing in fresh wolf skins procured from the hunters he let himself be chased through the woods by the wolf hounds of the Count of Carcassonne, and when the dogs caught him and practically tore him to pieces he had the huntsmen carry his mutilated body and lay it at the feet of the one he adored. Louve was not at all moved, and one cannot help thinking she may have been lucky not to have an attachment to one so unbalanced.

But not every tale of the troubadours is so romantic, and it is from them that some of the details have been handed down of how, outside those splendid and confident walls, the second hammer blow was dealt to the cause of reformation, or heresy, and thereby to freedom of religion, by the rapacious northern knights under the leadership of the unscrupulous legate Arnaldus Amalricus.

Only ten days after the slaughter at Béziers the fearful army of the Albigensian crusade stopped before the intimidating walls of Carcassonne. The fortress was held by a strong garrison commanded by Raymond-Roger de Trencavel, Viscount of Béziers and Carcassonne, a young man of only twenty-four, strong, handsome, utterly fearless and chivalrous, the ideal not only of the troubadours but of all the people of the Midi and of those who had flocked to Carcassonne to fight or die at his side. Not many weeks had passed since he had been summoned to Montpellier and ordered to give up all heretics, refugees and Jews who enjoyed freedom in his domains. Alone of all the nobles of Europe he faced the papal authorities with the challenge that he would offer home and food, shelter and clothing and the defence of his own sword to all who had cause to flee, or were in want. It is no wonder that the young Raymond-Roger was the object of hatred of the legates and that his stand caught the imagination of the threatened people of the Languedoc.

This Viscount was a skilled warrior as well as a hero, and when war was unleashed upon him without warning he swiftly and rightly decided that whether or not Béziers could withstand an attack it was Carcassonne that could hold up the flood tide of the invasion. Had he been at Béziers on the day of the terrible assault things might have turned out differently for that unfortunate city, but there can be no doubt that his decision to lead in person the defence of Carcassonne was the right one. He had only been there a few days when news of the fate of Béziers began to sweep across the land ahead of the invaders, and the country people fled to the stronghold, bringing with them their families but also driving their stock and hauling in great quantities of provisions.

In spite of deep wells bored in the hill, water was a serious problem for the crowd of tens of thousands of refugees which now supplemented the garrison, but of other supplies there seems to have been plenty. It soon became clear to the crusaders that there was no chance of taking the city by assault. Nor could they undertake a lengthy siege, for the crusading knights were only bound to serve forty days. And besides, Raymond-Roger himself led the most destructive sorties, laying about him with his battle-axe to deadly effect. His troops loved him and under his command Carcassonne was as secure a stronghold as any heretic could have.

Yet attack the crusaders did, and for two weeks without ceasing the onslaught continued. Raymond-Roger was always to be found where danger threatened and as assault towers and scaling ladders were laid against the walls he himself would counter-attack and hurl the besiegers down to the ground below. Taking off his helmet he was there for all the people of Carcassonne to see, and many a woman would have died to save such a hero.

At the end of two weeks it was clearer than ever that the fortress was not going to be taken. The invaders had suffered heavy losses, and if many of the townspeople had been crushed or maimed by the stones hurled from catapults, the number of mercenaries and knights whose corpses lay in the moat, or who were dying from scalding with boiling water must have been immense. The time had come to try other means, and the legate Arnaldus Amalricus now invoked his moral principle that it was not necessary to keep an oath made to the enemy of God. What could be easier than to ask for a parley, guarantee the young Viscount safe conduct, and then seize him as a heretic?

And so the knights were persuaded to invite Raymond-Roger de Trencavel to their camp. Certainly the heroic young Viscount could not have been duped by the legate himself, and probably some of his fellow nobles were deceived into inviting him in all good faith. However that may be, he was seized and loaded with chains. Bereft of its valiant leader, the city surrendered.

Raymond-Roger was taken into the fortress and shut away in a dungeon. A few months later he died, as imprisoned enemies so frequently do. His wide possessions in the Languedoc were forfeited, and awarded to an eager new owner in the person of Simon de Montfort, the most brutal if sincere leader the occupying forces could have had. The great crusade had won a victory which disposed of the most dynamic leader among its opponents, and set the seal on its future success as a war of extermination.

During the siege, the countess managed to escape in disguise, taking with her their two year old son Raymond II de Trencavel, whom she took to Spain where he was brought up by his great uncle, the King of Aragon. In 1240 he returned in an effort to avenge his father's death, but Louis IX sent a relieving force in the nick of time and Raymond had to retreat. Worse still, he was made to follow the King on his crusade to the Holy Land, to renounce his great name of Trencavel, and to be no more than the Count of Béziers. And in the Holy Land the tragic young man died. Carcassonne's disaster was completed.

Naturally, a place such as Carcassonne would not be complete without a tale of buried treasure. It is said, and actually believed by some, that the treasure of Solomon's temple in Jerusalem was stolen by the Romans (which it certainly was) and taken to Rome, where Alaric I got hold of it when he took the city. When the Franks were on the warpath he decided to save it by throwing it down the well of the Cité. And there it may, or perhaps may not be.

Impressive though the Cité is when viewed across the town from the canal, or when bathed in floodlighting above the river Aude, for the famous fortified stronghold to be seen in its true, stern, romantic and tragic glamour it ought to be approached from the south, by the path GR 36. Winding through the sharp and creviced rocks of white eroded stone, this track skirts the Montagne d'Alaric, drops through scrubby pines where cicadas compete in a non-stop zizzing contest, crosses the motorway on a bridge and curves through the outpost vineyards of dark red Corbières. Suddenly, round a bend, one is faced by the mighty ring of walls, their towers frowning suspiciously upon the walker in case he may be an agent of the enemy, come to spy out the best site for building a seige tower. Or perhaps he is just another troubadour.

Eastward, this same path meanders through forest, across the scented and arid scrubland of the limestone hills, through irises and broom, cystus and rosemary until, after four or five hours, it has climbed 2,000 feet to turn southward to head for the Pyrenees. But from the beacon on the summit another path drops quickly over Alaric's northern shoulder to reach the village of Moux.

It was a hot day of September when last we walked that way with friends. The dwarf yellow and the larger purple irises were long since over and the pinewoods were parched after nine months of drought. Not a trickle was to be found in any stream bed. Never mind, we assured each other thirstily; if we hurried we should have plenty of time for a beer or two at Moux before our bus arrived.

The only place for a drink in Moux was shut. We could hear a radio playing upstairs, but no amount of knocking, calling, rattling the door or throwing pebbles at the upper windows brought any response. Whoever was there was sleeping the deep sleep of the new vintage of Corbières. But the sight of four thirsty walkers sitting forlornly at the two small pavement tables gradually began to interest the villagers. One brought the news that in a vintner's yard further down the street there was a hose connected to a water tap. No, he had not tried the water. This was the Corbières country where water was used, not drunk; but it should be safe he said.

A grandmother on holiday from Bordeaux enquired of the locals, some of whom thought the landlord had gone to a football match at Lézignan, others that he was in a drunken sleep upstairs. These did him an injustice, for presently the innkeeper, who resembled the huge strong man with cropped hair in early Chaplin films, drove up in his car, fresh from the football match.

But there was to be no trade, for a Spanish labourer in the vineyard came panting down the street, carrying a bottle of his own wine. We must drink he said. The poor, thirsty English, of course they must drink. It was unthinkable to walk all that way and find the inn closed.

At that moment the bus arrived. We had time for a large and grateful gulp each of Corbières while the bus waited indulgently, the publican scowled, the lady from Bordeaux beamed, and the Spaniard smiled his pleasure at making these strange pale-faces his guests.

North eastward from Carcassonne it is only 30 minutes along the narrow and twisting valley of the Orbiel to the four ruined castles of Lastours. The reason for building four strongholds within a couple of hundred yards was purely geophysical. The impregnable site high above the river is topped with four rocky knolls, each just large enough to accommodate a very restricted fort.

A young mason perched high on scaffolding was carefully pointing the stonework of one of the ancient keeps. Having myself panted up several hundred feet of narrow track on the steep face of the hill, I asked him how he brought up the cement and scaffolding. By mule perhaps? Or were his supplies lowered by helicopter? He laughed, and patted his own broad shoulder. But he liked the work, and when he had finished that tower he would probably be moving on to the next. He was proud of his pointing and of Lastours too.

The four fortresses were once a stronghold of the Albigensians, and the names of the ruins are evocative of the days of the troubadours – Cabaret and Fleur Espine, Querthineaux and Tour Régine – but in fact the ruins themselves recall even more vividly the terror spread by Simon de Montfort.

After the surrender of Carcassonne the strongpoints of Lastours provided a permanent threat to de Montfort, so he decided to reduce them immediately, and no doubt to slaughter the heretics who lived in them and whose leader, Pierre-Roger de Cabaret, held out so defiantly. In 1209 he attacked them ferociously but without success — as anyone can well imagine who sees their position. Then in the course of a sortie into the surrounding country Pierre-Roger succeeded in capturing the new lord of Saissac who had been installed in that fortress by de Montfort when he reduced it and seized the properties of its then owner, who was loyal to Raymond-Roger de Trencavel.

Thwarted by de Cabaret, who alone was left unscathed in the neighbourhood, de Montfort decided to soften him up by sending to Lastours the survivors of his attack upon the village of Bram, a few kilometres further along the canal beyond Carcassonne. There "the scourge of God laid upon the enemies of the Church" (as he imagined himself to be) put into action his strategy of subduing the Languedoc by terror. When the peaceful little town of Bram refused to hand over its heretics he attacked it, and after three days broke down the defences. The garrison consisted of rather more than one hundred men, and de Montfort ordered that they should have their noses and lips cut off, and their eyes gouged out. Only one man he graciously left with a single eye, so that he might lead his fellows to another town and strike panic into the hearts of its defenders when they saw the kind of man they had to treat with in Simon de Montfort, now also the new Viscount of Béziers, and Carcassonne too. That such a sight would fill people with terror is certain, but it was actions such as these more than theological disputations which aroused the hatred of the Languedoc and turned the war into a struggle to the death, without mercy for any.

The arrival of the pitiful procession of the mutilated had the desired effect upon the defenders of Lastours, and they surrendered. Nevertheless, the seigneur had a valuable asset in his prisoner, de Montfort's protegé, and he was able to use his captive as a bargaining counter. He succeeded in wringing from de Montfort honourable terms for surrender – terms which, surprisingly enough, were actually kept.

My once very great affection for Carcassonne has had a tendency to decrease in proportion to the number of English drop-outs and German *Halbstarke* (half-strongs) who seem to find it a profitable place in which to drop out or be *halbstark*. But there is no denying the splendour of the Cité, and it is worth penetrating past the rows of tourist junk shops to the furthermost corners, especially when they are putting on the show of the *Médiévales*, a sort of giant son-et-lumière enterprise staged in the huge open-air theatre. The time we saw it the period chosen was the fateful first half of the thirteenth century, and the obvious temptation to lay on a bloodcurdling siege of Carcassonne had been well resisted. On the way in we passed stalls of crafts of that period, and there was even a pleasantly mixed aroma of dust and straw and manure. Entertainers were on the go, swordswallowers, a jester or two, men with a performing goat, and fire-eaters or flame-throwers who took a draught of some suitable fluid and blew it out alight as a long searing flame like the dragon on the petrol-station sign. I wondered what the fluid was that could be handled or mouthed in this way without apparently causing either burns or inebria.

All this was only to whet the appetite for the display projected on the curtain walls to the accompaniment of more than an hour of music from a choir ranged up the steps in suitable medieval gowns, and a consort of strange period instruments. The Berry Hayward Consort was playing upon such instruments as *saz*, *cornamusa*, *zarb*, *chalumeau* and *bendhir*, the programme informed us, but for that we were none the wiser, yet the sound was excellent, even if I doubt that so much thirteenth century music has survived or that notation was by that time perfected. .

The last time I left *Thames Commodore* in Carcassonne, neatly moored tight against the building of the Ponts et Chaussées, one of the lesser breeds that had come to prey upon the boats decided to steal her. Obviously there can be little future in a midnight voyage from a location only one hundred metres from a lock barring the route in one direction, and five kilometres from another in the opposite, so I can only presume that the intention was to run her up the cut and strip her of her contents. Having smashed a hatch to get in, the thief had started up the engines and cast off, but like most such individuals he was hopelessly inept and succeeded only in backing her into the corner of the basin before the noise of the impact aroused another boat-owner and the miscreant jumped ashore and fled.

Unfortunately, the boat had struck at a place where the wall sloped at a very gradual angle, so that was the end of two propellers and shafts, and maybe the dream of a second Rolls-Royce for some unfortunate underwriter. When we returned aboard I dipped quickly into the port basin to feel the damage under water, and even with immediate disinfecting and dosing by Ingrid, I picked up in those few seconds enough dysentery to keep me in bed for a couple of days. I wondered what the sickness rate must be among the youth of Carcassonne who spent the entire Fourteenth of July climbing greasy poles and performing other antics which invariably ended in a splash in the mixture of mud and hire-craft effluent which made up the contents of the harbour.

X

St Sernin and St Roch – Guirauda of Laurac – Dominican
country – Riquet finds the water – hydraulics at St Ferréol – up
to the summit – fateful murders at Avignonet – Montségur –
the twin bridges – Toulouse the rose-pink city – the fate of
Simon de Montfort.

A t Carcassonne the great expanse of vineyards comes to an end. Here
and there an isolated patch of vines may be seen, but the countryside is
no longer so arid and it is other crops which grow in fields to either side of
the canal as it continues its climb toward the summit. Fields of sunflowers
shine yellow in the dawn as the flowers start once more to twist their necks
at a regulation fifteen degrees per hour toward the distant evening. Individually the blooms are not particularly pretty, but in a mass they can be
impressive. It is a countryside of little villages and manors and prosperous
farms, but the rocky knolls are gone, and so are those southern trees the
umbrella pines.

Beyond Bram some of the locks have intriguing names. There is the Écluse de la Criminelle, but I have been unable to discover just who this
wicked woman might have been. Next but one is de Guerre, but here again
one can only guess that the name might recollect the fighting in the area
when the Languedoc revolted unsuccessfully against Richelieu in 1632, or
it might be derived from an earlier fight, involving the English, for in the
Hundred Years War that wicked nation was engaged in burning and sacking, besieging and wrecking all along the valley.

Then comes the lock of St Sernin or Saint Saturninus, the first bishop of
Toulouse, who was probably martyred under the Decian persecution but
whom legend places still further back in time as a disciple of John the Bap-
tist and companion of St Peter in Rome. The story tells that when Saturninus was passing the capitol at Toulouse the portents failed and the augurs
could get no results. Furious, the pagan priests seized Sernin and demanded that he should sacrifice with them, and when he refused to do so
the idols fell at his feet, shattered in a thousand pieces. For this, Sernin was
tied to the tail of a bull which was about to be sacrificed, and dragged round
the town by the enraged animal. He is commemorated in the splendid
church of St Sernin in Toulouse, which set an architectural fashion which
was to spread right across the Languedoc.

The canal is climbing quickly here, and another six steps in rapid succession lead to the bottom of the four-step electrically operated ladder of St
Roch, at the entrance to Castelnaudary.

St Roch himself was a young man of Montpellier who, it is said, was born with a red cross marked on the left side of his belly, an undoubted sign that he was destined to be a healer. In fact, it was St Roch who first broke through the custom of burning the clothes of a leper and driving the sufferer into the country as an outlaw, sworn to speak to no man down wind, to visit neither church, nor fair nor market. After years spent in tending the lepers in the Languedoc, Roch returned to his native town, and when asked who he might be he answered only that he was a poor pilgrim. Tragically this led to his being thought a suspicious character, perhaps a spy. He was arrested and imprisoned, and five years later he died in gaol without ever having disclosed his identity.

St Roch is not uncommon as the patron hero of churches in the Languedoc, and he is distinguishable in church windows and statuary by having a dog as his companion. It is said that when stricken with disease and nearly dying of hunger in a forest he was visited every day by a dog, which brought him a loaf that it had stolen from its master's table. Intrigued by the dog's behaviour in taking the bread, the master one day followed it, discovered the sick Roch, took him home until he recovered, and became his close friend.

The chapel of St Roch is beside the flight of four locks, and was built along with the other canal installations. In former times the passengers on boats had forty minutes or more to wait while their ship ascended or descended the steps, and on Sundays they were all disembarked and a mass was put on for them in the canalside chapel of St Roch, to fit the timetable of the post boats.

The St Roch locks lead up to one of the most beautiful canal basins in the world. Once again the genius of Riquet can be seen, for here he had no long pound to take up the shock of the quantity of water used to bring a boat up the flight. Instead he made his port basin so immense that it would serve as a suitable reservoir, and in fact it is more than one kilometre in circumference. One side has trees to shade the waiting barges, and across the water the town of Castelnaudary clusters on a hill and reaches down to the edge of a basin which is as large as a lake.

Castelnaudary is not another Carcassonne, not by a long way†, and if the latter was the seat of heroics during a medieval siege, the former is the modern training base of the French Foreign Legion, whose white pill-box caps can sometimes be seen among the jostle of the market day crowd. Maybe the town spilling down the rise above the basin was more handsome before the wicked English sacked it in the fourteenth century, for in later years it

---

† Lefranc de Pompignan once wrote "We will begin with Castelnaudary and say nothing about it."

became little more than a succession of truck-drivers' halts and grimy garages and tyre depots until it was mercifully bypassed and allowed to become a more normal and in no way extraordinary French town. But it prides itself on three culinary specialities. One of these is *cassoulet*, a sort of inferior pork-and-beans stew which I suspect to be what the Foreign Legion is trained on so that anything that comes their way in Chad or French Equatorial Africa will taste delicious in comparison. The other two are called *alléluia* and *gloria* respectively, and what these are like if eaten in their entirety I do not know, for after one bite I fed them to the swans, wondering afterwards if my action might have been observed by a member of the French Society for the Protection of Birds, who would have me hauled before the tribunal of the first instance for wilful cruelty.

Without Riquet's basin Castelnaudary would be nothing, and the great sheet of water is its one great asset. Not only is it the base of the prosperous Blue Line which began an embryonic life after my talk in 1963 to the Midlands Branch of the Inland Waterways Association, but at its western end where the wine barges used to load there is a charming waterfront that would delight many a painter, and just short of it one can admire the artificial island cunningly placed there by Riquet and thickly planted with trees to form a windbreak so that the horse-hauled craft would not be driven ashore by the howling wind.

It was in 1681 that twenty-three boats were hauled into the basin from the west in solemn procession. Commissioner d'Aguesseau was aboard, and with him was a whole orchestra of harps and violins to play martial music. As they moved out over the water the convoy was met by another flotilla, that of Archbishop Bonzy of Narbonne, which had come up the locks of St. Roch. With him were several other bishops, no doubt enjoying a day on the canal which had enabled them to destroy the churches of their opponents, and they ranged themselves behind the Archbishop as he solemnly blessed the waters of the Grand Bassin.

Castelnaudary is the capital of the Lauragais, but that was not always so. A small and rather jumbled village further from the canal bears the name of Laurac and was once the leading place in the area in the days when Castelnaudary was nothing more than Castellum Novum. Occupying its private pyramid mound it was a much safer place, but when artillery made hilltop sites less advantageous, Laurac became displaced by the newer town in the wide agricultural plain below. Today it is no more than a forgotten village of humble homes clustered on the slope below a rather dilapidated fortified church.

Yet Laurac was the home of Blanche de Laurac, one of the most famous of all women perfecti of the Cathar Church. Her daughter Guirauda de Laurac was the chatelaine of Lavaur on the northern side of the plain now crossed by the canal, and no woman was more widely loved and respected than she. In an age of intolerance, Guirauda gave home and food, charity and security to all who were persecuted, and within her town of Lavaur could be found Arab teacher and Jewish rabbi living in peace and tolerance and friendly disputation along with a population predominantly Catholic. Coming from a staunchly Cathar family, Guirauda also opened her gates to the Cathar perfecti, and so inevitably excited the envy and fury of Simon de Montfort.

One day in the spring of 1211, there could be seen flocking toward Lavaur the peasants whose homesteads had been burned, the outlawed seigneurs who supported the Cathar cause, Catholics who could no longer tolerate the cruelties instituted by the crusade, and the perfecti hounded from place to place ahead of the invading army of the northern knights. Guirauda took them all in to her town and her brother Aimery prepared to lead the defence.

Lavaur had not long to wait. Soon the forces of de Montfort were en-camped around the hill, with the crowd of enthusiastic pilgrims in atten-dance. The Catholic canon went out to ask what it was that de Montfort wished, and was told that all non-Catholic fellow citizens were to be sur-rendered. As at Béziers, the people of Lavaur rejected the demand, declaring that they would see themselves dead before they did such a thing.

And so the assault began. The town was well stocked with provisions and bravely defended. Week after week the garrison resisted, repelling attacks, burning the assault engines and the piles of timber in the moat, and making deadly sorties under the leadership of Guirauda's brother. But the town could not withstand for ever the impact of the rocks hurled by the catapults and trebuckets. At last the wall was breached, and the knights of the north and the mercenary rabble poured in.

The women and children and the Catholic priests were stripped and locked in the church. Of the male citizens, many were murdered, and no quarter was given to the Jews, or to any whom Guirauda had taken into the town out of her charity. Her brother Aimery who had so heroically led the defence was hanged, and eighty knights with him – until the gallows col-lapsed and de Montfort had their throats cut. Four hundred Cathars, either perfecti or alleged to be so as an excuse to get rid of them, were led out to the meadow. Men and women alike, they were piled upon an enormous pyre and burned at night, whilst the zealous pilgrims who followed in de Montfort's wake celebrated around the fire by singing their familiar hymn with immense joy. *Cum ingenti gaudio* they burned their fellow men, the chronicler relates. Beneath the clear darkness of the Languedoc sky the frenzied strains of plainsong drowned the crackling of the branches flicker-ing in the flames. 'Come, Holy Ghost, our hearts inspire, And lighten with celestial fire', and in the blaze the four hundred Cathars perished without a sound.

As for the noble Guirauda, known through the Languedoc for her charity and her kindness to the poor, de Montfort's men stripped her, dragged her out of the gate and threw her down a dry well. Then they hurled stones on her until she died, and next morning they filled the well with rubble. The people of the plain still tell that on a night when the moon casts only a faint light, and the air is still, you may hear from somewhere beneath the ground the voice of the gentle Guirauda de Laurac singing a melody of long, long ago.

A sign-post at the top of the St Roch locks direct the traveller to the "*Hauts Lieux des Dominicains*". And if the Lauragais was once Cathar country there is of course a direct connection, for it was that fact that eventually brought about the founding of the Dominican Order in that same area. Early in the thirteenth century the King of Castille decided upon a political marriage between his son and a Danish princess. A Spanish bishop was sent to Scandinavia to negotiate the contract, and taking with him a young monk named Dominic Guzman he set out over the Pyrenees. The party stayed overnight at Toulouse, a city with many adherents of the Cathar religion, and Dominic came to be boarded out with a heretic. This was a fateful encounter, for it determined the young sub-prior to spend his life in attempting to put down the heresy, and it was eventually to give rise to the Inquisition.

The Danish alliance was duly arranged, but the negotiations proved to have been a waste of time, for when the bishop again travelled north to fetch the princess he found she had died. The bishop and his sub-prior Dominic again returned to the south, arriving at Montpellier just when the legates were gathered there to discuss the eradication of the heresy. One of these men was Arnaldus Amalricus, later to be the butcher of Béziers; another was Pierre de Castelnau, one day to be assassinated at St. Gilles. As a result of the meeting it was decided that Dominic Guzman would be accompanied by two of the legates in an effort to deal with the heretics by sheer force of reason and argument. The Cathar Church had the support of the people of the Languedoc because of the sincerity and simple living of the ministers. These men were poor, they tolerated no ostentation or extravagance, they preached, so the deputation of the Church of Rome decided to try to beat them at their own game.

The two legates with Dominic as their companion set out to preach in poverty. In fact the legates soon tired of the effort of persuasion, or perhaps of the poverty, and the mission collapsed. Only Dominic remained to carry on with dogged determination, and he was very different from his fellow missioners. Back in his student days he had sold his books and belongings in order to relieve suffering during a famine, and to match this sincerity he had a nature which positively welcomed hardship, and suffering. But now, as he went his way alone from village to village and castle to castle, preaching to sceptical audiences, the founder of the order of the Preaching Friars could certainly never have dreamed that seven and a half centuries later, in the mid 1960s, the tale of his encounter with the Albigensian heretics would reach the Top Ten of pop discs, sung as the song 'Dominique' by the Belgian nun "Soeur Sourire". For that particular hit was no love song but a bit of ecclesiastical history:-

> *Dominique – nique – nique*
> *S'en allait tout simplement,*
> *Au Dieu, pauvré, chantant.*
> *En tous chemins entre lieux*
> *Il ne parle que du bon Dieu.*

And just to set the tale squarely in its period one of the verses dates it precisely to the reign of King John 'Lack-Land'.

> *A l'époque que Jean-sans-Terre*
> *D'Angleterre était le roi,*
> *Dominique notre père*
> *Combattit les Albigeois.*

Dominic did indeed walk from place to place in poverty, and perhaps chanting too, and it was in the Lauragais that his work was concentrated. With the approval of Rome he set about his uphill task of conversion by reasoning, and the house where he resided is still to be seen at Fanjeaux, south of the canal.

The strategy by which St Dominic attacked the heretics did not consist merely in coming in simplicity and poverty. His object was to reason the people out of heresy by sheer debate. The Cathars respected a man who came with neither scrip nor purse, travelling on foot, and they were often ready to mount a contest. A panel of local judges would be appointed, and the theological case for both sides would be debated in front of the local population. At the end of the argument the judges were expected to pronounce their verdict. But no verdict would have converted the people themselves, and in fact the success of the mission was very slight. No doubt this was partly because the Cathar perfecti were very able and sincere men, but it was galling to Dominic to find that he could debate for two weeks in a single protracted discussion and perhaps achieve not one single conversion. It is remarkable that he carried on, drinking only water and eating nothing but bread, living in the open to outbid the piety of the Cathars, and always preaching, preaching, preaching. If in the four years of quiet before the murder of Pierre de Castelnau he had only a handful of conversions to show for his efforts, this was perhaps because nothing could persuade people to rejoin a Church which was riddled with corruption and which threatened them with fire and sword if they thought for themselves. Eventually, Dominic founded his Order of the Preaching Friars, the Dominicans – the followers of Dominic or perhaps the *domini canes* as they liked to think of themselves in medieval symbolism, the dogs of the Lord guarding the flock of sheep from the onslaughts of the devil. The first monastery was founded at Prouille, down the road from Fanjeaux.

If the area south of the canal is Dominican country, that to the north is inseparable from the memory of Riquet the canal builder. Sixty kilometres of aqueduct was the almost incredible measure of what he had to achieve before the canal itself was even a possibility, but once he had hit upon the simple fact that the feasibility of a coast-to-coast waterway depended upon whether a sufficient amount of water could be made to flow to the neighbourhood of the Stones of Naurouze he turned his attention to the Montagne Noire, the nearest area of considerable rainfall.

After exploring the forest, Riquet decided to concentrate first upon the River Sor. It flowed away northward, in quite the wrong direction to be of direct use, so Riquet decided to divert the river, or as much of it as he needed, and he accordingly planned an artificial watercourse which would lead the Sor water round the western edge of the mountains to strike the course of the Laudot. Here the water from the southern slopes would be picked up also, and a feeder channel would conduct the combined amount all the way to Naurouze. This watercourse from the Sor to Naurouze is known as the Rigole de la Plaine. It is forty-five kilometres in length.

And yet Riquet wanted still more water, so he decided to cut a second feeder on the south side of the mountains, the Rigole de la Montagne. This was to start from the Alzau brook, tucked deeply away in the recesses of the forest, and in winding along the spurs of the hill at a slight gradient it would pick up several other streams on its way until after 20 kilometres it would be divided into two branches. One of these would discharge into the Sor some miles upstream of the point where the first rigole left it, and in this way the supplies from the southern slopes would reach the Rigole de la Plaine. But the other branch was to dive by tunnel under the hill in the village of Les Cammazes, and by ducking under the watershed deliver its water into the valley of the Laudot. The tunnel was constructed by the great military engineer Vauban, and it is still in use for its original purpose. It is provided with a path alongside the watercourse and one can walk through the hill beside the stream.

Having brought the water into the Laudot valley Riquet's next step was to block the valley with a mighty dam and so provide an immense reservoir. His idea was that during the summer months the water of the Alzau and its neighbours would take the right hand fork and swell the Sor during its period of least flow, whereas in winter the Sor could look after the whole canal and the Rigole de la Montagne would accumulate a store behind the dam and so provide a bank of water to be drawn upon in case of drought. This notion was a brilliant one. Three centuries have now passed since Riquet cut his rigoles in the slopes of the Montagne Noire, and throughout that time the canal has nearly always been well provided with water even when other waterways in less arid areas of the continent have been short of supplies. In 1985 an eight month drought which caused innumerable forest fires also emptied the reservoir of St Ferréol and the canal had to be closed in its higher levels above Carcassonne, but that was exceptional. So good were Riquet's calculations that in three hundred years the only modification has been that in 1776 a second and smaller reservoir, the Bassin de Lampy, was added to cover the additional needs of the branch canal to Narbonne.

Having first planned the Rigole de la Plaine to his satisfaction, Riquet then thought of making it navigable. Around the market town of Revel, behind the Black Mountain, there was a rich plain from which surplus grain was exported to the surrounding areas. If the feeder were made large enough, this harvest could be carried down to Naurouze on the flow, and there loaded aboard the larger craft of the canal. To this end Riquet actually built a loading basin near Revel, and added fourteen small locks between there and Naurouze. Special narrow craft of shallow draft were built, but before the main line of the Canal du Midi was opened Riquet wisely abandoned the scheme, realising that the most important function of his feeders would be hard to maintain if the interests of local shipping conflicted with sudden demands from the main canal for large quantities of water. The locks of the rigole were dismantled, and Revel's port was to remain without shipping.

To milk the Montagne Noire was a real stroke of genius. The hills rise to more than twelve hundred metres and moisture laden winds from both seas strike the area of hills, rise, cool by adiabatic expansion, and drop their water on the needles of the conifers and the leaves of the deciduous trees which make up the forest. Even in high summer the woodlands are damp and the streams usually rushing with water. It took us some exploring before we found the little hamlet of La Galaube and the pathway which plunged down into the damp woodland to follow the Alzau as it tumbled between mossy boulders and fallen tree tunks sprouting juicy clumps of fungi. After a few minutes the brook emerged into a neat trough of masonry set in a piece of ornamental park with specimen trees and lawns and seats, quite the last thing one would expect to find tucked away in the forest, but reflecting yet again the good taste of the Baron de Bonrepos. A granite slab commemorated Riquet's solution to the water problem of the canal, and from beside it the Rigole de la Montagne led away in a most determined fashion, its water rippling as clear as glass to disappear among the trees on its way to the parting of the waters and Les Cammazes, beyond which it would emerge on the further side of the ridge to join the Laudot. Yet most impressive of all is the Bassin de St Ferréol where the valley is closed off by the largest earth-filled dam in the world, eight hundred metres in length and thirty high.

France is so filled with saintly place-names that (as I have already mentioned) I never travel through its canals and rivers without a hagiography, a sort of bird identification book of saints. Perhaps it is often just curiosity, but also my interest is tinged with the delight of discovery of people I had never heard of, men and women such as Irenaeus and Blandina to whom we owe much of what is left of fineness in our civilisation. Yet it was only recently that I acquired a catalogue which identified for me within certain limits St Ferréol, one who previously had eluded me. But now I know that he may have been the man who was sent by Irenaeus of Lyon to evangelise the area around Besançon and who was martyred about the year 211. But one cannot be sure, and it does not really matter. From January 1970 the list of saints has been rigorously pruned to leave only one hundred and eighty out of the forty thousand contained in the original Roman calendar, of whom no less than four others were Ferréols.

To walk round the lake, complete with trip boats and a sailing school, takes an hour. And as usual, Riquet's attention to detail matched up to the era of the Roi Soleil. Handsome seats carved of granite are set along the top of the vast embankment of the dam, which at its foot reaches a thickness of some seventy-five metres. Below is a park landscaped into watercourses and cataracts fed by the overflow of the Rigole de Ceinture, which curves round the outside of the lake to sport and gambol among the glades, with stepping stones leading invitingly from point to point. As a splendid final touch the head of water feeds a tall and graceful waterfall in the park below, and a powerful fountain jet leaps twenty metres into the air to drench the ornamental trees with its drifting mist.

The vast dam was built as three parallel walls. The space between them was filled with earth and rubble, and the result was something very solid. But the water from the reservoir had to be drawn off at the lowest point, and by penetrating into the darkness of a cavity set in the bottom of the bank, between creepers and roses and ornamental shrubs, we were able to see the trio of giant taps through which the whole of the waters of the reservoir can be released as a flood or as a trickle, to swell the supplies which will eventually surge into the canal at Naurouze and feed all the canal on either side of the summit, from Toulouse on the Garonne all the way to Carcassonne upon the Aude.

From Castelnaudary the canal meanders about as though in no hurry, and after nine kilometres it passes a monument standing in a field to the left. This commemorates Les Saintes Puelles, who gave their name to the nearby village. Although they are sculpted in clothes of flowing seventeenth century style their tale lies much further back in history, contemporary with St Sernin of Toulouse. They were two girls who were hunted for having received and hidden the remains of a fellow Christian who had been murdered for his faith. They took refuge in the village, where they were eventually overtaken and killed. Still within the parish of Mas-Stes-Puelles is the final lock of the ascent, the Écluse Mediterranée, 184 kilometres from the lighthouse of Les Onglous, and five kilometres ahead and just before the double bend to the Écluse Océan which begins the descent towards the Atlantic, the Rigole de la Plaine comes pouring in over a little weir in a small bay on the right. It was there that we stood when Mlle Eveline Riquet de Caraman unveiled the handsome plaque which now adorns the wall of the spillway.

At Naurouze, as elsewhere, everything is majestic. The waters of the Montagne Noire run in fresh and clear after tripping through a mill to work the machinery and pausing to move more slowly through a stately basin, which was to serve as a port for the small ships of Revel which never came. There are alleys and seats, specimen trees, sluices and walks, and everywhere the crystal water rippling in its bed, splashing and laughing at its achievement in having found its way through so many miles of trough to the summit of the Canal Royal.

To see the basin of Naurouze as it should have been, but never was, one has to turn to the *Proceedings of the Royal Society* for 1670, where a description is given of the plan for "a great basin octagonal oval-wise, 200 fathoms long and 150 fathoms large, which shall be surrounded with 72 houses to be raised on arches. This basin shall receive all the waters which the deriving channel is to convey thither from the Black Mountain, to be distributed by the Royal Channel to both seas. In the middle of this basin shall be a Colosse, representing the King standing in a triumphant chariot drawn by four sea-horses, holding one foot upon a globe, and a trident in his hand, as marks of his greatness by both sea and land. And then a stream of water, issuing as from a source under the chariot, shall as 'twere be beaten back, and disgorge itself through the throats of serpents toward the four parts of the world, represented by as many rivers, which shall also pour out of their urns a prodigious quantity of water, to show that the graces which the liberality of the King plentifully diffuses to all his people, do pass through the hands of the Lord Colbert."

Alas this statuary was never built, but there is still plenty to see. Behind the basin and across the meadow are the Stones of Naurouze, a pile of blocks so unexpected that it is hardly surprising that they should have been regarded as of mysterious origin. It is said that Naurouze was a giant, way back in prehistoric days, and that he was engaged in carrying a load of stones out of which it was hoped to build Toulouse, but the long ascent to the top of the pass so exhausted him that he dropped his burden. The stones were broken in pieces, and the debris has remained there ever since, with the result that Toulouse had subsequently to be built of brick instead. And very beautiful that result has been.

So striking is the pile of giant boulders standing alone upon an open landscape, that it has always been associated with legend and prophecy. Even the 16th century astrologer Nostradamus brought them into his catalogue, predicting that when they should piece themselves together the end of the world would be at hand. More curiously, it was to this place that Marshal Soult was summoned to sign an armistice, and the cease-fire was signed by the Duke of Wellington at the table in the lengthman's cottage near the spillway. That was before the obelisk to Riquet was erected, for it was not until after the Napoleonic wars that the site was acquired for a memorial by those descendants of Riquet fortunate enough to have escaped the guillotine. Ambassadors, officers, counts and gentlewomen, their names are all there on the monument, and on one face is a handsome medallion of the Baron de Bonrepos himself.

The descent from Naurouze to Toulouse is a run of less than one day, and on the whole it is not interesting. A motorway runs close to the canal, and the day-and-night hum and smell of the traffic has done much to rob the countryside of its former gentle peace. Not that it has always been free from trouble, for however mellowed the land may appear it has twice been ravaged by the English. In the nineteenth century came the Iron Duke. In the fourteenth it was the Black Prince who marched past the Stones of Naurouze to pillage the hamlets and sack Castelnaudary whilst the Black Death was wiping out one third of his subjects back home.

Océan lock marks the beginning of the western descent. At the first double lock beyond it a minor road crosses the canal and the nearby motorway to the village of Avignonet-Lauragais, not in itself notable but a fateful place in history, as is commemorated on a tablet in the church. For followers are not always like their leaders. The mission of Dominic began as one of preaching, but he had not long been dead before two of the Brothers Dominican at Toulouse were appointed as the Inquisitors. There was to be no more of the gentle Dominic sung by Soeur Sourire. *Au Dieu, pauvré, chantant* had had its day, and the Dominicans Arnald and Seila were sent out to interrogate, to root out heresy by threat of sword and stake without reference to any authority of law, civil or ecclesiastical, and the area around Toulouse and Castelnaudary was one of the earliest to experience the system of terrorization by informers, by interrogation under solitary confinement, and by every means which in our own day we would associate with brainwashing and the torture techniques of a police state.

In the now vanished castle of Avignonet the tribunal of the Inquisition was sitting to investigate the beliefs of Albigensians brought before them, when they were surprised and murdered by men of the area who had sworn

revenge for the cruelties they perpetrated. The attack was supported or initiated by those who had retreated to the fastness of Montségur, and it was
the factor which led to an immediate decision to exterminate that stronghold and slaughter all who were in it. In 1243 the siege of Montségur was
begun, and as the new year opened the hill had already been beleaguered
for many months. Yet so impregnable was the steep hill that within the
church upon its top there lived many *perfecti* and their families, together
with others who took their part. The top of the hill was defended by no
more than three hundred armed men.

Over this community presided three men. The spiritual leader was the
saintly Bishop Bertrand d'En Marti, and the defence was under the cap-
taincy of Pierre-Roger de Mirepoix, aided by Raymond de Perella, the lord
of Montségur. Against them were ranged the several thousand soldiers of
the investing forces together with such military experts as the Bishop of
Albi with his siege catapult. Although the defenders might have been
starved into submission it seems improbable that the top of the hill could
ever have been captured except by treachery. After ten months of frustration the French bribed guides to show them a secret approach route, and
with their enemies at the gates the defenders knew that they could no longer
hold out. It was agreed that there should be a truce of fifteen days, at the
end of which the fortress would be handed over. The soldiers would go
free, or with only the lightest penances – though in fact they were mostly
destined to die in chains in the gaol of Carcassonne. The heretics too, like
the Christians at the time of the Roman persecutions, had merely to
acknowledge their errors. Perhaps it was expected that the fortnight's reflection would enable them to do so without much difficulty.

But that they would not do. At the end of the truce the fortress of
Montségur was handed over to the possession of the pope and his French
servants. Disarmed, the soldiers went innocently on their way to betrayal.
Of the Cathar Church, more than two hundred men and women were still
alive, among them the ageing Bishop Bertrand and several deacons, and a
number of volunteer defenders who had asked to be received into it within
the period of the truce, although they had no illusions as to what this would
mean.

Among the heretics were at least three women, of the family of Raymond
de Perella. His daughter was one of them, the young and radiantly beautiful
Esclarmonde, whose name alone is a reflection of the light she spread upon
the world. Her own mother and her grandmother were with her, and these
three staunch women were symbolic of the three generations which had
lived through the tragedy until this day when the resistance of the Cathars
and the existence of the Languedoc were finally extinguished.

Unresisting, the Cathar Christians were fettered, roped together, and
dragged brutally down from the remains of their fortress church. They laid

themselves quietly upon the pyre, and in one great blaze which flickered across the valleys they were burned. Perhaps the scent of the resin helped to mask the smell, and the roar of the fire to drown their groans. Meanwhile the friars and clergy stood far enough upwind to be safe from the heat so that they might chant their plainsong of holy devotion and piety, and the French knights chafed at the irritating way these heretics had of being so poor that there was no loot to be had.

The church of Montségur is still there today. Roofless, its massive walls have stood since 1244 on the summit of a peak which until recent years none could be bothered to visit. At the foot of the precipitous rocks beneath it there is a meadow where for centuries sheep have tolled their little bells as they have safely grazed, or some hardy village peasant has sweatily scythed the campanulas and gentians and anemones which spot the hay with patches of vivid colour. This pleasant slope is none other than the Champ de Cramatchs – the field of the cremated – where the fearful act took place which was to draw the curtain for ever over the freedom and tolerance which once the troubadours of the Languedoc had sung, and for which Guirauda of Laurac and many others had already met their death.

Toulouse is known as the Rose City. The buildings appear at first sight to be built of a very fine red sandstone, but it is brick. All those from before the skyscraper era are of the same material, and the mere colour of the place gives it a real beauty. But to the boatman, Toulouse is first of all the city where Riquet is remembered. The canalside road near the station is the Boulevard de Bonrepos. In cafés the *crocque monsieur* open sandwich of the rest of France is called a *Crocque Riquet*. A statue of the baron is at the head of the Allées Jean Jaurès, one bridge east of the railway station at Matabiau, and his tomb is at the foot of the massive central pillar of the cathedral of St Étienne where a plaque of black marble describes him as 'the beneficent genius who created the prosperity of the Languedoc'.

Riquet's greatest memorial however, is the canal itself. Toulouse was already a large city when he laid out his waterway, and he intended to connect the canal with the city moats so that the ships could load or deliver at many points. But the city fathers obliged him to keep his works outside the confined of their great Tolosa, and he had to skirt its perimeter to reach the Garonne below the city. One and a half centuries later Toulouse was threatened by the allied armies, and the canal became the defensive line which served successfully to hold at bay for a while the English forces under Wellington. But the city continued to spread, with the result that Riquet's canal now courses through an outer and decidedly dingy part of Toulouse, an area of motor repair shops and small factories.

Riquet's port basin was originally the harbour where the ships handed over their cargoes to smaller craft of lesser draught which would pass down the river on their way to Bordeaux, but so swift and shallow was the course that twenty Garonne craft were needed for the cargo of a single canal barge. Riquet himself urged that the waterway should be continued to the estuary, but it was not until 1838 that work was put in hand for the Canal Latéral à la Garonne. The feeder for this waterway greatly improved Riquet's port by entering at a bridge designed as a twin of his original. Side by side the two canals run in through the Ponts Jumeaux, the graceful arches of which are separated by a flamboyant sculpture in Carrara marble, showing the province of Languedoc as a seated woman ordering the sprites of the arts to join the Garonne waters to the Canal du Midi by a new canal. The cherubs are hard at work, digging locks with pick and shovel and fitting the lock gates, while the Mediterranean and Atlantic look on in puzzled surprise. This piece of decoration serves also to remind one that Riquet's canal was not constructed as a barge waterway but as a ship canal, and that it is merely the case that sea-going ships have now outgrown it. For caravels it was large enough, and the marble used in the Ponts Jumeaux sculpture was shipped to the site direct from the Ligurian coast aboard Genoese trading vessels.

I like Toulouse. Even if one cannot penetrate by boat right to the centre as one can at Strasbourg or Metz or even Paris, the Canal de Brienne which acts as a feeder for the waterway westward to the Atlantic is a hospitable place in which to lie for a few days without being disturbed by too much road traffic – the port of Riquet now being insufferable since it was converted into a roundabout. Of course the rose pink city is becoming over-boutiqued and supplied with trashy shops for the sort of young Frenchmen who wear such tight trousers that one is left in no doubt about the details of their anatomy, but there is a dignity about Toulouse which is appropriate to a place that once was a capital. It is very Languedocian, but in some ways also very French.

Once when we arrived there it was a Saturday morning and as we were running out of francs I was beginning to wonder whether we should be obliged to feed at some place that would take an American Express card, a prospect that is not always welcome.

"Where do you come from, Sir?" A honeyed smile and when I say Jersey there is a quick wink to the kitchen boy, and before I have a chance to add *"Non, non. Pas New Jersey mais le vrai Jersey.* Opposite St Malo, the Anglo-Norman Isles", the lad is off to the *boucherie chevaline* (or *hippophagique* as it is so smartly called in our Minervois shopping village of Olonzac) on the assumption that we are Americans and so will not realise that our tournedos will not be Rossini except in price.

So we were delighted to see in the Syndicate of Initiative (the delightful and misleading French term for a tourist information office) a notice to the effect that the following banks, and there were five of them, remained open on Saturdays to oblige visitors by changing money. Splendid. I wrote down the addresses and off we went.

We visited all five. The grilles were down at four of them, but at the fifth the front door was open because two charwomen were mopping down the marble steps.

Surprised, we returned to the Donjon where we had seen the notice.

"Can I help you?"

"Well...er...yes, I hope so."

"Hm, hm?" The girl was all smiles and a dash of Chanel No 5.

"You see that large notice about the five banks being open on Saturdays? Well, they aren't. We have trailed round to all five. They are shut."

She smiled winningly. "I know. It is several years since they were open on Saturdays." She must have been somewhere exciting to get that tan, I thought.

"Several years? Then why do you have the notice up? Is it just to annoy foreigners?"

"No, no, no, no, no. But we cannot take down a notice unless instructed to do so by the chief of the Association of Syndicates of Initiative..."

"Who never visits your office?"

"Perhaps..."

"Or not for several years. Well, thank you so much for your help."

That is what I mean by Frenchness. Obedience to a superior, however illogical the situation might become. I remembered the customs chief at Givet who had once exclaimed to me in despair as he looked up at the ceiling, "*Il y a un homme plus grand que moi!*"

My experience of Syndicates of Initiative has never been very encouraging. They seem in small towns to be closed until next August and only then to be open as a receptacle for the less bright young ladies of the locality. I have written to the French Tourist Information Office in Piccadilly to ask what were the means of reaching by public transport the small town of Sault de Provence where I wished to begin a week's walk. The reply was the latest edition of "Love France for her Many Faces," devoted entirely to relaxing in Brittany. ("Love France for her many faeces," a friend once remarked to me as we walked up a city towpath under several bridges which seemed to serve mainly as conveniences.)

And more recently when we were going to spend Christmas at our little house in the Minervois I had an idea that they were doing Traviata or The Marriage of Figaro in Toulouse and I thought we might go. But in France it is impossible to discover from a newspaper anything more exciting than who is the duty chemist at the weekend within a very small area, so I wrote to the Donjon and asked them for the programme of concerts and opera for the following month. The reply was a leaflet "Come trout-fishing in the Pyrenees in summer"!

Nevertheless, I love France dearly for her many aspects, and up at the top I have always found people helpful, or some of them. Monsieur Georges

Normand, the former head of the Commissariat Général for tourism was so grateful for the kind words I had used about the country that he would hand me out free rail passes, and even added once after a few aperitifs that if he were responsible for dishing out Legions of Honour he would award me one as a great ami of his country. However he was not the hander out of decorations, so I just had to make do with the Certificate of Capacity as a captain on internal navigations, a document which would normally be obtained only after strenuous study, examinations both theoretical and practical and, so far as I recall, a certification from a priest as to lack of moral turpitude, but which was permitted to be issued to me merely in exchange for half a bottle of Scotch.

The hire craft era had not begun when first I reached Toulouse by water. The year was 1963, and the Port de l'Embouchure still had a two-step lock leading out into the Garonne where now there is nothing but a busy roundabout for road traffic. Barges came past almost every hour, but yachts were rare, and as the season was ripe for the fashion houses of Toulouse to present to the public a display of their summer creations, the modistes saw the splendid opportunity of having their latest elegance in yachting wear modelled and photographed upon the only business-like boat of sea-going appearance which had turned up in the port of Toulouse for months past.

'*Soyez élégantes de bâbord à tribord*', the *Dépêche du Midi* exhorted its feminine readers, and to show that it could really be done the attractive Karole and handsome Tony dressed in everything in turn which might prove that even aboard ship one could be a '*loup-de-mer chic*' a dandy old sea-dog, male or female. Splendid tailored trousers of immaculate white were to be kept for the fashionable ports of the Costa Brava, and this we could readily believe. The photographs certainly showed a charming girl in spotless elegance with one finger delicately looped under the *Commodore's* mooring line, but I wondered whether one would really look so beautifully turned out after a hundred locks of the Canal du Midi, and a hundred scrambles up slippery walls to the lock sides above or down to the boat below. One might also have an attractive *thé schirt* for *le five-au-clock* on the open waves. Indeed, after a morning of seeing how smart we could really look if only we were to put our minds to it, we set off in humility towards the town, realising that our clean clothes were not quite as *élégant pour descendre à terre* as those displayed upon the *Commodore's* foredeck before a startled gathering of bargemen.

If one had no other reason for admiring Toulouse one could at least be grateful for the fact that it was here that the brutal Simon de Montfort met his overdue end. He was riding round the walls during the siege when some women working a catapult on the battlemented tower of the church of St Sernin fired a large stone which, according to the record of the time, "struck the Count Simon upon his helmet of iron in such a fashion that his eyes, brains, teeth, skull and jaws flew quite to pieces, and he fell to the earth utterly dead and bloody". Every church bell rang, the besieged danced with delight, and even today one can only wish that the incident had happened a few years earlier.

St Sernin's is famous in its own architectural right, and justly so. Yet it has its typically French contradictions, the time of Sunday mass coinciding with the bustle of a busy market up against its walls with traders shouting their wares with such electronic amplification as to drown the sound of organ and choir within. It was formerly a major halt for pilgrims on the road to St. James of Compostella, and its whole arrangement is designed to accommodate the long shuffling processions of pilgrims in their weird shell-decorated cloaks filing through the nave and from transept to transept. Already they had passed by way of St Martha's at Tarascon, through St Gilles and by the abbey of Psalmodi near Aigues Mortes, chanting their pilgrim song:-

> *'Voyez les beaux genêts,*
> *Le romarin qui branche*
> *Et d'où sort si grande odeur.'*

But the great odour awaiting them at St Sernin's was not that of rosemary. For their delectation there had been collected an all-time world-beating collection of relics. If Charlemagne furnished bits of six apostles that is already something, but every other revered person is also there, it seems, in bits. The skull of Thomas Aquinas is a particular pride, and so are the pieces of St Edmund King and Martyr and Monsieur Vincent. I have forgotten the total of saints who are represented by parts of their bodies, but I think it was one hundred and eighty-six. Not surprisingly, from this great boneyard an indefinable but thick and musty atmosphere seemed to steam upward into the nave, and if there was one feeling which it was almost impossible to experience, that was any sense of reverence for the truly great men and women, here remembered not for what they were in their lives but as a source of molars and toenails. Just to add a final touch of the ludicrous there was no need even to have a living guide. I paid for a ticket, and a disembodied voice – that of Ste Cassette, no doubt – recited the whole catalogue of the chamber of horrors in an unearthly and metallic voice which rasped through the tracery to vanish in the dust of the vaulting above before completing the loop and beginning all over again.

In Riquet's Port de l'Embouchure we had reached the end of his canal, but knowing that the hamlet of Bonrepos-Riquet was to be found somewhere in the direction of Albi I decided to visit the place and see for myself the chateau and park where Riquet had planned and experimented until finally his great work of linking the two seas was put in hand. Perhaps I expected some sort of National Trust mansion with an entrance ticket and a sales kiosk, and volunteers well versed in all the details graciously explaining the details of the house and furniture whilst making sure that nothing of value was left unguarded in the presence of the ambient plebs. But no, I found the chateau, which Riquet had built in 1670 when he pulled down an earlier one on the same site. It looked in a very sad state and was not open to the public. Down in the nearby village of Verfeil they told me that an old army officer lived there all alone. He had no money to keep it up, and the state did not help. He was away just now, so of course I might wander through the grounds to see whatever I could. There was none to object.

So I did. It was an excursion into a jungle of rotted tree trunks and knotted creepers, but any experimental locks and watercourses which most certainly once existed had vanished without trace under centuries of storm, leafmould, neglect and decay. One huge ornamental urn still stood on a pedestal, but that was all. I walked over the thistle-clad lawn and crossed the ha-ha, trying to imagine the place in the hey-day of Riquet's wealth, but it was not easy to see anything other than just one more mellowed, faded and collapsing French manor of brick.

Riquet's wealth – yes. That has always been an enigma. I have already mentioned his involvement in the horse-trading of the bishops, but it seems that he must earlier have had some way of amassing money. Tax men have of course never been popular, and the salt tax which was one of Riquet's main concerns was regarded as iniquitous. And yet it had to be paid if one were not to risk being condemned to the galleys for attempting to evade the tax or if one produced one's own salt by furtively boiling down sea water. It is possible that Riquet was humane enough not to wish villagers to be sent to such a fate, or perhaps he merely wanted to avoid the end of another collector of the salt tax, who was strangled and thrown down a well, but it seems that after some initial trouble and rioting he exercised a more gentle hand and raised money for the crown and himself in an easier way. He is said to have taken to forging, in his own chateau, and in this way to have managed to keep up his payments to the king and at the same time to amass enough money to live in style and build the waterway which was his one abiding passion.

The evidence is that a leading official in the Armagnac was caught minting money, and in the course of his questioning before being burned alive he revealed the names of his accomplices, one of whom was Riquet. Although forging and minting seems to have been common among the aristocracy, Riquet went in fear for his life, but after a while it became evident that he was not on the hangman's list. It was probably the royal interest in his canal which saved him. And whether or not the unfortunate man who alleged that he was an accomplice was telling the truth, Riquet seems afterwards to have kept to a strict path of financial honesty.

Nevertheless, his very large fortune must remain a mystery. For large it certainly was, even if he died with two million pounds of debt. The total cost of the canal was some fifteen and a quarter million pounds, and of this seven millions came from royal sources through Colbert, and a further six from the States of the Languedoc. The remaining two millions were provided by Riquet personally, some of this amount having been borrowed.

It was at Bonrepos that the Baron made his calculations. He worked out, or perhaps just guessed, that two men leading six horses could convey three tons by cart. A boat operated by two men could transport three hundred tons. To move this amount by water instead of by land would therefore save the wages of two hundred men and the maintenance of six hundred horses. Even if land transport should improve and roads become better, there would still be a great advantage on the side of the canal.

Considering again the horse, he reckoned that as a pack animal it could carry two hundredweight for ten hours a·day, but ten times that amount if attached to a cart. On the other hand, if plodding along the towpath it could move sixty times as much as by cart. It is interesting to compare his theoretical figures with those of modern waterways engineers, who reckon that the same horsepower that can shift one ton by lorry can move three tons by rail and twenty by canal.

By any standard, Riquet's achievement was astonishing. He had planned, initiated and brought to a successful conclusion the most ambitious engineering work since the time of the Romans. Perhaps the finest praise is that contained in the words of Vauban, who declared that he would have preferred the glory of being the author of that work than of all that he had achieved during his own life.

XI

The Montauban branch – Bayard and Maugis – the great flood
– the Christ of the parousia – Mozart by night – Castets-en-
Dorthe – Guyenne becomes English – the Dordogne and the
Isle – St Émilion – the end of Talbot.

A t Toulouse, Riquet's epic Canal du Midi has run to it end. So has the
best part of the scenery on the crossing from sea to sea, and because the
waterway runs decidedly northwestward the romantic atmosphere of the
south is already giving way to something less exotic. The rest of the course
to the Atlantic tidal water is on the whole less interesting, the opportunity
for excursions is much less, and it is unlikely that any would want to linger
long in the unspectacular countryside once he has visited Moissac and
perhaps Montauban.

The Canal latéral à la Garonne is what its title indicates, even if sometimes it is several kilometres distant from the parent river which supplies it
with water. In 193 kilometres it descends 53 locks to the tidal reaches of the
Garonne at Castets-en-Dorthe. It is a particularly uninteresting waterway
in its upper reaches, for it runs hard beside the main road and railway at
least as far as Grisolles, four hours and nine locks down the line. But at last
the railway veers away as the road has already done, and the canal shakes off
its matter-of-fact straightness and adopts a more rural course with noticeable bends if little else in the way of variety.

Just before Montech a side-branch aims off to the right. It leads down a
stately avenue of trees and through a few creaky locks to the city of
Montauban and provides altogether one of the better side trips available in
southern France, even if one can no longer steam proudly through the city
but must end the journey in a deserted but clean canal basin tucked away
out of sight behind the gasworks. This is the same basin round which an excited crowd gathered on a December night in 1843 to see the great marvel of
water flowing in to flood it to a depth of almost three feet. Little by little
and week by week the level was raised, and when it was evident that the
banks would stand the strain barges were allowed to use the waterway. In
June a boat arrived from Sète, laden with wine, a fact which demonstrated
that the city really was in contact with the outside world and even with the
Mediterranean. An official opening was called for, and the Minister of Public Works was towed down the cut from Montech in a great barge
pavilioned in splendour and steered by sailors in ceremonial dress. He ar-

rived after dark – it was November – and his ship was locked down into the
Tarn to steer through the city accompanied by a floating military band.
Flags, torches, a guard of honour and a banquet were laid on, and the canal
was well and truly opened.

The next step was to introduce a passenger service. The ship *Irma* was
built and launched at Montech, designed as a postboat for the
Montauban-Toulouse run. Of delicate lines and slim figure she was
launched in sober fashion, with a service of blessing at the Montech basin
which is now mudded and derelict. She proved to be an extremely fast run-
ner, and with five relays of horses she could cover the distance to Toulouse
as fast as the stage coaches and for half the price. Considering that she had
to negotiate twenty-one locks she must have been swift indeed.

Montauban was now determined to become a centre of shipping.
Another postboat was added, and the city campaigned successfully for
locks into the Tarn at Moissac. Ships could then reach Bordeaux quickly –
even if the return journey up the canal was not so quick – and the city
fathers next turned their minds to the idea of canalizing the Aveyron, which
joined the Tarn below the city. The winding course of this beautiful stream
with its castles set high on shoulders of rock was comparatively steep, for in
the 140 kilometres above its junction with the Tarn it fell 100 metres and
some fifty locks would have been necessary. The calculation of the costs
was still in hand when the Grand Central Railway arrived and slew the navigation before it was born. Montauban's days as a great port were gone for
ever.

Montauban has its own place in one of the great epic tales told by the
troubadours as they travelled from castle to castle in the middle ages, for it
was here that Reynaud and Allart, Guichard and Richard, the four sons of
the Duke Aymon, had their fortress. Perhaps most of all one associates
their mighty deeds with the forest of the Ardennes and the valley of the
Meuse, but with such a magic steed as Bayard they covered the spread of
western Europe easily enough. There is even a Bayard's Leap in the north
of England.

It is at Montauban that many of the deeds of valour of the brothers took
place. For years the four young men were fleeing from the great Charlemagne, whose nephew had been slain when playing chess with Reynaud.
He had cheated, and Reynaud had snatched up the chess board and struck
him such a blow with it that he split his skull down to the top vertebra.
Eventually the four fugitive brothers obtained permission from the King of
Gascony to build a castle on a hill above the River Tarn at Montauban, and
thither of course came Charlemagne with his twelve mighty knights and an
army of soldiery and men at arms, determined to get even with them.

Fortunately, the four valiant lads had a cousin without whose help they
could never had stood out against the massed might of the great Emperor of

the Franks. His name was Maugis. As a baby he was snatched away by the terrible Saracens, but he ended up in Sicily where he was brought up by the very competent fairy Oriande, who taught him a lot of useful tricks before sending him on to study under the magicians of Toledo. When at last he found his four cousins again he presented them with two gifts which were to prove of great value; the horse Bayard, which could gallop as fast as the wind, and the famous sword Flamberge, a blade so sharp and strong that it would pierce the stoutest armour.

Charlemagne's siege of Montauban continued for many a month. Provisions ran short, but Bayard would bite open one of his veins and fill a stable bucket with his blood to nourish the warriors and Reynaud's wife and two infants, regenerating the full quantity overnight. There were sorties and sallies, and men-at-arms fell like grass under the scythe before it was decided to have recourse to mortal combat between the two mightiest warriors, Reynaud the son of Aymon, and the redoubtable Roland, hero of the great rear-guard action of Roncevaux, that same Roland who was later to die of a broken heart in his castle overlooking the Rhine.

Such was the clash of their arms that the whole country was shaken by an earthquake, but the two heroes proved so equally matched and mutually invincible that they decided to call a halt, shook hands and promptly became the firmest of friends. Regrettably, however, Richard the youngest of the brothers had been taken prisoner through the treachery of one of Charlemagne's men, and the Emperor ordered him to be hanged at Montfaucon, in the north. The protests of Roland, of Turpin the Archbishop, of Ogier the Dane and all the mighty men and lords and knights of the entourage were of no avail. Richard was taken off to his execution. But Maugis had not been trained in vain by wizard teachers. He had with him an ointment which, when rubbed in to the skin, gave him the ability of flying like a bird. Acting as an aerial spotter he flew over Paris and Montfaucon and directed the other three sons of Aymon riding on their lightning steed to the scene of the execution. Already the executioner had placed the noose around Richard's neck when with a bound Bayard was at the foot of the scaffold, the trusty blade Flamberge flashed, the executioner was cut down, the rope severed, and to the cheers of the crowd Richard was swept up to the four-seater steed and carried away as fast as the wind to Montauban.

Charlemagne did not take well to being tricked, so he invested Montauban again, but one night when he was asleep in his imperial tent Maugis came bounding silently in on the back of the faithful Bayard, immobilised the Emperor with a magic drug and carried him off into the castle. Charlemagne was no better pleased with this adventure, but in spite of his storming and fretting the four sons of Aymon knelt before him and asked for an end to the warfare. At last the Emperor gave in to their request, and meanwhile Maugis had left Montauban for the Holy Land. As a pilgrim with cloak and scrip he felt he must expiate his lapse of etiquette in laying hands upon the great first Emperor of the Holy Roman Empire.

Montech, where the Montauban branch leads off from the main canal, is also the scene of the world's first water-slope, that at Béziers being the second. I must admit that when I saw it being built I felt confident that it could not conceivably work. A plunger shoving a puddle and a barge up a quarter of a mile of canal bed – was it conceivable that the device would operate without losing so much water that the boat would be stranded? So it was with some scepticism that I jumped out of my bunk when I heard a barge approaching, and hurried over to watch.

The operation was faultless. A barge came in, the watertight gate of the canal was lifted into position, the great shield on the end of an arm dropped behind the ship and the two big locomotives on either side of the slope started their motors and began slowly to separate their puddle and push it ahead. The water that leaked round the edges during the whole ascent was hardly enough to fill a bucket.

The water-slope is in fact the only point of interest all the way to Moissac. Montech is merely a derelict factory and even the romantically named Castel-Sarrasin has nothing to distinguish it from any other town of no consequence. But locks come thick and fast, and after twenty-two from the port basin at Toulouse the canal runs up to a mighty aqueduct as it turns toward the town of Moissac. Thirteen huge stone arches carry the canal across the River Tarn, and their solidarity once stood the town in good stead. That was in 1930, when one of the most violent inundations in modern times brought the floodwater surging down the Tarn with such force that the railway viaduct just upstream was snapped off and swept away. Overnight, the main line from coast to coast was broken, and in place of the bridge there was now a gap of two or three hundred metres of whirling and sucking muddy turmoil. Surprisingly, the canal bridge, which offered much greater resistance to the stream, was left quite intact.

The watercourse of the aqueduct happened to be broader than was necessary for the barges, so the engineers had the canal drained off and the towpath of the northern side broadened with blocks of concrete. Upon these a railway track was laid, and at either end of the aqueduct a length of line led away to rejoin the railway. When the work was complete and the canal refilled with water six weeks after the interruption, the first pair of locomotives steamed cautiously along the towpath beside the canal to test the new track. They weighed 180 tons apiece, and hauled a further nine wagons loaded with earth and stone. The bridge held without a tremor, and for another two years all the trains passed over the canal aqueduct, their speed limited to five kilometres per hour. As the barges made sometimes six, or even seven if unladen, there were occasionally some exciting races, with the ships only a foot or two from the wheels of the coaches. The lock-house just beyond the aqueduct was in use for some time as a temporary railway station, and the keeper told me that it was not unknown for a passenger alighting at Moissac to step out into the lock.

The night of flood was a disaster for Moissac, for the remains of the collapsed railway viaduct held up the vast quantities of floating debris and uprooted trees to form a dam which raised the Tarn still further so that it broke its bank and surged through the town to sweep away any house in its path and drown the inhabitants. This is reflected in the street name Rue de l'Inondation, and the covered market which was a gift from the City of Paris to the stricken community. Further upstream in Montauban the town bridge built in the early fourteenth century had wisely been provided with holes and high arches to reduce the pressure of floods and it held, yet many people were marooned in their houses or drowned. The path which leads along the high retaining wall of the river from the canal basin to the town passes beside an emotionally moving memorial to a young canoeist, Adolphe Poult, who took out his little craft and succeeded in saving three hundred and seventeen people before his canoe was overset and he himself was drowned.

The first time I steered over the aqueduct into Moissac it was in the wake of another storm, which had felled a number of trees into the canal further ahead, so the lock-keeper recommended that we should stay until the engineers had dealt with the blockage, a task which would take them several days. But for this fortunate event I would perhaps not have had the chance to experience something in Moissac that has remained with me ever since.

There are certain things which one may come upon unexpectedly but which nevertheless hit one so violently that life is never quite the same again. It is illumined with a new light, a fresh certainty, an increased wonder, and awe, and thankfulness. Two such things have burst upon my awareness, and curiously enough I discovered them both by canal and have returned to each of them more than once. The first is the polyptych painted by Matthias Grünewald which is now in the Unterlinden Museum, not far from the canal basin in Colmar. The other is over the doorway of the abbey at Moissac.

The abbey of Moissac is alleged to date back to the time of Clovis in the sixth century. Legend relates that when in 506 he had beaten the Visigoths in battle three angels appeared to him, bearing the architectural drawings of an abbey he was to erect in Quercy and was to dedicate to St Peter. Unfortunately, the apparition vanished without identifying the building site more closely, so Clovis climbed to the top of the hill behind Moissac and cast his javelin with all his might. Fortunately his throw fell well short of the Tarn and landed in a marsh, and there he built the abbey.

However that may be, the abbey was certainly there in 847, the year when the Viking ships sailed up the Garonne as far as Toulouse, laying waste and sacking and pillaging as they went, for they destroyed the abbey of Moissac on their way. Rebuilt, it was affiliated to the famous foundation of Cluny. This second building with its famous cloisters had survived nine centuries, in spite of the attacks upon the town by Simon de Montfort, the occupation by the English, and their expulsion a few years later by the Duke of Anjou, until the French Revolution, when it became in turn a barracks, a gunpowder factory and a forage store. Later, the great court of the cloisters was to be pulled down to make way for the Bordeaux-Séte railway when reason began to assert itself again and the Fine Arts Commission intervened to preserve from complete destruction the finest work of romanesque architecture in France. And there it still is.

I make no apology at all for saying that to stand before the door of the abbey and be confronted by the Christ of the Second Coming can be a tremendous spiritual experience. He and his whole vibrant entourage of seraphims and elders and evangelists come from a century before the Inquisition burned two hundred Albigensian Christians in the town. He is not a Christ of hatred, nor is he a figure of passion or a mere man of sorrows exalted to wear a saintly dressing-gown, but a person of utter authority and of a power that would be terrifying were it not for the complete calm and serenity with which he is opening the new age of justice and right. There is a halo behind his head, made up of a formal cross and a dozen thistles, but it is not the halo which makes the Christ truly royal. Nor is it the grandeur of the kingly robe. It is the face, of a Christ who is infinitely great. The twenty-four elders are almost breaking their necks in the suddenness of their amazement at his appearance and the rebecs on which they were about to play a well-practised song of welcome dangle unplucked from their hands. Only the two angels in attendance have an air of superior knowledge, as though they have known all along that it will be like this when time has come to an end and existence run into a new dimension.

There is no anger in the face of the Christ regnant, no humility and yet no pride. He stares one straight in the face as he has done others since 1130. He is a Christ who cannot be deceived, but who understands what it is to be human and bound within four dimensions. He forgives, but he will have no compromise with evil. Absolute justice and glory is portrayed above the door of the abbey church of Moissac, and it was done by a man unknown. More important than his identity is the certainty that this central figure of the parousia is not one that any man could have thought up. I am certain that it is authentic, and can only have come from a genuine vision of the truth of eternity. Like Grünewald's Crucifixion in Colmar it is the work of a man who had seen it, who had been allowed to travel through dimensions of time and space to glimpse the ultimate reality and to record it for others for all time, and in such a way that its dynamic power is never forgotten, never lost, and can survive the worst a human revolution can do.

The first of my visits to Moissac coincided with the celebration of the nine hundredth anniversary of the abbey's consecration after the Viking desecration. It was already dark as we took our seats beneath a five hundred year old cedar in the lawn of the cloisters, and the warm night was so breathless that the air did not stir the scented needles of the cedar or cause the least flicker of the candles. We were to have Vivaldi and Bach and Mozart, and if there had been nothing else to delight us at Moissac it would have been worth the journey merely to be introduced to Mozart's Double Concerto for Flute and Harp.

The concert began with Vivaldi, and the orchestra, which had come from the university of Tübingen, seemed to be curiously ill at ease, not in their playing but over some matter which we in the audience could not guess. The first movement of the Mozart was followed by only the swiftest break before the second began, and when the piece reached the third movement it seemed to us that the conductor was definitely accelerating. The tempo increased still further, and we were surpised to see the maestro glance at his watch. The horns horned, the harpsichord tinkled as fast as its jacks would pluck, and the string players sweated in the warmth of their energetic bowing. At last with a grand flourish the conductor brought the orchestra into the final chord, sustained it for a moment, then cut it off. And even as we began to applaud we realised why *allegro* had had that night to be more *allegro* than ever. With a roar like an inter-continental ballistic missile, the SNCF sent the Marseille twelve coach night mail thundering by, immediately behind the musicians.

When in the previous century the Fine Arts Commission had intervened to save the cloisters, the railway was cut through the town just the same and was merely moved a few hundred yards further back toward the hill. Lesser abbey buildings were demolished, and a rock cutting was chopped in the stone immediately behind the corner of the cloisters. Trains from the west would steal up unheard to approach through a tunnel, and there was almost complete silence until the locomotive burst screaming into the open air, shaking the abbey to its foundations. But the conductor had been told of the timetable, and he managed it, with three seconds to spare.

Beyond Moissac the canal continues pleasantly but undramatically through Valence d'Agen, a place which provides an elegant course of lawns and trees and walks to please the bargeman, but nevertheless turns its own face the other way. It has changed too much for the plan of an English fortified strong-point to be discernable any more, but it is said locally that hard by the old church English knights lie buried in all their armour since the days of the Black Prince.

Another three locks, and the waterway passes round the side of a cliff overlooking the remarkably unattractive town of Agen, with a grimy goods yard and a cathedral restored in the worst period of restoration. Beyond it comes the half kilometre long aqueduct which takes the canal flying over the mighty River Garonne in great style, but for the rest of its way to tidal water the lateral canal has little in the way of excitement or scenery to offer. One long straight section follows another, the flat line broken only by very plain concrete bridges. The towns lie away to the side, clustered by the river which was navigable for flat boats in the middle ages and in the time of Riquet. As late as the last century an enterprising Monsieur Jollet of Toulouse built a passenger vessel, the *Clémence-Isaure*, with a draught of only eleven inches. She was to be able to navigate the river under all conditions, and she worked up from Agen to Toulouse in about fifteen hours. When the river was reasonably high, barges could float down the stream instead of using the canal, and this is why locks were provided to connect with the stream at Moissac and Agen.

There have been disasters on the canal. At one point there is a monument to the victims of *Le Gascon* in 1908. *Le Gascon* was a steam barge, I was informed. Hardly had the ship passed under the village bridge when there was an explosion which shook the houses, wrecked *Le Gascon* and hurled all five men a board her into the air with such force that their shattered bodies descended on the further side of the trees beyond the towpath. Further ahead another explosion is commemorated, but a more recent one. The memorial is to the crew of a petrol tanker which was somehow sparked off at that point. How it happened was never known, for of the boat and its crew even less was left than of *Le Gascon*.

At Castets-en-Dorthe the canal ends in a grass banked basin with a tide lock into the Garonne. When first I went that way there was great activity at high water because so many barges were wishing to pass out, or were arriving on the flood. But one day there was another activity, the same duck-chasing that one can see on 14 July in the port basin in Carcassonne, and one which in Britain would probably not be allowed. Or at least it would cause demonstrations and protests, and to my mind rightly.

I had already realised from notices tacked to the trees that there was to be a great duck race, but I could not easily imagine what that could be, or how it would be conducted. Could they be genuine ducks, I asked the man who was pulling the handle of the beer pump in the village pub.

"Why not? On the feast of St Luke one makes always the race of the ducks. It is very amusing."

I do not know what it had to do with St Luke, but about mid-morning the younger inhabitants of Castets began to crowd the canal banks. Then a row-boat put out from the shore and took up a station in the middle of the broad water between ourselves and the waiting barges. In this boat were a boy who did the actual rowing, an old village father with a mysterious bulging sack, and the local constable, in his shirt sleeves and with trousers rolled up above his knees, but wearing his pill-box hat as a symbol of the firm law and beneficent order conferred upon the country of France by her police.

A loudspeaker crackled over the water. "The first duck is presented by the community of Castets to those born within the parish boundaries and not more than fourteen years of age."

The older youths and girls stepped back and the younger ones crowded along the banks. A dozen or more dived into the canal and waited, afloat.

The old man in the boat was the duck-keeper, and untying the neck of his sack he pulled out a muscovy, holding it by the shoulders of its wings. He handed it to the constable, who stood up in the stern and heaved it high in the air, watching with arms out-stretched as the bird fluttered down to the water. At once the boys and girls were racing for the duck, which sat on the water watching them out of the side of its head as though trying to remember everything its relations had told it about the St Luke celebrations. The leading boy was approaching swiftly with a crawl stroke and now he was near enough to shoot out a hand to grab. But the duck was not there. As he lunged, the bird rose to its feet and flapped splashing along the water to sit down a few yards further up the canal. Several boys were swiftly in pursuit and others plunged in from the further bank. The muscovy looked quickly, saw itself hemmed in, and upending its stern it dived neatly below the hunters to surface again close to the bank.

But with primaries trimmed to prevent it flying right away the duck could not escape for ever. After a chase up and down the reach it was at last seized by a boy, who conveyed it struggling to the bank. The duck was his – to carry home for dinner if it was a male, or to keep as a pet, or as a layer if a female.

It is a regrettable fact that the French are extraordinarily casual in their attitude to creatures other than their own domestic animals, and it is only recently that a society to promote the protection of birds has begun its difficult task in the face of a population used to blazing away at larks for the supposed delicacy of their tongues, at thrushes to make paté, and at any other bird just because it moves. In the year that I wrote this, hunters on the west coast tried to blow up with a bomb those who were demonstrating against the shooting of migrants, and a man who remonstrated with two men for coming into his garden to shoot at the small birds was promptly shot dead by them. *La chasse* dies hard in France, so the habit of chasing birds which cannot escape is perhaps not surprising.

Other ducks released were for girls only, or for the under eighteens, or open for general competition. One of them was quickly caught by a good swimmer who approached along the canal bottom, reached up, and grabbed the astonished bird by the feet. The next was nearly landed on three occasions but always struggled free from its captor before the shore, and raced away to start all over again. I thought it a cruel sport and I did not like it any the more when I saw it again many years later at Carcassonne. The sixth duck had just been thrown aloft when we moved up to the lock to start dropping down to the tideway an hour before the ebb, so that we should be sure of plenty of water over the shallows further down the river.

The banks of the Garonne are high and tree-covered so that one does not realise without scrutinizing a map that one is gliding down an impeccable wine-list. Chateau Yquem and Sauternes, Barsac, Loupiac, Graves and St Médard are only a few of the vineyard areas the boatman has merely to imagine before the bridges of Bordeaux come into view, a city generously spread round a long bend in the river, laid out in the grand style and with all the dignified appearance of a capital city, which is precisely what it used to be. However, the English can take no credit for its appearance, for they had been thrown out of Aquitaine (which, never being very good at languages, they called 'Guyenne') centuries before the magnificence dawned. Yet they were certainly responsible for the early development of the port, which only recently has suffered a decline and handed over some of its role as a terminal for the West African trade to an extension of its own port further down the Atlantic coast. The reason for this change is partly to be found in the long and sandbank-infested estuary of the Garonne, known as the Gironde.

The origin of the English connection dates back to the Plantagenets. The last Duke of Aquitaine died in 1137, and his daughter Aliénor married Louis the Young, the future Louis VII of France. However, the King was a rather monkish individual and she was excitable and amorous. He regarded her as so frivolous that he managed to have his marriage annulled, and rather unwisely kicked her out along with her exceedingly large dowry, which included the Périgord, Toulouse, Auvergne, and several other slices of the south and west of France. So, when a few weeks later she married Henry Plantagenet their combined territories exceeded those of the French crown.

The next blow was that Henry soon became King Henry II of England, and she Queen Eleanor, so a great part of France slipped away into the control of that dreadful country, Perfidious Albion. This was not a situation which the French monarchy could tolerate for ever, even if it took the crown nearly two centuries before it made up its mind at last to snatch back what it could. Thus began the Hundred Years War.

By this time, however, the inhabitants of Bordeaux and the Aquitaine were thoroughly used to being English, and seem to have had no objections. On the contrary, instead of niggardly and extortionate rulers they had long had masters who had given them charter upon charter, freedom and privileges which the French monarch would never have allowed them, and a vigorous trade with England. The English quickly became addicted to the *'vin clarté'* of the area, the clear red wine the English merchants and importers called 'claret' which was as near as they could get to the correct pronunciation. The wool trade also flourished, and import duties and excise were unknown. So, when the Hundred Years War came to an end and England was defeated, there was no cheering in Bordeaux. The first heyday of the city was over.

My first voyage down the Garonne ended at Bordeaux, where the life of the old original *Commodore* under my command also came to an end. But aboard her successor I thought it could be interesting to try to reach the spot where the Hundred Years War had ended, and even if the Gironde was as dull an estuary as one might expect I steered down it to its confluence with the Dordogne and swung round to starboard at Bec d'Ambès to take the rising tide to wherever it might lead.

The mere name of the Dordogne conjures up a picture of a rippling river cut deep in limestone, its twisting course trickling shallow past cliffs riddled with caves where once our ancestors tried their hand at painting wild life on the walls. Those glamorous upper reaches are only accessible to the kayakist or the walker, but further down the river is used by a modest amount of commercial traffic – the occasional coaster of two or three hundred tons, and a rare barge instead of the many sailing vessels which once sailed down it to carry the wines to other lands. At the confluence by Bec d'Ambès the river is more than a kilometre in width, and the first place on the way upstream is Bourg-sur-Gironde. Wondering why a town definitely sur-Dordogne by several kilometres should be named as on the Gironde I asked the captain of a refinery ferry which we used as a temporary landing stage, and he explained simply enough that Bourg used indeed to be on the Gironde, but so much silt came down the Garonne and the Dordogne that the tapering tongue of land between them grew fast. So fast that one could almost see it moving. The confluence was continually being pushed downstream, and given enough time it would reach the sea.

Already at Bourg there was a surfeit of lampreys. Indeed, of all the rivers in the world the Dordogne is the one for lampreys, just as it was in the days of King Henry I. The lamprey is curious in its habits, and so are the lamprey fishermen, of which there seemed to be hundreds. Each had a boat which he rowed across the river, all the while paying out a long net which floated. The shipping channel seemed to be the favourite hunting ground, and wherever there was a little man in a little boat there was sure to be a net stretching from him to a lamp floating on a piece of cork a hundred yards or more distant. Lamprey nets are expensive, and I took good care not to foul one.

For the first 20 miles above Bourg the scenery was undramatic, and there was not a quay or jetty, nor indeed anything but a few ancient wooden wrecks stuck in the bushes on the bank. Then at Vayres the Dordogne changed its habit and became more mindful of the eye of the beholder, starting with the splendid spread of the Chateau de Vayres, its neat lawns and topiary falling down to the river. It was only five miles now to-Libourne, once a flourishing port and a place which carries its English connection proudly in its name – for it was called after its English governor Roger of Leyburn. Libourne is now a market town with only a quay where railway sleepers from the Périgord are loaded into the barges which just occasionally remember to come and collect them, and inviting though this jetty might appear, it provided the most uncomfortable night's mooring in the world, for it was set exactly at the place where two strong tides met, the fast ebb of the Dordogne already twisted and swirled by the thick buttresses of the handsome Louis XVIII toll-bridge being struck violently in the ribs by the ebb of the River Isle which ran in past the town. Combined with an evening surfeit of *Lamproie à la Bordelaise* and an overdose of nearby St Émilion the resulting swirls produced an acute sense of paranoia. I discovered that it was much better to moor along the quays of the old port in the River Isle and eat the lampreys in peace.

Libourne might be the end of the run for the faint-hearted, but even if the buoyage ended there I thought the adventure had hardly begun and I would take *Thames Commodore* up to the limit of navigation. Precisely where that limit might be was a matter of opinion, courage and the passage of time. My oldest *Guide de la Navigation* (1888) gave ten locks, the first of them just before Bergerac, for at that time barges of one hundred tons, horse-hauled from the bank, traded for grain and wine as far up as Limeuil, nearly a hundred miles up from Bec d'Ambès. The edition of 1922 gave the same limits but stressed that transport was not very organized. Towage was by oxen conducted by the proprietors or their domestics and the price was to be a matter of negotiation, taking into consideration the number of oxen and boats, the weight of the lading, the prevailing difficulties of navigation and the level of the water. The locks were now ruined, and although the 1965 *Guide* showed navigation as possible up to within seven miles of Bergerac staunch, the limit in 1971 was stated to be just short of Flaujages, sixteen miles nearer the sea. Even this proved optimistic.

I decided first to tackle the River Isle, which was comparatively short. My guide stated confidently that it was navigable all the way to a lock – which was presumably in ruins – twenty miles up, at Laubardement. Earlier there had been forty locks and one might have gone all the way to Périgueux, but that was a few decades ago. So, when the flood began to run up past the staging I set off up the river.

The Isle was narrow and winding, and as trees had collapsed into the river from both banks the course was up the middle. For the first ten twisting miles there were no difficulties other than fishing derricks manned by fishermen in a wine-deep slumber. Not until the bridges at Galgon did I have to await an extra foot of flow, and then *Thames Commodore* made a gentle and relatively easy passage up past Savignac to St Denis-de-Pile, where more extensive shoals put an end to her voyage.

At one point a soldier appeared on the bank, waving and shouting and behaving with the sort of unbridled hysteria that the English boatman expects from foreigners.

"*On tir*," he yelled. "*On tir!*"

This was surely the occasion, I thought, to strike the defiant attitude of Sir William Lucy in Henry VI. "Tis a mere French word; we English warriors wot not what it means." Without reducing speed I retaliated with the loud hailer. "Then one must cease," I called.

The soldier set off at a run, crashing through the undergrowth to warn that once again the unreasonable English, the scourge of France, were up the valley. Fortunately he reached his fellows in time, for as we swept round a sharp bend to where the targets were ranged along one bank and the snipers on the other, not a shot was fired.

Next day it was the turn of the Dordogne. I knew that the tidal effect ran up to beyond Castillon, so I began to consider how we were to find the channel in what looked to me a somewhat muddled stream. Obviously I had only to ponder the habits of oxen and domestics to realise that the channel must once have been within ten metres of the right bank. Superimposing on this piece of information the fact that the course was last dredged in 1925, I had a fair idea of where the deep water would be – namely just where I did not expect it. All the same, everything went well, and in no time we were up level with St Émilion, seven miles above Libourne.

France has many little towns which are more curious than one could conceive until one has actually been there. Minerve is one, and St Émilion is another. Clumped on a collection of limestone hillocks it consists of a mass of ruins of abbeys and convents constructed both on the surface of the ground and beneath it, the stone being soft enough to cut away in blocks so that both the quarries and their product could be used. It has a 'monolithic' church about one thousand years old, which has three naves and is entirely hollowed out of the hill, the tower alone being added all by itself on the surface above, constructed from the stone excavated from below. This church is also the scene of the judging of the last year's wine by the jurats in their scarlet ermine-trimmed robes, to ensure that it comes up to the appellation controllée standard.

Among the ecclesiastical ruins a little town of vintners has grown up, and one of the wine chateaux on the edge of the town is Chateau Ausone, alleged to have belonged to Ausonius, the Roman poet who was tutor to the sons of Constantine, the first Christian Emperor, and whose statue stands beside the Moselle at Neumagen, where Constantine had his summer residence.

As for St Émilion, he seems to have been an 8th century monk who came from Brittany and lived as a hermit deep down in a small cave. Local belief somehow mixed him up with a fertility deity, so it was formerly alleged that married but childless women had only to take a seat upon the stone slab which had served him as a bed in his little cavern, and within a year they would be certain to give birth.

Another ten miles, and my guesses as to the habits of oxen and servants were still proving correct. Then beyond St Jean-de-Blagnac I kept fairly close to the port bank, and taking it gently came up to the town of Castillon-la-Bataille without running aground, even if our slight wash broke here and there on shoals or sunken logs to the side.

Castillon proved to be a sleepy little town on a steep rise above the Dordogne. At its foot lay an old steamer converted to a crane-stage for the gravel lighters. Once this vessel had carried convicts to the Ile de Ré prison, but like the handsome ox-drawn sailing barges still moored in the stream it now had a quieter life and offered a hospitable mooring to any boat improbably penetrating thus far up from the distant Gironde. But we were still not at the limit of navigation, and although the tidal effect at Castillon was small I decided to wait until next day before going further ahead. In fact there proved to be only three miles more before the river shoaled at Lamothe-Montravel so badly that there was no choice but to turn round. As recently as five years earlier the *Guide de la Navigation* had given a further twenty miles of navigable river, but that was little enough compared with the original length of 414 kilometres or 260 miles above Bec d'Ambès, even if much of it was described as 'raftable' with a minimum depth of about ten inches – good enough for canoes, but certainly not for ourselves. Even if we had only made a total of rather over fifty miles up from the Gironde, the sight of a ship creeping up the stream was enough to bring children streaming from the village schools along the river.

On our way up we had passed the memorials to the great defeat suffered by the English. One marked the site of the actual battle and the other, right by the disused towpath where servants no longer goaded their oxen, was erected on the spot where were slain the Great Earl of Washford, Waterford and Valence; Lord Talbot of Gooding and Urchinfield; Lord Strange of Blackmere; Lord Verdun of Alton; Lord Cromwell of Winfield; Lord Furnival of Sheffield; the thrice-victorious Lord of Falconbridge, Knight of the noble order of Saint George, Saint Michael and the Golden Fleece, and the Great Marshal to Henry VI. Curiously enough, these were all one man, for they were the various other titles of the aged John Talbot, Earl of Shrewsbury, who had been governor of Guyenne for an astonishing span of fifty-three years.

I had earlier had a particular interest in Talbot, dating back to my days as a geneticist, for he provided rare evidence of the faithful reproduction of a dominant gene throughout all or at least many generations. Usually it is a difficult matter to trace inherited characteristics back over the centuries because few people know for certainty even such mundane facts as whether their great-great grandfather was bald, or left-handed, or could roll his tongue sideways. The exceptions are found in families which for various reasons were so notable that they were painted or sculpted over centuries, such as the Hapsburgs. There is nothing remarkable in the Hapsburg lip as such. It is not unique. But it can be traced in that particular line just because as rulers they always sat for painters.

Talbot had an interesting and unusual dominant gene which caused phalangeal synostosis, which means that the joints of his fingers were fused so that they could not bend like those of most people. This is known because his corpse was returned to England to be buried in the parish church at Whitchurch in Shropshire. The tomb bears one of those fashionable effigies of a knight recumbent, and whether from observation or personal knowledge or hearsay the sculptor faithfully portrayed him with unbending fingers. The same effect can be noticed in some of his descendants fourteen generations later, a fascinating testimony to the faithfulness of chromosome copying at cell divisions, for a little calculation of the kind in which geneticists like to indulge would indicate that the gene must have been reproduced more than seven hundred consecutive times between the days of the thrice-victorious Lord of Falconbridge and his descendants in our own time.

It is interesting also that when the tomb was renovated in 1874 the coffin was opened for reconstruction – or maybe just out of that morbid curiosity which drives people to peep at the remains of the dead – and the fingers were found indeed to have the peculiarity I have described. Another fascinating discovery was that a church mouse had penetrated the hole made in Talbot's skull by a French battle-axe and had built a nest out of leaves torn from the Book of Common Prayer. That the mouse was a good Anglican cannot seriously be doubted. A Presbyterian or Congregationalist mouse would not have touched the book, even for making a bed.

As to the battle which put an end to the Hundred Years War and sealed the fate of the English dominions in France, it was notable for two other reasons, the complete success of French strategy and the fact that here for the first time the day was decided by a new-fangled weapon, artillery. Guyenne had by then been largely reconquered by France, but knowing that the inhabitants were restive under the oppressions of Charles VII, King Henry VI of England instructed the Earl of Shrewsbury to recapture it. Swiftly Bordeaux was retaken, and Castillon also, but the commander of the opposing French forces, Jean Bureau, decided to settle the matter once and for all in a single engagement. The plan was to construct a well protected camp, and lure Talbot to attack.

The French army of ten thousand men was rapidly installed in a camp protected at the rear by the small river Lidoire and its cliffs. The front and sides were contained by about a mile of ditch hastily dug and filled from the river, and so designed that its zigzags gave the possibility of cross-fire. Trees were felled along it to obstruct any leaping by English cavalry, and in the centre was a deep nick which appeared to the English (as was intended) to be a gateway.

The English advanced and rushed into this funnel, unaware that no less than three hundred pieces of artillery were concealed along the banks on either side. Fired at from both flanks the English were forced back on each other, yet in spite of their terrible losses they endeavoured to storm the supposed gate. But it was too late. A few more salvos and they turned to flee. And at that moment a force of Breton horsemen, cunningly concealed at a distance, descended at full gallop and attacked them with their lances.

The English left four thousand dead upon the restricted field, their commander Talbot among them, and those that escaped were quickly overtaken at Castillon itself and elsewhere. The day of the heavily armoured knight on his war horse was over, and so was the English hegemony over all French territory except for Calais, even if the local inhabitants may have regretted it. As Charles the Dauphin says in *King Henry VI*, 'All will be ours, now bloody Talbot's slain.'

So ended the English rule which extended far into the Midi. And there ended also my own exploration by water of the southern part of France. Lamothe-Montravel was the furthest point to which it was possible to penetrate by inland waterways, many hundred of miles and more than three hundred and fifty locks from the Scheldt, which was our favourite point of entry to the continent because of the beauty of the passage of the Meuse through the Belgian and French Ardennes which lay ahead.

Waiting for water enough over the shallower reaches below Castillon, it was time to return, not to England but to the Canal du Midi and the Minervois, and at an age when one may have less certain balance – because it is not possible to take a dredger into the semi-circular canals of the inner ear – and when one might find it definitely unpleasant to fall off a high lockside onto a boat below as I once had done on the River Doubs many years earlier, it was nearly time for us both to give the signal "Finished with engines" and enjoy the wonder of the Midi from our terrace at Montouliers, perhaps the most delightful of all the villages of the Minervois. The wandering line of plane trees at the edge of the plain below conceals and reveals nostalgically the long pound of the Canal du Midi winding toward Béziers or Carcassonne, and looking across our vines toward its curving line of green our thoughts often stray, lock by lock, from the Saône and Rhone to the Gironde, across the incomparable Languedoc made accessible to us by the ingenuity of that indefatigable man Pierre-Paul Riquet, Baron de Bonrepos, and by "*Thames Commodore*", the little vessel aboard which we travelled the length of his waterway so many happy times, and without which we would never have discovered the enchantment of that sunny, wine-drenched area of France.

Index of People and Places

(For ease of reference people are listed in italics)